*Entrepreneurs and Politics
in Twentieth-Century Mexico*

ENTREPRENEURS AND POLITICS IN TWENTIETH-CENTURY MEXICO

Roderic A. Camp

New York   Oxford
OXFORD UNIVERSITY PRESS
1989

Oxford University Press

Oxford New York Toronto
Delhi Bombay Calcutta Madras Karachi
Petaling Jaya Singapore Hong Kong Tokyo
Nairobi Dar es Salaam Cape Town
Melbourne Auckland

and associated companies in
Berlin Ibadan

Published by Oxford University Press, Inc.,
200 Madison Avenue, New York, New York 10016

Oxford is a registered trademark of Oxford University Press

Library of Congress Cataloging-in-Publication Data

Camp, Roderic A.
  Entrepreneurs and politics in twentieth-century Mexico / by
Roderic A. Camp.
    p. cm. Bibliography: p. Includes index. ISBN 0-19-505719-8
    1. Businessmen—Mexico—Biography. 2. Elite (Social sciences)—
Mexico—Biography. I. Title.
HC132.5.A2C35 1989 338′.04′0922—dc19 [B] 88-28745 CIP

9 8 7 6 5 4 3 2 1

Printed in the United States of America
on acid-free paper

To Mamacita

Preface

Some of the sources in this book deserve special explanation. The focus of this study is the relationship between the private sector and the state in Mexico since 1920. Most of the available literature does not comment directly on this issue. Although I will place the Mexican case in the appropriate context of the available theoretical literature, the majority of which stems from the experience of Western, industrialized nations, Mexico's unique pattern demands alternative sources. As is true in many areas involving political research in developing countries, original sources of data must be created. The most important among these are oral interviews with entrepreneurs and politicians.

Two decades of field research in Mexico have guided me in this unusual quest. In particular, my research perspective has been strongly affected by my previous work on the relationship between Mexican intellectuals and the state.[1] I have learned several important lessons about the value of oral interviews. In the first place, a topic involving even a short historical perspective requires that interviews involve multiple generations of Mexicans. I have been able to converse with three generations for this research, many persons in their seventies and eighties, and others in their late twenties and early thirties. This range is critical, not only because of the breadth of perspective it provides, but because different generations offer widely differing views.

I also learned from my previous studies that an examination of a relationship between any two social actors involves at least two, and often more, perspectives as elites examine each other, since the groups themselves are divided from within. I have therefore interviewed seventy-five Mexicans from both the private and public sectors, persons selected on the basis of their age, ideology, insight, and influence during the years from 1982 to 1986. Many of the insights obtained from my study of intellectual life, both methodological and analytical,

proved appropriate to this project. As I have done with earlier research, I drew on eclectic reputational and positional criteria to select
individual subjects. I believe I have developed a special rapport with
elite Mexicans that allows them to discuss many controversial subjects
frankly and emotionally.[2]

In addition to insights obtained from a large sample of political
and entrepreneurial elites, I developed **a biographical data set** on
entrepreneurs as part of a long-term project to test the presence of a
power elite in Mexico. In the late 1960s I embarked on the collection
of biographical information on postrevolutionary political leaders.
Those data have been continuously updated and expanded, and now
include some 2,850 complete cases of prominent politicians since
1884.[3] These data are part of what I call the Mexican Political Biography Project and will be cited throughout the text as (MPBP). In the
1970s I added data on Mexican intellectuals and their relatives, and in
the 1980s I constructed two additional biographical data banks on
leading military officers and entrepreneurs.[4] Collecting data on entrepreneurs proved a difficult task, much more so than for politicians and
intellectuals. Although not as closemouthed about themselves as Mexican career military officers, entrepreneurs have published very little
about their lives and rarely allow themselves to appear in published
materials.

To provide the most useful collective portrait of entrepreneurs in
the Mexican Entrepreneurial Biography Project (MEBP), I included
individuals who were stockholders, founders, managers, and board
members of the 200 leading firms in Mexico from 1920 to the present.
Because I am also interested in their associational affiliations, and the
connection of private-sector interest groups to the state, I considered
the names of presidents who ran the leading entrepreneurial organizations, including the Coordinating Council of Entrepreneurs (CCE),
the Mexican Bankers Association (ABM), the Mexican Employers
Association (COPARMEX), the National Federation of Chamber of
Industries (CONCAMIN), the National Chamber of Manufacturing
Industries (CANACINTRA), the National Chamber of Commerce
(CONCANACO), the Mexican Insurance Association (AMIS), and
the Mexico City and Monterrey Chambers of Commerce. All
members of the elite Mexican Council of Businessmen (CMHN) were
also considered for inclusion. I also added to my pool of leading
entrepreneurs the names of Mexicans mentioned in analytical works.
The data set is cited throughout the text as the MEBP.

The biographical data provide an empirical and insightful picture of the makeup of Mexico's leading entrepreneurs, regardless of origin and generation, revealing important trends over time. Finally, a data set on leading Mexican firms complements the biographical information and the firsthand interviews, with variables on ownership, board membership, group membership, ranking, and sectorial representation. These data helped to establish the nature of linkages between entrepreneurial families, and between politician-entrepreneurs and traditional businessmen. Although the data are incomplete because of the unpublished nature of financial information in Mexico, the basis for some empirical conclusions is established.

The thrust of this work, however, is humanistic. The sources provide a rich mine of new information, but they cannot unearth all the answers, nor do they establish the tone of this book. Instead, it is my hope that many fresh ideas concerning the relationship between the private sector and state will be offered, some based on these new sources, others speculative in tone. While Mexico's characteristics are unique, many valuable comparisons can be made with other Third World nations.

Pella, Iowa   R.A.C.
May 1988

Acknowledgments

The research for this book has taken place over many years. My own institution, Central College, has provided numerous travel grants to Mexico. In 1983–84, I spent a year in Washington, D.C., on a fellowship from the Woodrow Wilson International Center for Scholars, allowing me to pursue extensive research in the Library of Congress. I would also like to thank the staff at the Hispanic Division for their help, and my assistant, Quynh Thai.

Much of the original research in this volume owes a debt to two Mexicans: Miguel and Tatiana Basáñez, who through their hospitality and assistance made possible many fascinating interviews. I also owe a debt of thanks to Ernesto Canales Santos, who arranged for numerous conversations with leading members of the Monterrey Group. Finally, I received helpful comments from Miguel Basáñez, Sylvia Maxfield, and Luis Rubio on various chapters.

Contents

Entrepreneurs and Politics
in Twentieth-Century Mexico

1

Introduction

Perhaps no group in the twentieth century has attracted more controversy than entrepreneurs, the leading lights of capitalist development.
Academics in general, and liberal academics in particular, remain
suspicious of entrepreneurial motives, bringing this emotional baggage
to their analysis of businesspeople. The uncomfortable feelings academics share about the business world explain their attraction to the
study of economic decisionmaking from both a public and private
perspective, the crux of scholarship in the field of political economy.
Whereas scholarship offers plenty of studies on economic ideology
and the impact of foreign investment on government decisionmaking,
the paucity of studies on the structure of the private sector—the
characteristics of its leading entrepreneurs, and most important, its
political relationship to the modern state—is noteworthy.

Interest in the political role of the private sector, from the point of
view of politics and sociology, derives from two broad theoretical
perspectives. The first of these, elite theory, came to scholars' attention
through the work of Gaetano Mosca and Vilfredo Pareto. C. Wright
Mills popularized their ideas, especially the concept of a "Power
Elite," that is, a small set of interchangeable economic, social, political, and military leaders who govern a society.[1]

Younger theorists have continued to debate the validity of this
interpretation. Critics of power elite theories have found Mills' original interpretation overdrawn and simplistic. Some of those who now
subscribe to the existence of a power elite believe that the United
States is characterized by many separate elite groups, and that these

3

only come together sporadically.[2] Others, notably W. G. Domhoff, provide evidence to suggest that the political and economic elite in the United States is a socially cohesive class.[3] Students of Third World cultures have found elite theory highly attractive. The first major North American student to apply this theory to Mexico was Robert Scott, who in the mid-1960s suggested that Mexico was "governed by a power elite of interlocking political, economic, and status leaders whose interests and attitudes overlap sufficiently to assure a considerable degree of cooperation, but it is neither a closed nor a functionally specialized elite."[4]

Another set of theorists have sought to establish the role of groups vis-à-vis the state. Borrowing from interest-group literature, state theory in European Marxist interpretations, and decisionmaking analyses, these researchers have tried to classify political systems and describe the role groups, including the private sector, play in formulating public policy. For the Latin American region, authoritarian, bureaucratic, and corporatist political models have been most popular.[5]

This book applies a collection of methodologies, descriptive and empirical, to test many assumptions about the role of the entrepreneur in twentieth-century Mexico. Collective biographical data on the social background and economic experience of a broad group of Mexican entrepreneurs are made available for the first time in this book. Valuable perspectives from firsthand interviews, representing the views of entrepreneurs and government officials, are interspersed throughout. Portraits are drawn of typical Mexican entrepreneurial types and the institutions they represent. Both are presented in the larger and unique context of the Mexican state and general political process.

Elite theory neglects many important questions about the entrepreneur. The most serious weakness of collective elite biography is the dearth of information on social background. As Philip H. Burch has suggested, a "careful investigation of the social origins, economic linkages, and general recruitment patterns of a nation's top decision makers should itself reveal much about the relative power of different groups and classes in a society."[6] Later chapters analyze, in considerable detail, many of these characteristics. Establishing the connection between the individual entrepreneur and the firm he represents further enhances the value of elite data.[7] Economic data about Mexican firms is not public. Since 1982, some information has been made available about publicly held corporations, which are a small minority. Nevertheless, where possible, data have been collected on the most important firms, board members, and owners.

In his extensive examination of North American elites, Burch concluded that "one matter that is often slighted in elite studies is that of key family and kinship ties. There are very few references to such links in the general literature on the subject, . . . one searches in vain for any examination of kinship ties among elite figures in American business and government."[8] The reason for this omission is simple. Family background data are the most difficult of all biographical information to obtain. And data are plentiful in the United States compared to Third World countries. I have worked two decades to acquire background data on Mexican elite groups, especially their family ties, and the results of that research are presented in the following chapters.

Traditionally, researchers assume a high degree of cohesion within the business community. Business leaders are, indeed, often divided along such lines as firm size or economic sector, but other variables, often more important, also come into play. Yet the only study of Mexican domestic entrepreneurs, until recently, was that of Flavia Derossi, who collected original information on an important group of industrialists. And she herself admits that her work omits financiers, bankers, and government officials, who in Mexico are at least as important as industrialists.[9] Furthermore, geography plays a significant role; firm location explains many of the attitudinal differences among business leaders' relationships to the public sector.

One of the characteristics of public and private leadership that has fascinated elite theorists is the acclaimed interlock between private- and public-sector elites. Evidence for this exchange in the United States has been well established. In Mexico, however, it has been suspected, and even asserted, without firm evidence.[10] Some Mexican analysts believe ties between private- and public-sector leaders are only natural, enhanced by a similar lifestyle stemming from a shared standard of living, common social activities, similar educational backgrounds, and ultimately, intermarriage.[11]

Social linkages do play a significant if undeterminable role in the relationship between governmental and private-sector leadership groups. As several students of entrepreneurs suggest, it is worth examining the professional and social organizations of economic elites in order to identify similarities among leading leading entrepreneurs and other elites.[12] Moreover, the structure of professional organizations themselves, their ideology—especially their beliefs concerning the state—their leadership, and their position in the larger political arena provide additional insights into the direction and function of entrepreneurial groups.[13]

Elite theorists point to many deficiencies in the literature on entrepreneurs and their group relations. State theorists, though relying on a longer tradition extending back to classical interpretations of the role of the state, are equally divided in their views of the state and its functions. In the first place, social scientists use the term state rather loosely. This is natural given its ambiguity. One of the complaints one can make about this literature is theorists' unwillingness to define the state in a concise, concrete manner.

Plato suggests that the state is conceived out of the needs of humanity since no individual is completely self-sufficient. As for defining a state, he seems to argue that when people come together to supply each other's needs, they—as a group—can be termed a state.[14] Here the difference between a society and a state is unclear. Nineteenth-century theorists, articulating a vocabulary and set of conditions more compatible with the present, provide a more enlightened description. According to Engels, the state is the product of society, which itself is a contradiction of class interests.[15] Expressed more precisely, the state "pursues goals and allocates values for the collectivity."[16]

This book attempts to explain how one group of overriding importance in society relates to the state. Conceptually, then, our complex task is to separate a part (the private sector) from the whole (the state), and describe the interactions between the two. The key element in private sector-state relations, as Hegel explains, is sovereignty.[17] That is, state functions and power stem from the whole of society. Expressed differently, the state pursues a course of action sustained by the idea of a society's common good.[18] Describing who defines the common good becomes the problem for a political analyst.

Recent theorists suggest five possible relationships between the state and other political actors. The first interpretation is that the state merely provides an open arena for various groups, including the private sector, to struggle for supremacy in choosing the common good; the state plays no role in these conflicts. A second view, increasingly popular, conceptualizes the state as an active arbiter to whom social actors appeal to settle their conflicts. Many political elites themselves, and Mexicans are no exception, find this interpretation attractive. A third conception, favored by traditional Marxist theorists, is that the state favors elites, especially the private sector, in their conflict with the masses. Naturally, labor groups and class-conscious masses support this view. The traditional "power elite" concept coincides with it. A fourth interpretation reverses the argument, suggesting that the state favors mass interests. In Mexico, as we will see, many private-sector leaders believe this interpretation accurately describes the basis of their relationship to the state. The final view is that the state, while autonomous in its relations with any group, is committed to manipulating all social groups, especially the masses and the private sector. Because its purposes often seem contradictory, this interpretation has been labeled the contradictory state theory.[19]

The role of the state in Mexico arises from numerous historical peculiarities, the most important of which is that, compared with its northern neighbor, its role is all-encompassing. As David Brading makes clear, prospective entrepreneurs have offered their talents to the state, rather than constructing interests confrontational to it.[20] Historians point to the Spanish heritage to explain this larger state role, but the indigenous contribution should not be ignored. Religious and secular decisions were intertwined, and authoritarian characteristics of indigenous elites were compatible to and supportive of the European influences introduced in the 1500s. It is accurate to say, therefore, that historically "Mexico has been conditioned to governmental intervention (through the Church, Crown or State) in the nation's economic activity."[21]

Mexico's independence from Spain in the third decade of the nineteenth century introduced philosophic influences that explain the contradictory nature of the present Mexican state. By the 1850s, a philosophy known as Liberalism had emerged as a dominant political force, superimposed on a half-century of chaos, violence, and civil war. The essence of this contradiction has been beautifully expressed by Karl Schmitt:

> a new doctrine of political relationships . . . stressed individualism as against corporatism, and equality of citizen rights as against group privileges. The tenets of this theory, soon to be called Liberalism, advocated the equality of citizens before the law and the guarantee of certain rights in the face of state authority. The two doctrines—state authoritarianism vs. individual rights—seemingly conflict, but the theories were blended in a peculiar fashion by the intellectuals and political leaders who came to power in independent Mexico.[22]

Liberalism, with its inherent contradictions, was codified in the 1857 Constitution, a document remaining in effect until Mexico's present constitution emerged from a decade of social revolution.[23] The 1917 Constitution, instead of correcting the elements which historically gave birth to a contradictory state, further codified and legitimized them in the legal foundations of modern Mexico and in the minds of the post-1920s generations. One leading Mexican theorist concludes:

> In sum, the Constitution of 1917, which outlines the essential features of the new State, is clear testimony to the contradictions which the political-military-bureaucracy—its creator—had to deal with. So, in some parts of the Constitution we observe the classic precepts of liberalism, in others they are denied. In the same way, the equal rights of all citizens are recognized, as well as class antagonism. And it is precisely to prevent this irreconcilable antagonism from destroying society in a senseless war that the intervention of an "impartial arbiter" is proposed, a power apparently rising above the fundamental classes of society which is in charge of regulating the dispute. This "arbiter" is the State.[24]

The Mexican state, today, not only because of what it has done, but because of how it has been conceived, is a dominant force. In societies where the state plays a forceful role, politics itself becomes all-encompassing. Octavio Paz, Mexico's leading intellectual of the older generation, could say that politics dominates the culture and the economy.[25] Mexicans' perception of the state has progressed so far that it is embedded in elite mythology. If there is a common dogma among the intellectual, the member of congress, and the ideological jurist in Mexico, it is the dogma of the ontological preeminence of the state over civil society: the *estatolatría*.[26]

Before embarking on an analysis of the private sector as a social actor attempting to direct or thwart state policies, we need to briefly understand how outside observers, and Mexican public officials themselves, see the role of the state. Most recent analysts characterize the Mexican state as either semiauthoritarian, corporatist, or autonomous.

Political authoritarianism, especially in the Mexican context, implies that decisionmaking power is in the hands of a few leaders, that leaders are selected or approved by the executive, that the state controls social groups, and that political participation is limited.[27] The Mexican state is not truly authoritarian because it is often flexible in its response to different group interests; it allows for substantial change in its leadership; and recent structural reforms, however limited in scope, have expanded the number and influence of social actors, both inside and outside the political arena.[28]

As a subcategory of the authoritarian description, some authors have focused on corporatism, the concept that the basic unit of politics is the corporate (usually occupational) group, not the individual. Some characteristics of the corporate model also appropriately describe the Mexican state.[29] In the context of the relationship between the state and the private sector, the outstanding feature in Mexico is that the most important social actors—namely entrepreneurs, urban labor, peasants, and bureaucrats themselves—belong to state-initiated associations over whose governance, demands, and even leadership the state has exerted a degree of control.[30] Dale Story's recent work on business organizations suggests that while certain corporate characteristics seem valid, on the whole the Mexican private sector does not readily fit into the corporatist theory.[31]

Increasingly, the Mexican state is also being described as autonomous by scholars like Nora Hamilton, although she herself believes state autonomy is limited. She argues that a state demonstrates autonomy when it pursues goals other than those of the dominant social actors, when its decisions cannot be attributed to the direct or indirect influence or intervention of a dominant social actor, or when the dominant social actors cannot prevent the state from acting contrary to their own interests. Hamilton very specifically says that state autonomy exists only when the dominant social actor—in this case, the private sector—"cannot constrain state actions which may threaten its interests or even its existence, that is it [the State] transcends structural boundaries by eliminating old structures and creating new ones."[32] As will be seen, the 1982 decision by President José López Portillo and a handful of close advisers to nationalize the banking system represents a classic decision of the state which altered the boundaries of the private sector and its relationship to the state and other social actors.

If the state acts autonomously, in whose interest does it act? Observers of the Mexican polity believe that within the executive branch the state itself has developed its own version of the public good. An underlying belief in Mexican society that the state has the responsibility for establishing the pattern of economic life gives the state considerable leeway in formulating its own views. Susan and John Purcell suggest that the state's version of the public good be called the state interest, rather than the public interest, because it is essentially formulated by political elites and includes as a major component the maintenance of political control by the present elite coalition.[33] Thus, the state itself, when its own interests are at stake, will act in a way that significantly influences the relationship between the public and private sectors.

Some theorists argue that the Mexican state is limited in pursuing an autonomous role because the individuals who make up the leadership of the state, especially the executive branch, themselves lack cohesion. Cleavages within the state have been outlined by many political analysts.[34]

Sophisticated Marxist analysts now admit that an autonomous state is possible, especially when major social actors are in disarray. They are not willing to admit that the private sector ever loses complete control over the state, only that it has less control than traditional Marxist theory usually ascribes to it.[35] Supporters of this interpretation believe that the private sector (the capitalist class) is in an advantageous position because it can exert more influence over the state through individual actors than can the masses, whose resources are not equivalent. Because Marxist theorists believe the state automatically supports private-sector interests, they argue that other social actors representing the masses must be unified so that they can oppose both the state and the dominant entrepreneurial groups.[36] In Mexico's case, however, at least from the state's viewpoint, the private sector is not an ally. The state works to keep both the masses and the private sector divided so that it can operate from a position of political strength in settling conflicts, imposing its own vision on society.

In Mexico the relationship between the state and the private sector is complicated by the fact that the executive branch, or bureaucracy, is itself a social actor of as much importance as the private sector or organized labor. The bureaucracy uses state resources to implement its own interests. The bureaucracy's role as a political actor has been ignored because observers confuse the Mexican state's commitment to capitalist development, an unquestionable direction since 1940, with its commitment to a capitalist class. As Miguel Basáñez argues, it is committed to the former, but not the latter.[37]

The viability of this bureaucratic leadership will continue as long as it is not recruited from other dominant social actors such as the private sector.[38] Peter Smith, for example, believes they have been separate social groups.[39] (Unfortunately, Smith's data for economic elites is taken directly from Derossi, who studied only industrialists. Consequently its value is limited.) A receptive environment also favors the perpetuation of a "state interest" and a group capable of its successful advocacy in Mexico: the government's patronizing attitude creates a belief on the part of the average Mexican that one should accept the state's help, rather than control that help.[40]

Of these several sets of theoretical interpretations, this work most closely follows the argument that Mexico has a semiauthoritarian political system, and that none of the popular political theories adequately explain its unique features. It does indeed, as Dale Story has argued, have certain corporatist qualities, apparent even in the private sector. But the authoritarian, corporatist, or bureaucratic models are too monolithic to describe Mexico's political reality accurately. Within this eclectic, semiauthoritarian framework, this work supports the view that the contradictory state theory fits Mexico. I have provided evidence throughout that the private sector is just one of several important social actors to which the state responds. Further, the state generally acts in its own interest, and even though its goals often favor the private sector over other groups, this is not necessarily in response to private-sector influence. Neither politicians nor entrepreneurs see the private sector exerting such an influence on the state.

Conclusions

This work examines the relationship between the state and the private sector from a political historian's point of view and consequently relies on political rather than economic analysis. A plethora of books on Mexico's economic development exist that combine economic data with political-economic analyses. My purpose is to focus more deeply on the relationship between the domestic private sector and the state, and to raise political questions about that relationship.

The literature on state theory and political economy helps to identify important questions in analyzing structural characteristics of the relationship. However, the qualities of this relationship are influenced not only by frequently examined economic variables, domestic and international, but equally by significant and unexplored characteristics such as elite attitudes, historical experiences, traditional roles, societal concepts of the state, and other conditions flavoring individual and group behavior.

How politicians and entrepreneurs view the state, and how those views affect the relationship between them are among the issues to be addressed. Throughout this analysis, both groups' views toward each other and toward their own roles rarely stray far from their inherent values as to the state's role in society. With each variable considered, the attitudes of both public and private actors must be considered, since their relationship is not determined by each operating in a vacuum. I hypothesize that since the private sector is the stepchild of the state, their initial relationship and the dependence it engendered, at least psychologically, have never been quite severed. This characteristic is an essential ingredient in the mixture of Mexico's private-public ties, and conditions patterns of behavior within the two sectors.

A second condition that continuously finds its way into the relationship between businesspeople and the state is the influence of the United States. I find the cultural impact (some might call it imperialism) significant, a subtle quality pervading the minds of all elite Mexican actors. North American entrepreneurial attitudes about social responsibility, political activism, and innovation are a more difficult influence to describe than economic investment and control. All these attitudes affect, in significant ways, the views of Mexican entrepreneurs toward the state. I sense that this influence has strengthened the view of the more radical and younger entrepreneurs who are pushing the Mexican state beyond its traditional political limits. These entrepreneurs have provoked divisions within their own ranks, and consequently, Mexico's business community is undergoing a redefinition of its role, especially in relation to the state.

A composite portrait of any elite group usually clarifies other societal characteristics; Mexican entrepreneurs are no exception. I explore many questions raised about the business class, both inherently and in their relationship to leading politicians. With new data extending back into the nineteenth century, I wish to answer some timeworn questions historians have raised about the origins and family ties of multiple generations of Mexican entrepreneurs. I offer the hypothesis that leading Mexican entrepreneurs are not as open to new recruits as are their political counterparts, that like prominent intellectuals they have been affected very much by immigrant families, and that place of birth and adult residence strongly determine the cultural values of future business leaders.[41]

One of the characteristics of North American capitalism that elite theorists always have found fascinating is the extent of the exchange between economic and political leaders. I believe, contrary to some scholarly observations, that the exchange or interlock between Mexican private and public figures, as Smith surmised, is relatively limited. Where it exists it is often obscured from view. It differs across the private-sector leadership according to economic sector and other variables. Most importantly, certain types of entrepreneurial groups, namely bankers, have had a predisposition toward positive ties with the political class. In Chile agrarian capitalists played this role.[42] Moreover, I hypothesize that changing educational patterns extending from primary to graduate school levels will alter the behavior of both groups and their relationship to each other.

Naturally, one area all social scientists are interested in is the extent to which individuals and groups affect a society's decisionmaking process. I suspected, from earlier work on Mexico, that the private sector was among the most influential groups. But my initial hypothesis about the role of the private sector is affected by what I discovered about the role of politicians as independent-interest groups. Additionally, I explore what businessmen believe about themselves, their influence on the state, and the nature of their political role. These findings lead me to reassert the importance of personal values and attitudes in group behavior.

I originally believed that Mexican entrepreneurs had the most cohesive and influential institutional resources for altering policy decisions affecting the private sector. I encountered a far more complex pattern of behavior. As a capitalist society develops, it creates institutions to channel various group demands to the state. Mexico's institutional structures, such as interest-group organizations, inherited characteristics from the larger culture. Institutional structures are superimposed on strong cultural patterns which never disappear, and organized behavior conforms more to traditional patterns than to modern, superficial institutional constructs.

Mexico's economy began to expand rapidly in the 1960s, suggesting that firm ownership and operation were changing from traditional family control to modern corporate administration. Institutional patterns, I found, were again deceptive. With data on prominent families, board membership, and ownership, I encountered many surprising patterns, some of which countered my preliminary hypotheses. The family, it seems, remains a crucial variable in the control and operations of major industrial groups and, consequently, the relationship between the private sector and the state. Firm size also has a tremendous impact on private-sector attitudes toward the state.

Finally, although the focus of this book is on the domestic private sector, it does consider the political impact of multinationals on the relationship between the private and public sectors. I found, to my surprise, after completing the research, a substantial gap between perception and reality on this question, and that perception may carry more weight than reality. Hopefully, these and many other mysteries will be resolved in the following pages.

2

A Brief Historical Sketch
of Private Sector–State Relations

The relationship between any two groups of leaders and the sectors they represent is unlikely to remain static during six decades. Throw in a revolution and its consequences in a postrevolutionary period, and the environmental context becomes more unsettled, flavoring both the direction and volatility of the relationship. This book focuses on the period since 1920, and the end of large-scale violence is a logical benchmark for beginning. However, Mexico's private-public sector relationship did not appear from thin air. As subsequent chapters document, certain characteristics of the Mexican entrepreneur's relationship to the state were already well established by the end of the nineteenth century. The following is not meant to be an original narrative, but rather a brief history of the recent past, suggesting significant features which will help explain, at later points in the analysis, some of the peculiarities in the structure of the business community and its ties to the state.

In the decade preceding the Mexican Revolution of 1910, a muted portrait of the relationship between the state and the private sector emerged. Unfortunately, historians have not yet provided us with a broad picture of Porfirio Díaz's relationship to the entrepreneurial class. We must rely on the work of regional scholars. According to Friedrich Katz in his analysis of northwestern Mexico, Díaz tried to separate political from economic power by encouraging controlled opposition among various competing groups. Díaz ultimately gave up these attempts, and the economic oligarchy eventually monopolized political resources as well.[1] Díaz's failure to withstand the pressures of regional oligarchies appears to have been widespread and, at least in northern Mexico, the source of much prerevolutionary fervor. Díaz made a fatal error in excluding the middle class. He gave too much power to Mexico's emerging capitalists, who were beginning to transfer resources from land into commerce, mining, banking, and manufacturing.[2]

Díaz misjudged in concentrating too many resources in the hands of one important group. His experiences provided an important historical lesson to the postrevolutionary leadership: the political and economic aspirations of a broad group of Mexicans must be fulfilled to maintain political stability. An obvious political imbalance, favorable only to the capitalist class, produces instability.

According to a political-economic view, Díaz also failed to develop the institutional mechanisms to sustain his ideology. Subsequent governments since the 1920s have institutionalized their leadership, their ideology, and their relationship to emergent political actors. In this respect, they were apt pupils of the prerevolutionary period. The fact that Díaz did not effectively institutionalize his governmental processes does not imply that the private sector lacked ready access to the state. According to Robert Shafer, consultation between business representatives and the state existed before 1910, but their communication increased notably after the Revolution.[3]

Shafer's interpretation has several interesting implications. In the first place, historians, both neo-Marxist and non-Marxist, seem to agree that the economic oligarchy's influence prior to 1910 was substantially more significant than since 1920, at least in the immediate postrevolutionary decades. Why, therefore, does Shafer conclude that consultation increased after 1920? Several explanations come to mind. First, private-sector forces in the prerevolutionary period were regional, not national. Second, the private sector's representatives were personal rather than institutional. Third, as will be shown in a later chapter, Mexico's capitalists were more strongly represented in the Díaz government than in any period after 1920. Capitalists, in effect, were making important policy decisions themselves, and therefore consultation with their political peers was redundant. Institutionalization benefited the process of communication and consultation after 1920, but did not immediately produce increased political influence.

In the initial phase of the Revolution, from 1911 to 1912, the

Madero family, wealthy landowners and investors in what later became major Coahuilan enterprises, took over Mexico's political leadership. Like Díaz, Madero shared power with many capitalists. In fact, fully 30 percent of his collaborators were prominent entrepreneurs, a figure higher than in any administration before or since. (MPBP) But once the violent phase of the Revolution progressed, entrepreneurs, like other affected groups, turned their efforts toward regional leaders. More than Mexico City politicians, these local leaders determined entrepreneurs' survival, political and economic, from 1913 to 1916.

A sense of institutionalization, reflecting a coherent, stable national leadership, slowly evolved under President Carranza, who, like Madero, represented the landowning class. But Carranza initiated a policy that had tremendous structural and psychological import for the state's relationship to the private sector. He achieved the capitalist class's support by returning confiscated estates to former owners, maximizing the political benefits to his administration by extending this policy over several years, and making sure only the federal government had this power.[4]

Carranza's actions from 1917 to 1920 introduced several important features to be built on by the post-1920 governments. He encouraged entrepreneurs to shift their dependence from regional and state leaders to the federal government. This policy was one of many that concentrated power in the hands of national authorities, contributing to a cancerous pattern from 1917 to the 1980s. Carranza's policy also established an economically dependent relationship between the two sectors, one that the state exploited for many decades to come. Under Carranza the state began acting as mentor to a youthful private-sector disciple. As it consolidated power, it doled out resources to nurture the nascent private sector.

In the 1920s, as the middle-class revolutionary leadership took political control, the relationship between the private sector and the state became more complicated. Some authors claim that entrepreneurial types were in charge of economic policymaking in these administrations, thus reducing the potential for conflict between business and government.[5] Actually, relations between the state and entrepreneurial groups during this decade were tense. Tensions emerged, in part, from the apparent contradiction in the 1917 Constitution between social goals and capitalism. [6] Moreover, President Obregón and Calles' land reform policies once again antagonized the traditional capitalist class, which Carranza had mollified. Calles' critical posture toward the Catholic church did little to facilitate good relations between the pro-Catholic entrepreneurial class and the state.

For the most part, however, while general policy goals during these administrations were characterized by contradictions inherent in the evolving revolutionary ideology, their overall economic policies essentially were orthodox. As Charles Anderson and William Glade argue, "they anticipated no radical departure in their planning from the economic institutions and practices prevailing in the industrialized nations."[7] They built on the foundation initiated by Carranza, putting in place those conditions necessary for capital accumulation and for the creation of a new capitalist class.[8]

Perhaps the most important contribution of the 1920s administrations to the private sector's well-being, and consequently to its relationship with the state, was government support of the banks. Realizing the importance of capital to development, the state created several public institutions to promote industrial growth. The state's "support to private banks is indicative of the government's importance in capital formation and of the linkages between the government and the private financial sectors."[9]

State intervention in banking was important for three reasons. First, it established a dependency of the expanding manufacturing sectors on government-supplied capital. Second, the banking industry itself became a key channel for an exchange of private- and public-sector leadership (MEBP). (The significance of this tie is developed later.) Third, and finally, state intervention in the banking sector also served as a model in later years for state involvement in manufacturing and mining. The Mexican state relied on and encouraged the private sector, intervening only when domestic entrepreneurs could not or would not carry out their economic responsibilities.[10]

Another critical element introduced in the 1920s, which would bear much fruit decades later, were the technocratic ideas of Manuel Gómez Morín and Gonzalo Robles, the former an important treasury official, the latter a close economic adviser of General Calles. Gómez Morín influenced an entire generation of future politicians as the dean of the National Law School from 1922 to 1924.[11] Gonzalo Robles, with the help of Daniel Cosío Villegas, established an in-house training program in the Bank of Mexico, from which many leading officials in the bank itself, the treasury ministry, and the National Finance Bank graduated. As Douglas Bennett and Kenneth Sharpe suggest, the orientation they received was one of "economic independence from the colossus to the north, industrialization, the importance of a middle class, primary reliance on the private sector, and the need for vigorous action by the state to create the conditions for private-sector investment."[12]

Calles' administration (1924–28) has been labeled a period of nationalistic capitalism, in which the banking sector served as an agent of Mexico's economic development.[13] It is ironic, therefore, that an important generation of foreign capitalists joined the pool of Mexican entrepreneurs during the 1920s and 1930s. Many of these immigrants were of Arab and Jewish origin, and came to seek their fortunes, following the footsteps of an earlier generation of Spanish businessmen.[14]

During the 1920s the state established itself as the supreme arbiter among competing interest groups. Labor, which was the most well organized, and enjoyed a favorable relationship with the state, tried to dominate it, but failed. By 1931, Calles' successor had implemented a new labor code that insured an increasingly large state role in resolving management-labor conflicts, and in dominating the only powerful competitor to the private sector, then and later—organized labor.[15] Although the state was internally divided, the state and the president, especially Calles, were perceived as all-powerful.[16] The popular image of a powerful state, and a president who embodies that power, would later plague entrepreneurs in their own relations with various administrations.

In the following decade, the most important event in Mexico was the world depression. Its impact on the evolving relationship between the state and the private sector in the 1930s was largely ideological. The alteration in the government's philosophy has been aptly described:

> In Mexico, the years of the depression challenged the implicit faith in the classical economic ideas, particularly in their application to governmental policy. It is true that Mexico never completely adhered to a laissez faire philosophy, but no new system supplanting the Classical and Neo-Classical (including Socialist) had emerged in Mexico, and the breakdown occasioned by . . . the depression of the Thirties, smoothed the path for a shift by Mexican economists to a national welfare approach.[17]

At the high point of the depression in Mexico, 1932, no major social or political changes were introduced, affecting either the private sector-state relationship, or economic policy in general.[18] What the depression did accomplish was to strengthen some leading Mexican economists' resolve to promote industrialization, to replace an export agricultural economy, a policy wholeheartedly pursued after 1940. Moreover, the immediate economic consequences of the depression created sufficient social pressure that by 1933, President Abelardo Rodríguez had introduced a number of policies that expanded the role of the state in social and economic matters.[19]

The key political figure in the 1930s was Lázaro Cárdenas, who introduced several changes modifying the relationship between the private sector and the state. In response to the doubts raised about the efficacy of orthodox economic policies, Cárdenas welcomed a new breed of economic advisers oriented toward Keynesian principles. Some observers credit Cárdenas with widening the antipopulist-populist economic split that has plagued Mexican political leadership to the present, and has weakened the state in its confrontations with the private sector.[20] The introduction of a Keynesian philosophic influence in government economic policymaking also increased the tensions between the private sector and the state, subsequently weakening the private sector's influence over the state.

Cárdenas made a second decision with a contradictory impact on the private sector—nationalization of foreign oil companies. The 1938 nationalization served as a landmark for later encroachments over domestic capital. More importantly, it consolidated state power vis-à-vis other significant political actors, reducing an extremely important foreign entrepreneurial influence.

Whereas Cárdenas' decision strengthened the Mexican state in the eyes of the populace and the private sector, it also strengthened the domestic private sector by eliminating a powerful, meddling, foreign economic influence. On the other hand, the long-term impact for the private sector was important in that it put into question the sanctity of private property, placing what became an extraordinary resource in the state's hands.

Cárdenas may have been more responsible for the institutional outlines of the present-day relationship between the Mexican state and the private sector than any other president. He set in motion or redefined three basic precepts of this relationship. First, he reformed the National Revolutionary party (PNR), the antecedent to PRI (Institutional Revolutionary party) established in 1929. He believed that the private sector should be excluded from the party. According to Shafer, Cárdenas would not have met with much resistance to this idea since business groups displayed little interest in the PNR's creation.[21] Thus, separation of the private sector from the electoral vehicle of the state's leadership was introduced in the 1930s. The only major political actors in the Mexican arena not openly recognized by the party are the private sector and the Catholic church. Although businessmen have always been permitted to join the party as individuals, they exert no influence through sectoral membership. Cárdenas' political decisions initiated the beginning of a structural as well as philosophical separation between the two groups, making it possible for government rhetoric to deny the private sector representation, thus relegating it to a second-class political status.

On the other hand, the exclusion of the private sector from formal party membership did not indicate that Cárdenas wanted to abandon them to their own fate. Instead, he visualized private sector-state relations occurring through alternative, state-controlled channels. He therefore revised legal guidelines requiring individuals owning certain types of companies to join formal business chambers. Even though there is some question as to the constitutionality of requiring Mexicans to join an organization against their will, this concept prevailed.[22]

Essentially, Cárdenas' decision had two consequences. First, it set in motion the pattern of institutionalizing relationships between actors and the state. Second, it reestablished once again the state's hegemony over the private sector, in effect controlling the form the private sector's representation to the government must take.

Finally, Cárdenas applied the same philosophy to other key political actors, including peasants and workers. His decisions toward organized labor were those most important to the state's relationship with the business community. Cárdenas created a national labor federation, the Mexian Federation of Labor (CTM), comparable to the business sector's national chambers. The private sector welcomed this type of intervention, believing the state could more easily control class struggles so as to benefit their economic interests.[23] But Cárdenas made an important distinction between labor and business.

Organized labor, through national federation membership, was automatically incorporated into the official party. This was done because labor was more influential than the private sector on the state's power in the 1930s, and its incorporation conformed to a populist image the leadership hoped to convey. The long-term consequence of this historic distinction was that organized labor and government legitimacy were intertwined, and labor's political influence on state decisionmaking was formally recognized by this structural arrangement.

The Cárdenas administration implemented one other decision affecting the private sector, a liberal immigration policy.[24] With the civil war in Spain and events in Europe coming to a head, Cárdenas opened up Mexico to a flood of European refugees. Many of Mexico's original entrepreneurs at the end of the nineteenth century had been of Spanish origin. A new influx of foreign businesspeople, who brought small amounts of capital and, more important, entrepreneurial skills and spirit, occurred in the 1930s. According to Carlos Abedrop, a leading banker, these people created numerous businesses.[25] They contributed to the speed of Mexican economic expansion. They also restricted the exchange between entrepreneurial and political leadership, since foreign-born entrepreneurs could not hold high political office.

In 1940 Cárdenas was replaced by Ávila Camacho, his hand-picked successor. That year marked a critical juncture in the relations between the private and public sectors, because it began a succession of Mexican presidents devoted to the proposition that industrialization is the key to modern economic growth.[26] The state attempted to promote private-sector achievements in economic development. For example, the government created tax incentives and channeled funds into industrial investment through official banks at lower interest rates than those prevailing in the domestic market.[27]

Why did the Mexican government move in this direction in 1940? There are several explanations. One argument suggests that Ávila Camacho's presidential candidacy symbolized an ideological expansion in political leadership. In particular, his administration was thought to have incorporated conservative groups, including private-sector allies, within the state.[28] It is true that some disenchanted conservative groups supported his candidacy, but far more of them opted to support his opponent, General Juan Andreu Almazán. Furthermore, once in power, Ávila Camacho did not substantially increase entrepreneurial types in the cabinet, compared to his predecessor. What he did do, however, was invite private-sector representatives to serve on the boards of directors of a new breed of state institution, parastate industries.[29]

One scholar claims that Ávila Camacho's regime took the advice of entrepreneurial leaders, yet describes the private sector as very weak.[30] This seems contradictory. Ávila Camacho's government did not pursue industrialization because the private sector wished it; rather, the evidence supports William Glade's view that "industrialization, with or without private capital, had by the mid-1940s entered the belief system of the day as a self-evident good. The private sector's efforts were welcome, but the state, too, forged ahead in this drive, encouraged by a labor movement eager for new jobs."[31] The problem for the state was that the private sector was not providing sufficient investment, and therefore, the state had to step into and fill a vacuum during this period.[32]

While Mexican economists point to 1940 as a benchmark year for the economy, 1946 is politically far more important. It marks the beginning of Miguel Alemán's administration, a regime having major consequences for business-government relations and political development. His administration is notable because the number of entrepreneurial collaborators reached a high point for post-1940s governments. Alemán also introduced the modern Mexican politician, who might be labeled a professional public figure. The Alemán prototype is well educated, a graduate of the National University, a lawyer, an urbanite residing most of his adult life in Mexico City, and, most important, a civilian.

These new career administrators accelerated the rate of industrialization in Mexico. To stimulate economic growth, the government expanded rather than reduced its role. Thus, Alemán and his collaborators were more willing to use the state's power to support goals shared by the growing business community.[33] As Wilkie suggests, Alemán and his successor expanded state action in economic life to the greatest extent in national history. At the same time, Alemán believed that foreign investment was necessary to augment domestic capital, and his administration provided a climate favorable to such investment. Foreigners' increased influence added an additional element to the private-public sector relationship. Contrary to common criticisms of Alemán, he did not sacrifice popular interests to industrialization or favor business interests to the neglect of the masses.[34] The most rapid period of social change in Mexico includes the Alemán years.

The image of Alemán favoring private-sector interests is as important as his actual results. Relations between the state and the private sector during this period generally were good because Alemán operated in a positive ambience toward private initiative. According to Mexican businessmen, he understood the needs of the private sector, and he sought to convey his government's view as supportive of Mexico's entrepreneurs. As a prominent banker suggests,

> the Mexican government in the immediate postwar period understood the situation perfectly, and began to help all these enterprises with tax laws, import taxes, investment money from the National Finance Bank, and associated with them as an investor if they didn't have sufficient

capital, in the steel industry, for example. It was a great effort to help the private sector, and the policy was initiated by President Alemán, and was continued up through the 1960s."[35]

Alemán also altered the balance politically by putting a lid on the growth of the labor movement, limiting their economic bargaining power and their political influence over the private sector's influence with the state.[36]

In the 1950s Alemán's immediate successor, Adolfo Ruiz Cortines, continued the same economic policies in many respects. He emphasized public investment as a stimulus for industrial growth.[37] But the power of Mexico's president to create a popular image for his regime is no better illustrated than by Ruiz Cortines. "His attitude toward the private sector" according to Raymond Vernon, "was distant and correct."[38] Therefore, it seemed to most Mexicans that the administration's ties to the private sector were less intimate than those of Alemán.

The positive and stable relationship between the two sectors so carefully crafted by Ávila Camacho continued uninterrupted until the late 1950s, when Adolfo López Mateos took office. López Mateos was a Mexican president in the populist mode, and he used the Cuban revolution to embellish his regime's credentials as liberal and nationalistic. But to the private sector his rhetoric was misleading, and private investment fell off in the initial years of his administration.[39] Sensing this, he made amends to the private sector, actively wooing their support. "In a series of major speeches through 1961 and 1962, the president and his principal lieutenants repeatedly emphasized the loyalty, respect, and support which the government was prepared to offer to Mexico's domestic businessmen. The efforts seemed to work. By 1962, the standard image of all the Mexican regimes since 1940 had been reestablished."[40]

However, during the 1950s the positive images both sectors shared of each other were colored by individual experiences. According to Eduardo Bustamante, López Mateos' secretary of government properties, leading entrepreneurs translated their distaste for politicians into important policy decisions. As Bustamante reveals in the next chapter, a prominent businessman turned down a major investment opportunity because he did not trust the government.[41]

In the 1960s, fissures appeared in the established relationship between the private and public sectors, caused partly by the fact that the attitudes and values of both groups began to evolve in different directions. Several segments of the public sector already had lost their initial faith in the Mexican entrepreneur. Furthermore, several groups in the private sector were no longer dependent on government help to survive.[42] The private sector's growth not only changed the nature of its financial dependence on the state, but also made it increasingly attractive to skilled professionals as a career option.[43] Talented Mexicans who were unrelated to first and second generations of Mexican capitalists opted for management positions in the private sector, providing infusion of new blood and ideas.

The early 1960s began an uncertain decade for the state-private sector relationship. In 1964, when Gustavo Díaz Ordaz became president, he took pains to reestablish entrepreneurs' traditional confidence in the state. His open support of private-sector investments, and his lessening of the rhetorical attacks on private education, helped create a positive image of the state.[44] Nonetheless, his government simultaneously expanded the size of the public sector, thus increasing the state's potential role as an independent force in its own self-preservation.

Díaz Ordaz's early impact on the private sector is minor compared to his actions in 1968, when student demonstrations were violently suppressed in the capital. The year 1968 is a watershed in Mexican politics. The events themselves are well known, and their immediate impact was not notable. Their long-term influence, however, is more important for the state and its relations to various political actors than any single event in the last three decades. In the aftermath of the student massacre in Mexico City, the middle class and the public leadership began to question the developmental model used since 1940. Moreover, Mexicans' faith in entrepreneurs, and their role in the traditional developmental model, was also tested.[45]

What 1968 did in a baldfaced manner was to raise, in a very public forum, questions about the legitimacy of the political system and its economic model. The dissatisfaction brought on by the events of 1968 cannot be attributed solely to one political miscalculation on the part of Mexico's leadership. As one contemporary observer of the early 1960s wrote, Mexico was already "approaching a new and difficult state in the relations between its public and private sectors, a stage both perilous and promising, a stage generated partly by the increasing political maturity of its people and partly by a growing dissatisfaction with the performance of the country's economy."[46]

The consequences of 1968 for the private-public sector relationship parallel the conditions characteristic of the intellectual-state relationship during the same period. Díaz Ordaz's successor, Luis

Echeverría, was most responsible for the changing relationship, and his behavior was grounded in the 1968 events. Laurence Whitehead argues:

> The overall character of the Echeverría administration—including its choices of economic strategy—cannot be understood unless the gravity of the 1968 legitimacy crisis is grasped. The need to recapture popular credibility after that confrontation cannot be used to explain or excuse every decision of Echeverría's administration, of course, but nothing it did can be properly understood unless that priority is seen as central.[47]

Echeverría's administration became preoccupied with questions about the economic model, and the role of the private sector as the key ingredient in the success of that model.

Most politically aware Mexican entrepreneurs share the view of analysts on the importance of 1968. In fact, they see the history of the relationship with the state as a pre- and post-1970 pattern. "For the first time in modern Mexican history, there was a possibility that Mexico would lose its political stability. . . . Echeverría was so preoccupied with this that he pursued a populist policy of huge government expenditures. The government began to contribute more than the private sector could to economic growth."[48]

To relegitimate the system in the eyes of the Mexican people Echeverría sought to pass off his government as propopulist, increasing deficit spending and expanding the public sector. On behalf of the working class, initially his administration increased benefits for organized urban labor, even supporting the expansion of independent union leadership in some sectors. But his administrators failed to win over the sectors he most sought to please. All segments of the working class were strongly dissatisfied with his economic policies.[49] When the newly formed independent labor leadership strengthened their position, he quickly reverted to politics as usual, bringing labor back into the government fold. He also increased public spending in the social sector, expanding programs in education, public health, and social security.[50]

In his more specific relations with the private sector, Echeverría added fuel to the fire by offending entrepreneurs with a variety of actions more direct than his support for selected popular groups. He introduced tax reforms and a law that would make stock ownership public. Private-sector organizations opposed both reforms, and the stock ownership law was not passed.[51] In another ill-conceived political decision, he intervened in a university dispute in Monterrey, after which both the rector and the state governor were ousted, upsetting entrepreneurs from the North.[52]

By expanding the role of state investment, Echeverría sent a message to the private sector that his government supported an exaggerated statist model of development, which the Right had always resisted. According to Newell, this led many entrepreneurs to curtail their investment in Mexico, thus weakening the economy and increasing the demand for public-sector investment to take up the slack.[53]

There is dispute over Echeverría's goal during this period. Was he truly interested in the welfare of the masses, or was he interested in restoring the legitimacy of the political system and the vitality of the state? The consensus is that he was attempting to revive the state's role as an arbiter among competing groups, especially organized labor and the private sector. To do so he sought support from intellectual dissidents, students, and even the army—all of whom, for different reasons, were disenchanted with political leadership after 1968.[54] Although he was somewhat successful in restoring limited support among these groups, his actions produced a response on the part of entrepreneurs that permanently changed the balance between the state and the private sector.

Echeverría's actions had many consequences for the private sector. In the first place, both the domestic and foreign business communities acted together to confront the public sector, exemplified by their efforts to change the leadership of the Mexican Council of Businessmen.[55] Secondly, and more importantly, entrepreneurs took economic actions to cripple the economy, contributing to a near political crisis at the end of Echeverría's regime.[56] According to many observers, the private sector became more unified in its opposition to government policy than at any time previously. This meant that it was more difficult for the government to play off one group of entrepreneurs against another, a technique long used by Mexican political leaders to dissipate businessmen's potential political influence.[57] Because of the post-1968 legitimacy crises, and the new policy directions taken by the Echeverría administration, the government was itself divided, making it a weaker foe of the private sector. And finally, another view argues that the bark of Echeverría's antientrepreneurial rhetoric was much worse than the concrete bite of any supporting policies, thus encouraging entrepreneurs to strengthen their own organizations.[58]

Echeverría attempted to alter or at least readjust the balance of power among business, labor, intellectuals, and the state. All analysts of the period agree that he failed, though each explains the causes differently. Some feel that the state itself was in a weakened condition because of the defection of support from traditional allies such as the middle class. A second explanation is that the private sector was in a stronger position to resist populist policies because it had grown in size and was no longer as dependent on the state as it had been historically.[59]

When Echeverría's term ended in 1976, he left Mexico in a political and economic crisis. His last-minute nationalization of lands in northwestern Mexico left business with a bitter taste of his propopulism, in word and in deed. Thus, when José López Portillo was inaugurated, relations between the private sector and the state were at their worst since 1920. The business community decided to take a wait-and-see attitude toward the new administration. Sensitive to the failures of his predecessor, López Portillo used his inaugural address to suggest his intentions toward the private sector. Most leading businessmen were impressed with the new president.

> With the administration of López Portillo, we thought everything would be different from his predecessor in the relationship between the government and the private sector. In his inaugural address he gave us the impression that he was sincere, that he had some charisma, in fact he made a magnificent impression on us. I believe the first year or two of his administration bore this impression out.[60]

The succession of political crises since 1968 had contributed to the decline in the Mexican political system's legitimacy. By 1977, the relationship between the state and the private sector had altered substantially. The state required the private sector's assistance to make its economic model perform effectively. It hoped Mexicans would connect the benefits of growth and employment to a positive image of the state. Moreover, as various political actors asserted greater independence from a politically weakened state, it desperately needed their political support.

To his credit, López Portillo recognized the key role the private sector would play, economically and politically, in the survival of the Mexican state. The difference between 1968 and 1977 is that in 1977 the economic crisis was severe, and both the private sector and organized labor were ready to use their power to modify government policy to their advantage.[61] The most critical decision López Portillo made was to change the government's rhetoric, to go after private-sector cooperation in an outward, positive manner. López Portillo illustrates the importance of a Mexican president's posture toward the private sector. The entire ambience in which a government operates is flavored by the president's attitude and behavior.

Economically the relationship between the state and the private sector changed during this period. Historically, immediately following the Revolution, the private sector had depended heavily on the state for financial support. In the long term the dependency had not been eliminated, but by 1977 the relationship was reversed, and the state had become economically dependent on the private sector.[62] Economic growth, through an alliance with the private sector, would legitimate the shaky position of the state apparatus. López Portillo's overt efforts to woo the private sector produced concrete results. Public investment soared, and so did private investment.[63]

The most critical variable in what happened economically and politically after 1976 was the rapid increase in oil production. Initially, López Portillo restrained himself from using oil resources to finance Mexico's development. That restraint was short-lived. As late as 1974, Mexico actually imported petroleum, but by 1978, petroleum accounted for one-third of all exports; by 1980, 66 percent; and at the beginning of 1981, 74 percent.[64] Public-sector growth expanded at a dizzying rate. Instead of relying on his newly formed alliance with the private sector to achieve economic growth, the president resorted to international borrowing and deficit spending. Not only did the public debt soar, but the private sector's own debt doubled from 1977 to 1980.[65]

The private sector, however, paid a price for its cooperation with the government. López Portillo sought, and successfully obtained, an entente with the more progressive sectors of the private domestic and foreign business communities. His initial success, combined with the extraordinary increase in oil revenues, revived internal unity within the Mexican state. On the other hand, divisions within the private sector grew sharper, and disagreements among various factions were publicly visible.[66]

One of the issues that provoked disagreement was to what extent and in what manner the private sector should cooperate with the state. López Portillo encouraged this debate with the introduction of electoral reforms in 1977. Essentially, the reform was designed to help legitimize his administration and the state itself by allowing smaller opposition groups to qualify for national elections. As Wayne Cornelius notes, the number of parties increased, and seven of them actually fielded presidential candidates. Voter abstention declined markedly.[67]

Political liberalization directly affected private sector-state relations. López Portillo's philosophy of expanding the opposition, particularly leftist parties, encouraged activist entrepreneurs to explore increased participation in the electoral arena. In the middle of his administration, certain businessmen seriously considered founding a new political party.[68] In effect, he opened up the political arena to more groups, heightened the ideological debate between left and right, and made entrepreneurs more aware of the importance of electoral political participation.

In terms of access to the decisionmaking process, the private sector, especially during the initial years of the López Portillo administration, gave him high marks. He intended to take Mexico into the General Agreement on Trade and Tariffs in 1979, but was dissuaded from doing so by opposing groups in the private sector. According to one expert, "the policy process in the GATT decision, including the national debate, showed that at times elite groups enjoy a substantial degree of autonomy vis-à-vis the state."[69]

After 1979 the quality of the private sector-state relationship declined rapidly, finally breaking down seriously with the president's decision to nationalize the banking industry. The nationalization and its consequences are analyzed in detail later, but as an event in the broad historical sweep of the relations between the two sectors, it is critical. Nationalization changed the economic, and therefore political, balance of power between the two sectors. The rapid growth of state-controlled enterprises, from 84 in 1970 to 760 in 1982, reflected public-sector expansion.[70] Complemented by the nationalization, the state becomes the virtual rector of the Mexican economy, relegating the private sector to a secondary role.

In 1982, when Miguel de la Madrid took office, conditions in Mexico were worse than at any point in recent history. The characteristics of the economic crisis are well known. Not only did the president face an economic challenge that seemed to many almost insurmountable, but the state's political power was at its lowest ebb. Thus, having very little political legitimacy, he was faced with restoring the economy's health, reestablishing private-sector confidence, and unifying the political leadership. Just two months after he took office, Emilio Goicochea Luna, president of the National Chamber of Commerce (Concanaco), would declare, "never before has the private sector had such difficulties communicating with the government."[71]

De la Madrid recognized the immensity of the problem, and the need to restore favorable relations with the private sector. He personally believed that the nationalization had destroyed the equilibrium between the private sector and the state.[72] In the first three years of his administration he repeated the conciliatory efforts of his predecessor, particularly in 1983. Again, the presidential style, public posture, rhetoric, and intent weighed heavily on the system. One of Mexico's leading industrialists asserted this fact nine months into de la Madrid's administration:

> Psychologically, in the last six months, the government has accomplished a tremendous amount, but concretely not very much. But of course his psychological achievement is a big one. His posture is positive and people can understand this. We are optimistic in the long run, and tolerant in the short run. And remember, the responsibility for achieving this economic recovery is not 100 percent the government's, rather it is ours and the people of Mexico.[73]

What de la Madrid achieved best was improved channels for communication. Even regional business groups sensed this change immediately following the presidential succession. As a leader of the state of México stated, "I have no problem communicating our ideas to the government. We have more opportunities in 1983 to do this than we ever had before."[74]

Improved communication and a positive tone alone were not sufficient to restore the traditional balance in the relationship between the private and public sectors. The structural conditions of the larger economic and political environment were so altered from previous decades that de la Madrid had an impossible task. Moreover, structural characteristics within the state and the business community were altered equally. The two were in such flux, structurally, that fluctuations in the influences of opposing groups—the pro- and antipopulist groups within the state, and political activists and nonactivists within the private sector—were bound to damage their relationship.

The broader outlines of the private sector's relationship with the state under de la Madrid are fleshed out in considerable detail throughout the remainder of this book, especially in the last chapter. To highlight briefly several policy orientations he initiated, and their consequences for business-state relations in the larger historical context is helpful here.

De la Madrid, like his predecessor, continued the policy of political liberalization. During important municipal elections in 1983, the Institutional Revolutionary party (PRI) actually allowed opposition party victories in several state capitals and the important border city of Ciudad Juárez. The party that gained most from the electoral results was the National Action party (PAN).[75] But as in the past, local political leaders, opposed to the liberalization policies imposed from Mexico City, abruptly put a stop to the reforms. Although opposition victories were no longer recognized after 1983—in fact, vote tallies were blatantly altered in 1985 and 1986—opposition leaders received a taste of their potential level of support. Businessmen sympathetic to the goals of PAN were not blind to the power of the average Mexican voter. Increasingly, as de la Madrid's administration continued, a vociferous minority began to view electoral opposition as a useful tool to pressure the government and ultimately to change the balance of power between the state and the private sector. The environment introduced by de la Madrid culminated in a competition for the leadership of PAN, and the victory of Manuel J. Clouthier, former president of Coparmex (Employers' Federation of Mexico) and the Coordinating Council of Businessmen, as the Panista presidential candidate in 1988.

The consequences of political liberalization went beyond the electoral arena. De la Madrid's response to public criticism was more open than his predecessor's, encouraging a plethora of critical editorials and articles in the mass media. Among the leading critics, often quoted in the media, were the leaders of various industrial and entrepreneurial interest organizations. Both quantitatively and qualitatively, the depth and range of business criticism grew. Groups like Coparmex had always been openly critical, but in 1983, semiofficial industrial organizations such as Concanaco organized a conference to protest both the nationalization of the banks and the exchange controls. The PRI actually ran advertisements in the media to defend their position against published private-sector criticism emanating from this conference. The official party actually claimed that these interest groups were not political institutions, nor were they appropriate channels for the expression of ideological positions.[76]

On an economic plane, de la Madrid also emphasized a number of programs encouraging reprivatization and/or liberalization of the economy. As his administration continued, the policies were inconsistent. He started off his presidency with a fairly orthodox austerity program in 1983 and 1984, but by the end of 1984, he felt pressured to pursue a policy of deficit spending.[77] Although his administration's message to the private sector has been mixed, the overall philosophy of economic liberalization was visibly symbolized by Mexico's policy reversal in 1985 when it decided to reopen negotiations to join GATT.

It is too early to evaluate the long-term impact of economic liberalization on private sector–state relations. Nevertheless, it is clear that liberalization has neither led to private-sector satisfaction with the government nor contributed to increased unity within that sector.[78] If anything, liberalization heightened the debate within the private sector, between those elements who believe Mexican economic competitiveness internationally is essential to future economic expansion, and those who favor continued state protection.

It can be argued that the pursuit of a mixed economic program that leans toward a larger private-sector role sends two psychological messages to the business community: first, that public-sector elites under de la Madrid, while not in agreement, believe the private sector must play the key role in economic revival, suggesting their own devaluation of the state's economic potential.[79] Second, although objective economic conditions such as lower inflation, fewer bureaucratic requirements, and cheaper credit have not been present, de la Madrid's administration has conveyed its confidence to entrepreneurs, boosting their morale at a time following the bank nationalization, when it has been at a low point in its history.

Conclusions

This brief historical outline paints only the broadest strokes in the complex picture of the private sector-state relationship in Mexico. This chapter cannot provide original data on the historical pattern, since that would necessarily be a book-length study. Instead, this sketch suggests that certain outlines of the relationship have been longstanding, unaltered by the passage of time.

An important feature, found elsewhere in the Western world, characterizes the prerevolutionary relationship between the state and the private sector: the interchangeability between political and economic leaders. The level of the exchange in Mexico is small compared to the United States, where an artificial separation between political and economic leadership exists at the local and national levels. The breadth of Mexico's leadership exchange is further limited by the fact that many individuals moving between political and economic careers are from the same extended family, tied by kinship relations.

The Revolution was essential to the private-public sector relationship in several ways. First and foremost, it affected the proximity of the economic and the political leaderships to each other, not only by substantially lessening the pool of economic elites holding national political office, but more importantly, by attaching a negative connotation to the exchange, from the point of view of both the public and the private sectors. In the postrevolutionary period, some of the outstanding builders of the private sector reaped their original fortunes in public life, but they were exceptional, as were their private-sector peers willing to contribute to national political leadership. The 1920s, therefore, sets the tone of the relationship between the Mexican business and political worlds. They are to be complementary, formally friendly, and collaborative in their relationship, but not essentially interchangeable in their values.

The Revolution set the tone also for these separate values. Mexico's political leadership emerged from the violent phase imprinted, by the Revolution and the provisions of the 1917 Constitution, with a populist streak. Politicians are not anticapitalist, for as the narrative suggests, they generally follow orthodox economic behavior typical of their contemporaries. But publicly they must polish their populist credentials, and one method for accomplishing this goal is to distance themselves, formally, from the private sector. This was accomplished by a twofold pattern. First, businessmen were not recruited into Mexican political leadership, which, if possible, flaunted its popular origins, even if after 1920 most politicians were actually middle class and urban. Second, they denied businessmen any formal relationship with the evolving political institutions of the regime, notably the official party.

In the 1930s, the state made an important concession in its relationship to the private sector, deciding that businesspeople must be incorporated, like other groups (except church officials) in quasi-official organizations. This decision was important for several reasons. Because the private sector was provided with, indeed required to participate through, formal channels for communicating with the state, its own independent organizations were slow to emerge. These voluntary organizations, such as Coparmex, seemed politically and economically redundant to many entrepreneurs. The private sector also found itself in the company of other important groups, in that its structural and institutional characteristics as a major interest-group actor were crafted by the state.

As Mexico faced World War II the outlines of the private-public relationship were well established. They included an artificial separation between the leaderships of the two sectors; a public, rhetorical posture on the part of the state downplaying the private sector's importance; a growing separation of the two sectors' values; a big-brother pattern, with the state as mentor to the private sector; a state divided between pro- and antipopulist factions whose attitudes to the private sector differed; and an economic situation in which the entrepreneurs were an incipient force.

From the 1940s through the 1960s these basic characteristics of the relationship remained largely unchanged. The one condition that began to alter the pattern was the increasing economic strength of the private sector. After 1968, however, the state's political legitimacy itself came into question. Political legitimacy became the overriding variable, fueling the battle for power between the antipopulist and populist forces within the state.

Each time the populist faction won out in these internal squabbles, it engineered decisions, such as the 1982 nationalization, that further alienated the private sector. The outlines of the relationship as sketched in the 1920s no longer were applicable in the 1980s, and even if both parties wished to restore the ambience of their earlier pattern, changed conditions made that impossible.

The state under de la Madrid reasserted itself as the orchestrator and director of Mexico's development.[80] In this sense, it wished to continue its traditional role as senior partner to the private sector. Whereas the state had greater control over the economy than at any point in the twentieth century, its political legitimacy was at its weakest point in fifty years. Thus, the state was more dependent on the cooperation of the private sector for its own legitimacy (as reflected in its ability to stimulate economic growth) than at any previous time. The state's dilemma was how to relate to the private sector while best increasing its own legitimacy.[81]

The irony for the Mexican state is that it has nurtured a private sector that no longer is a weak sister—it is much better organized today than when the original rules of the political game were formulated in the 1920s and 1930s. Private-sector leadership is divided into various factions. It no longer speaks with a united voice, thus complicating the nature of the relationship. Finally, the seeds of separating the private sector from the state—delegitimizing entrepreneurs by excluding them from overt political participation—have borne fruit, but not what the original political leadership envisioned. Whereas the politicians may have benefited initially from a weak private-sector image, they now suffer from the lack of a shared value consensus that resulted from that separation. As one regional business leader exclaimed, "government officials who run these agencies and business leaders should have much more direct exposure to or experience with one another. We need to have many more people in government who have some knowledge and experience in the private sector."[82]

3

The Mexican Entrepreneur

Most studies of economic development in Mexico, in examining government decisionmaking and its role in economic growth, have ignored the entrepreneur completely. It is valuable to explore the entrepreneurs themselves because of what is revealed about their role, self-image, and attitudes toward political life. Because entrepreneurs have contributed to the evolution of new cultural values and the modernization of structures essential to economic and political development, a more complete picture of businesspeople is helpful in assessing their impact on social change.[1]

Entrepreneurs' Role

Students of entrepreneurship are divided as to whether only organizations or individuals share its qualities. We commonly think of an individual entrepreneur as someone who competes, leads, innovates, and take risks.[2] But theorists argue that in the United States, the individual businessperson's entrepreneurial spirit is insignificant. Hugh Aitkens explains why:

> The term "entrepreneurship" refers to a kind of behavior which is characteristic of certain organized associations of individuals (usually business firms). It is only in highly exceptional cases that the presence of this characteristic can be imputed to the actions of personalities of single individuals. The general rule is that it is the *association*, not the individual, that exhibits entrepreneurship.[3]

Aitkens' interpretation fits contemporary industrialized economies well, but how accurately does it describe Mexico? He admits that typical characteristics of entrepreneurship differ in other cultures.[4]

One important conclusion of this study is that public, corporate ownership is a long way from dominating Mexican business. This economic fact of life, alone, gives the individual entrepreneur exaggerated importance in Mexico's economic decisionmaking. Family control over the business world alters the goals and therefore the very definition of a successful entrepreneur. In countries like Mexico, a businessman tends to "consider business not as an impersonal activity of 'economic man' directed at maximization of profit but as an extension of his family's drive for social status."[5]

A further distinction, extrapolated from general cultural differences between Mexico and Western industrialized nations, is that Mexican entrepreneurs' attitudes toward the state are the very core of their self-definition. History provides an important explanation of why North American and Mexican entrepreneurs' views of the state do not coincide. Mexico did not have a genuine entrepreneurial class until well after the 1910 Revolution, nor did Mexican labor share a strong class consciousness until the 1920s. In the United States and Europe these two groups grew on their own initiative, whereas in Mexico the state played a leading role in their formation.

A firm's history may illustrate North American entrepreneurship better than an individual businessman's biography, but a collective portrait of select Mexican businessmen says more about business values there than would knowledge of several firms. Such a portrait suggests that Mexicans see themselves as competitive, innovative risk-takers, lacking in future orientation. As one long-time accountant noted, "a typical Mexican attitude is to work for today."[6]

An effective way to define the Mexican entrepreneur is to ask representatives of the business community to describe their own role. They repeatedly name three roles. First, as one prominent business leader argued, that "the private sector should provide employment, that is their foremost activity."[7] Second is the accumulation of resources or, as simply put by some, earning money. The third definition is more sophisticated, introducing some ethical concerns: the entrepreneur has a responsibility to produce a quality product and to see to the welfare of employees. Rómulo O'Farrill, president of the largest television chain in Latin America, identified fundamental goals for the Mexican businessman: "First, he has to make sure what he produces is of good quality and can be sold at a competitive cost. Secondly, when he takes control of a company he also assumes responsibility for the relationship between the employees and the employer as well as employment."[8]

No leading entrepreneurs interviewed contradicted the idea that they should acquire resources and create employment. The most critical characteristic for understanding the relationship between the state and the private sector, however, is businessmen's view of their larger environment and the role they should play there. Entrepreneurs' opinions on this differ substantially, suggesting a decisive division. Two opposing interpretations have been clearly expressed. The minority view is argued by Jorge Sánchez Mejorada, past president of the powerful Coordinating Council of Entrepreneurs: "Regardless of what businessmen are attempting to do they should never forget that other social problems exist, because entrepreneurs need to understand in Mexico, as elsewhere in the world, that they are living inside a society which exists around them and they cannot operate in a vacuum."[9]

Such an attitude seems logical and sophisticated. But the older generation, those who still dominate private-sector decisionmaking, do not share Sánchez Mejorada's interpretation. These Mexican businessmen do not concern themselves with a sense of social consciousness, nor do they believe that it is an entrepreneur's valid role. Gabriel Alarcón, founder of one of Mexico's largest newspaper firms, is an unreserved advocate of the traditional view. "I think the function of the Mexican entrepreneur very simply is to create employment and earn money. This is his role, his role is not to be involved in politics. . . . The politicians should run the government and we should run the private sector."[10]

Mexican entrepreneurs do not provide a homogeneous self-portrait on their social role or mission. Like the public sector's, the private sector's composition is not monolithic. The reasons why entrepreneurs see themselves differently, and consequently see their relationship with the public sector from differing points of view, stem from their entrepreneurial function, their size, their place of residence, and possibly their economic activity.

The single most decisive division within Mexico's private-sector leadership stems from the individual entrepreneur's task—as manager or capitalist. It has been argued that as economies develop, professional managers replace the possessor of capital in key positions.[11] It has been suggested, however, that the views of capitalists versus administrators differ widely. Federico Ortiz Alvarez, a career employee who attained the presidency of the Celanese Corporation, explains.

I think in a sense that the difference between being an owner and a professional administrator is that the latter will work for a firm regardless of who the owners are. They see the firm as a means of redistributing wealth as well as creating it. I believe this is the mission of a responsible administrator. It is important to have a social mission, to distribute wealth as well as generate it.[12]

If most Mexican administrators are concerned with a social mission, their potential conflicts with the state increase, since the mission requires them to consider more carefully the state's role in the distribution of wealth and, consequently, their relationship to the state in pursuit of this goal. Some observers believe that the most successful Mexican entrepreneurs are those who recognize the importance of external, social and political forces, and try to manipulate them.[13]

Other Mexicans believe that size of firm affects entrepreneurs' social attitudes, and consequently their views of the state. As the chief counsel for Latin America's largest industrial firm suggested, "the small entrepreneur does not see the government as a competitor, although they have complaints about the government's behavior. The large entrepreneur, on the other hand (and there are two types, one which sees a mission in their country, and the other one which does not have a concept of a social mission) has a different attitude."[14]

One of the difficulties of making generalizations about Mexico's private sector is that it does not share the degree of centralization that characterizes national political leadership. In certain regions, business communities have evolved under special historical conditions, including distinct local attitudes toward the government. A business leader of the state of México believes that "the conception of the people of the state of México about the role of the government is quite different from that in Guadalajara or Monterrey. I think it has to do with the people here and their proximity to the Federal District. . . . The cooperation between the industrialists and the government is quite good, but it is unique to the state of México."[15]

Among industrialists, geography plays a divisive role. Derossi believes, for example, that proximity to Mexico City is an important determinant of private-sector behavior and attitudes toward government. She divides industrialists into three groups. The first, the central, dependent group, located around Mexico City, relies heavily on government support, resulting in a dependent relationship with the state. A certain love-hate attitude between the public and private sectors emerges as a consequence. Derossi's second group of industrialists, including the Monterrey Group, reside in outlying regions and are independent of Mexico City. Her third group reside away from Mexico City, but are economically weak and dependent on the government.[16]

It has been suggested that entrepreneurs' economic activities affect their attitudes. Again, information is available for industrialists only. Dale Story found that three-fourths of the industrialists interviewed exhibited a strong sectoral consciousness.[17] No indication exists that entrepreneurs in retailing versus those in manufacturing, for example, have differing views on the issue of a social mission. My own interviews demonstrate, however, that attitudes toward the state might well be affected by the economic activity of the individual entrepreneur. Before 1982, bankers experienced the closest relationship to the state, so it is likely that their attitude toward the government differed from colleagues in other economic sectors. The consequences of this special relationship will be developed in a later chapter.

Entrepreneurs' Self-Image

The nature of self-image, another aspect of portraits of leading businessmen, is equally important. Their positive or negative feelings about their occupation affects their relations with other societal groups. Several authors have cited studies to support the view that Mexican businessmen feel comfortable in their society and good about themselves. Derossi argued that because Mexican society placed such emphasis on economic development as a fundamental national goal, entrepreneurs believed themselves to be making important contributions to development.[18]

Surprisingly, the overwhelming conclusion from my interviews is that businesspeople believe that other Mexicans view them with disdain, and consequently they suffer from a poor self-image. This self-image consists of several components. According to one scholar, the persistence of inequalities in Mexico's development is blamed on *malos mexicanos* (bad Mexicans), usually members of the private sector.[19] No better example exists of this interpretation than the blame José López Portillo placed on the banking community in his 1982 State of the Union address announcing their nationalization. One Mexican businessman comments:

> When we talk about the private sector in Mexico many people use terms related to business, businessmen, and entrepreneurs in a pejorative sense. For example, did you see the article today in the paper quoting the former president in a forthcoming interview blaming the private sector for all of his problems. I think this is ridiculous.[20]

Still another source of negativism is the sense of inferiority many Mexican businessmen share toward foreign firms' export capacity and technological quality.[21] As one expert concluded, their inferiority is psychological, not economic or technological.[22]

Intellectuals are one group whose view of entrepreneurs contributes most persuasively to their negative self-image. Intellectuals exert considerable influence because their evaluations pervade Mexican mass media and higher education. The Mexican intellectual's view of businessmen as ruthless, money-grubbing opportunists is critical.

> This viewpoint is of considerable importance, not because it invariably corresponds with the facts, but because it is so widely believed, particularly by the literate and educated intellectuals of Mexico. This simple and pervasive image painted by the Mexican intellectual conditions the strategies which the business groups feel obliged to use in dealing with the government, and it conditions the public responses which the government feels obliged to make to any overtures by the group. Though the image does not prevent the Mexican government from dealing intimately and continually with individual leaders of the business world, it does require that government negotiations with the business class as a whole should be publicly cloaked with a certain reserve.[23]

A pervasive, negative image of businesspeople conditions not only the actions of entrepreneurs—and even government officials—but, equally important, the entrepreneurs' self-image. They perceive that the public's view is negative.

How did the Mexican public obtain such a negative impression of the private sector? One astute entrepreneur believes that

> in general, they think we are opportunists because unfortunately the private sector has never defended itself in an institutional way, by emphasizing the value of commerce and industry in Mexico. Whenever a problem occurs we are the ones who are blamed for it. After many years of criticism, the average Mexican now has a very unfavorable opinion of the private sector. We should fund a constructive campaign to promote the good qualities of the private sector.[24]

Another prominent businessman, a former director of the National Chamber of Commerce, known for his outspoken criticisms of government policy and the government's posture toward business, suggested a different but complementary explanation. His thesis is that when entrepreneurs defend free enterprise in Mexico, they often must attack the government. Thus, it can be said that the concept of free enterprise itself really does not have a negative image, but rather that the process of defending it has made private initiative a bad word to the average Mexican.[25] When stated this way, the significance of the historic role of the state becomes apparent. In other words, if the state's role had never loomed large in Mexico's economic development, the private sector would not find itself confronting the government every time it defended its own actions.

Some individuals view Mexican entrepreneurs unfavorably because of their arrogant relations with government officials. Immediately following the revolutionary years, some Mexican entrepreneurs thought many government leaders were uncultured. Believing them incompetent, prominent entrepreneurs delegated their negotiations with politicians to lower-level employees. Politicians have not viewed entrepreneurs in a favorable light because entrepreneurs expressed their distrust of them in an open and direct fashion. This attitude is illustrated in a revealing anecdote from Eduardo Bustamante.

> When I was in public life, I had a very interesting experience with the Fundidora of Monterrey. For years this business maintained a monopoly over the steel industry. . . . The government eventually started Altos Hornos, and later helped the Peña Colorado Mining Company in the state of Colima begin operation of a steel mill. The Monterrey Group wanted to buy Altos Hornos. Eugenio Garza Sada asked me, as the minister in charge of government-owned enterprises, if I would sell. I said absolutely not because we needed competition. Instead, I offered him the opportunity to become the second largest stockholder in the new Peña Colorado operation. He replied very arrogantly that they were not interested. When I asked him why, he brusquely told me that they did not trust the government. I was insulted by his remarks.[26]

Values of Entrepreneurs

The entrepreneurs' self-definition has revealed some significant characteristics of how they define their role and the breadth of acceptable functions. Since a special concern here is the relationship between the private and public sectors, it is useful to examine the attitudes of the business community, and to a lesser extent the political leadership, toward three major concerns: to what extent are social responsibilities an appropriate concern of business; to what degree should the government participate in economic life; and to what level should the political participation of business increase.

One issue that has sparked constant controversy in Mexico is the degree to which the political and economic leadership is homogeneous. Normally this debate centers on the interchangeability of leaders between both groups. Yet another important measure of homogeneity is the consensus which exists between these groups' values. Two decades ago, Robert Scott was struck by the growing degree of consensus in the key values of the political and nonpolitical elites.[27] This consensus, combined with the shared values of three generations of politicians, are crucial to understanding Mexican political stability.[28] Scott made these observations, however, at the high point of Mexico's economic growth, before the intellectual disenchantment in the post-1968 era.

Business leaders seem to agree that before the 1970s, the private sector showed no interest in social issues. According to Emilio Goicochea Luna, businesspeople were only interested in producing more goods.[29] Another entrepreneur bluntly states that there "is going to be a revolution, but it will not be of a violent kind, rather it will take place in the thinking of the entrepreneurs. They will start to develop a North American attitude toward economic growth. We run a grave risk that the social interests will be ignored, and this will cause serious problems. In my opinion both the middle and small companies need to become socially conscious."[30]

The Mexican who has most frequently articulated this view is José María Basagoiti, an entrepreneur who represented the Mexican Employers Association, the most vociferous proponent of the private sector's increased social role. In a very emotional fashion, he described his vision of unrealistic Mexican entrepreneurs with their heads in the clouds. He labeled them impractical. His major thesis is that businessmen do not understand what is happening in Mexico because they do not comprehend the present social and political realities.[31]

His views are important for several reasons. In the first place, he and the organization he represents have come into conflict with the state. The state is not opposed to socially responsible entrepreneurs, but is afraid of the methods Basagoiti and others use to involve the private sector in social issues. Secondly, attempts to redefine the entrepreneurs' role increases tensions between the public and private sectors. Finally, his view suggests that Mexican businessmen's self-image is in flux, and that conflicts exist within the private sector. These inner tensions complicate relations between the private and public sectors, making politicians' assessment of entrepreneurial attitudes difficult.

Social responsibility can be such a key entrepreneurial value in a businessperson's self-definition and relationship with other important actors, that it is worth examining why this concept traditionally lies outside Mexican entrepreneurs' roles. One reason social responsibility takes a back seat to the traditional concepts of what a successful entrepreneur should be is that businessmen have not valued a knowledge of general socioeconomic conditions. The fifteen top reasons for entrepreneurial success given by Mexican entrepreneurs include only pragmatic management skills. General knowledge of the larger Mexican environment placed a poor sixteenth on their list.[32] "A famous author once made a statement which applied very well to the situation in Mexico, and that is that many of these people do not really have a nationality, that is they aren't really Mexicans, they are strangers in their own country. They essentially lack a sense of social responsibility."[33]

Another factor is that Mexican entrepreneurs conceptualize social responsibility in very narrow terms. Latin American business leaders tend to interpret social responsibility as medical and welfare facilities for their own workers.[34] They combine this view with their general hostility toward public-sector actions in the economy, seeing social responsibility as a strategy to combat the influence of the government.[35] A businessman who truly includes social responsibility in his self-definition is expressing a profound change in attitude about the overall purpose of private enterprise in society.

Finally, it has been suggested that businessmen with a sense of social responsibility are limited by their resources. As one entrepreneur suggested, "large enterprises have the luxury of having a social mission, but it isn't fair to criticize the medium-sized and small company owners for their lack of social concern. They are too preoccupied with earning a living and obtaining capital for their firm's growth. You never think of the larger picture until you yourself are in better circumstances."[36]

Of course, businessmen's denial of social responsibility is not the only explanation for their attitudes toward the state. It is necessary to examine how entrepreneurs and politicians see each other, their role in society, and the expansion of political participation. Mexican businessmen's views of the state in the 1980s can be summarized in one word: distrust.

It may well be that the entire decade of the 1980s will be characterized by economic conditions conducive to distrust. But historically such conditions are temporary. They do not explain the underlying causes for distrust, or the long-term tensions in the relationship between the private and public sectors. In addition to blaming the government each time the economy takes a turn for the worse, businessmen share a longstanding view of Mexico's government as dishonest and incompetent. As one Mexican suggested, "all of my friends and contacts, whether they are entrepreneurs themselves, or corporate lawyers and accountants, are critical of the government. They dislike the corruption, the inefficiency and the ineptness of the government."[37] Examples of these criticisms are legion, but underlying them is a more basic image businessmen have of government officials, stereotyping them as lazy and overpaid.[38] This prejudicial image makes it difficult to consider the state objectively.

The negative image government officials conjure up in the minds of businessmen has been around for decades. In the 1960s Derossi was quite surprised that Mexican industrialists gave politicians low ratings in prestige and in power. It is understandable that they could deny politicians prestige; how they could deny politicians' exercise of power is more difficult to explain. Derossi speculated that industrialists psychologically refused to recognize the power of their most important antagonist because politicians controlled them.[39]

After many interviews with Mexican entrepreneurs I realized that Derossi's speculation has a solid basis in the attitudes of certain businessmen. Many have a knowledge of their relationship to the government and think about the issues involved, but many others profess ignorance, among them some of Mexico's leading business figures. These same entrepreneurs were not shy or ashamed about expressing their unconcern. For example, Max Michel Suberville, chairman of the board of one of Mexico's most important retail chains, frankly admitted, "I am ignorant of the effect which the private sector has on government policy. I don't really know anything about it, it's not something that I think is important."[40]

Some of the difficulties between the private and public sectors can be explained by businessmen's ignorance. On the other hand, specific differences in important values may be equally important, especially if both parties are operating on a different wavelength. Perceptive entrepreneurs provided an insightful critique of two essential, interrelated values, liberty and the role of the individual. The Mexican entrepreneur's view of liberty has been best expressed in this statement:

> The trouble with the private sector is that they love their liberty, . . . but they don't understand the difference between their liberty and society's liberty. They will do anything to defend their own liberty as a group, but not society's liberty. This is incomprehensible. . . . The problem therefore is that the private sector's definition of liberty is not well defined within the general terms of liberty.[41]

This distinction stems from the historical relationships between vested interest groups and the state. These groups desired special privileges for themselves, unshared by society. In the nineteenth century, maintenance of these privileges led to bloodshed and civil war, when the state attempted to reduce the prerogatives of the Catholic Church. Since the 1940s, the business community has had an inherited concept of group versus societal liberty advocated for centuries by religious, military, and mercantile interests in Mexico. This inherited value system stands in the way of discussions among Mexicans. As one businessman explained, when entrepreneurs and politicians "become serious about a particular issue, there is a major distinction between the emphasis each of us gives to the importance of the individual versus the importance of society as a whole."[42]

Another important value that comes between the private and public leaderships is the extent to which the Mexican government has become involved in economic life. For one group of entrepreneurs the suspicion exists that the government is moving strongly in the direction of a socialist state. They even believe this tendency is part of the international socialist movement.[43] This view is most widely shared by a group of businessmen affiliated with the Mexican Employers Association. Their suspicions of state economic policies were reinforced by the 1982 nationalization of the banks. While this interpretation is important, it does not yet reflect the majority opinion among the business community.

Most leading entrepreneurs accept the fact that Mexico has a mixed economic system that has formed the basis for the informal coalition between the business community and the state.[44] Even in the 1980s, most businessmen still favor a substantial government role. As one company president argued, "a mixed economic system is legitimate and appropriate for Mexico. It is necessary . . . to bring development to my country. . . . We require help from the government or we cannot develop."[45]

Some entrepreneurs favor a mixed economy because they are financially dependent on the state. Their view is somewhat analogous to those United States firms who would like to see less government control, but yell loudly if the government removes a subsidy to them. A Mexican government official suggested that many businessmen believe it advantageous to have the government own stock in their firm.[46]

Most Mexican businessmen accept the de facto role of the state in the economy but are critical of government intervention. Dale Story, in his study of industrialists, concluded that four-fifths of them were critical of state intervention, especially nationalization of private firms.[47] In general, Mexican businessmen give two reasons against state intervention: it is excessive, and it competes unfairly with the private sector. A common example cited by entrepreneurs was Conasupo, the government's agency that subsidizes and sells basic foodstuffs. As Jorge Sánchez Mejorada explained to me, "one of the reasons why the private sector is very antagonized by Conasupo is that its retail stores do not pay taxes. This is unfair competition in the private sector's opinion. . . . For the most part, no one in the private sector objects to its regulatory role. What they object to is the fact that Conasupo owns many businesses selling in the retail market."[48]

The other attitude that most affects the relationship between the private and public sectors is how businessmen interpret the expansion of political participation and their role in it. John Womack, Jr. could say at the beginning of the 1970s that entrepreneurs strongly supported the concept of a "licensed democracy," characterized by constrained debate of the issues, limited criticism of the country's development policies, and safe political contests.[49] In other words, they were willing to restrain their own criticisms and support a system that in turn put a lid on other actors, such as organized labor, who would create obstacles to their vision of how Mexico should develop.

Historically, Mexican businessmen have not participated actively in political life. In her survey of industrialists in the 1960s, Derossi reported that only 6 percent belonged to a political party, and only 10 percent claimed membership in political organizations.[50] In the 1980s, in a poll taken by the Mexican government, 17 percent of the industrialists and 22 percent of the company presidents surveyed admitted membership in a political party. Of these, three-quarters were PRI members.[51] These figures compared favorably with some occupations, but on average, 30 percent of all Mexican occupational groups claimed party membership. Thus it is fair to conclude that not only have prominent businessmen traditionally been underinvolved in politics as measured by party membership, but they have lagged substantially behind other groups.

Entrepreneurs have not participated overtly in politics for many reasons. In the first place, it can be argued that active participation was unnecessary because of the overall economic policy direction taken by the government since 1946. Second, because the government organized business into formal chambers with direct access to the executive branch, participation was redundant. Third, their relationship with political leaders might well be enhanced by less rather than greater visibility, an interpretation with considerable merit.[52] Fourth, some businessmen who might be interested in political life claim they cannot afford to take the time to participate.[53] Fifth, Mexican entrepreneurs have traditionally used intermediaries, such as individual politicians or political groups and movements, as primary vehicles for political action rather than involving themselves personally.[54] And some businessmen, who can be described as idealists, take the extreme view that everything about the government is negative.

Businessmen can be divided into several groups on the basis of their views of political participation. There are those who believe that they should not be further involved in politics. In the 1970s, one of the leading figures who campaigned against the traditional attitudes of entrepreneurs denounced them as committing class suicide.[55] Michel Suberville articulated this lack of interest well when he stated, "I believe that we have enough contact with the government, but I don't think that this is really very important as we function in our way and they function in theirs. We don't really want to be involved in politics."[56]

A second group believes greater participation is necessary. One businessman comments, "A tendency exists today that the private sector should participate more heavily in politics. Even though we are professional businessmen and not really politicians, this tendency is real. These individuals are looking for a greater role for the private sector. However, I believe it is only a tendency, . . . and that the current system is adequate for our development."[57] Among those who favor increased participation, the basic issue is whether to influence the government from within, or to change or replace it from the outside.[58] The majority of my interviewees who favored increased participation believe it should be carried out within the present governmental framework. A Mexican analyst suggests that some of the larger industrial groups and banks (before nationalization) located in Mexico City favor this more conciliatory view.[59]

Some entrepreneurs believe that everyone should participate in politics, but as individuals, not as business organizations. Guillermo Cantú, director general of La Comercial Insurance Company, gave a rationale for this view: "Mexico has never had a clear identity. We also did not have a clear political identity after independence. The only way to improve and change this lack of identity was to have become more monolithic politically in order to preserve what identity we have. I do not believe we [business groups] should be involved politically ourselves to preserve this identity."[60]

Other businessmen who favor participation advocate another view. Although a minority, they are quite vocal in expressing their position and quite visible in their activities. These leaders support an increase in the number and influence of business interest groups. In the 1985 elections they financed candidates from the largest opposition party, the National Action Party (PAN), and some of their most articulate spokespersons ran for congress or governorships. Their most radical proposal, one having significant political consequences, favors the creation of a political party espousing a clear free-enterprise philosophy.[61]

Politicians' Values

Mexican entrepreneurs' views of the role of the state, the state's influence on economic development, and political participation shed much light on the nature of their relationship to the public sector. At the same time, we can obtain a more complete understanding if we consider politicians' views on these issues as well.

It is clear from dozens of interviews with Mexican political leaders that they favor a strong and well-defined role for the state in Mexican economic development. Although Mexican politicians are by no means unified in their views, which explains why government decisionmaking from time to time follows contradictory paths, a consensus is evident.[62] Contrary to some businessmen's fears, the majority of Mexico's political leadership has no intention of creating a socialist state. The philosophy that continues to dominate political thinking emerged most clearly under Miguel Alemán's administration in the late 1940s. Antonio Martínez Báez, his secretary of industry and commerce, objectively articulated the philosophy of this regime.

I believe that the Mexican Constitution provides considerable liberty for private industry, while at the same time allowing for equal freedom to eliminate the abuses of capitalism. Alemán operated within these constitutional provisions to create state intervention in the general interests of the people. The purpose of state intervention during this administration was not to benefit individual economic interests in the private enterprise sector. It is unjust to say that the Alemán regime had a philosophy of protecting capitalism and foreign investments to the detriment of the Mexican people. A more balanced analysis would reveal that the overall achievement of his administration was to prolong those legal regulations which confirmed a strong role for the government in the economy. This defined the legal position of the government vis-à-vis the private sector. Basically, the legal framework which defines this relationship has remained the same until today.[63]

Repeatedly, Mexican politicians have stated that they see the role of government as not the elimination of private property, but rather the maintenance of social equilibrium. If government exceeds this role, most Mexican politicians believe it will bring disequilibrium to the system, or confirm the worst fears of entrepreneurs, by becoming socialist. Other politicians use the provisions of the 1917 Constitution to rationalize their support for a mixed economy. Modern Mexican liberals think the state's role is to promote political stability and economic growth by using all available forces, private and public.[64] Mexican politicians believe that private initiative should be protected, and that the state should play a mediating role. A former cabinet member stressed that the role of the state as a stimulater of improved economic conditions should not disappear, but that the state must continue its role without becoming a dictator or absorbing the private sector.[65]

Leading politicians are severe critics of the system they represent. Rather than dwelling on corruption, perhaps out of self-interest, they focus their complaints on the inefficiency of a ballooning bureaucracy. Some even argue that a huge bureaucracy is worse than the evils inherent in capitalism because it absorbs power and can easily abuse its authority. They suggest that more sophisticated planning and more effective organization are the improvements most needed. Many think that government in the 1970s and 1980s has extended its control to too many industries for which it has no expertise. For example, a former secretary of government properties argued that "the government is not justified in intervening in an area in which private enterprise is failing, just to save jobs, because they don't have the expertise to operate such failing industries."[66]

In the 1980s the Mexican government legally and pragmatically altered its position in the Mexican economy. First, constitutional reforms were introduced that made the state the "rector" of the Mexican economy. Second, the 1982 bank nationalization initially placed 75 to 85 percent of the economic resources directly or indirectly in the hands of the government. As one public official admitted, these two actions have caused the public to believe that the private entrepreneur's activities are reduced and that the state is in control of the economy. From a political point of view, many consequences have occurred. Because the private sector criticized the government, the public began to think of entrepreneurs as reactionaries. Politicians publicly attacked them as unpatriotic, as bad nationalists, and worst of all, as anti-Mexican. Moreover, the government insinuated that they are tied to the Catholic Church, forming an alliance between reactionary interests.[67] Officials created an imbalance in the traditional alliance between the private and public sectors by publicly suggesting that the private sector had not carried out its part of the bargain.

On the issue of political participation, Mexican politicians again are divided, but a strong consensus emerges. The vast majority have a strong belief in increased participation and democracy. Their support for participation is qualified; they believe it requires a simultaneous increase in education, so that average Mexicans can exercise their responsibilities as well as their rights.[68]

Many politicians connect citizen responsibility with a belief that the present opposition parties do not have the capabilities to govern Mexico. President Miguel de la Madrid stated unequivocally in an interview that Mexico was not ready for a bipartisan or pluralistic political system in which the opposition would win. He argued that neither the Left nor the Right had the ability to govern Mexico, and that it was romantic to think these parties would be able to guide the country. Mexico was not ready, he implied, for the type of political system we have in the United States. Before this could occur, more time was needed for the people to be educated in civic responsibility. Therefore, while he believed in the right of the opposition to participate, and had consistently encouraged them to do so, he did not really believe that Mexico would have an opportunity to institutionalize a bipartisan system in the immediate future.[69]

Another fear political leaders express is that if the system is opened too quickly, political demagogues will abound. This may help to explain why Mexico's political leadership has not allowed the PRI to incorporate entrepreneurial groups.[70] However, a large number of prominent political leaders, while not referring to business specifically, believe that the government should propose a plan to encourage increased representation of various interest groups. Still others argue that the government should not make obstacles or difficulties an excuse for not expanding participation. If most politicians favor expanding participation, why have businesspeople been slow in responding to an increasingly favorable environment, and why have they been excluded from government plans? One explanation is that the private sector itself is afraid of increasing its participation overtly within the system for fear of losing its independence from the government. There is no question that the most powerful political rival to government in Mexico today is the private sector.[71] The further it incorporates itself into the governmental apparatus, the more dependent it becomes. This argument suggests independence is strength.

The public sector fears a strongly independent private sector operating in the political arena because that would throw other political actors off balance, making the state's mediating role increasingly difficult. Finally, some politicians find it difficult to encourage private-sector participation in opposition to the government because of a false but accepted understanding of what it means to be loyal to Mexico. In my study of intellectuals, I found that many government officials defined loyalty to Mexico as loyalty to the government or PRI. Even some entrepreneurs believe this.[72]

Conclusions

This chapter illustrates the importance of self-definition in the role entrepreneurs play in Mexican society. To understand clearly how any group defines itself, it is essential to comprehend how society as a whole views the group, since self-definition does not take place in a social vacuum. Certain historical characteristics come into play in the evolution and definition of entrepreneurial roles in the Mexican context.

The most important of these historical characteristics is the traditional role of the state in the economy, and state initiation of private-sector interest groups. Mexicans in general, and entrepreneurs especially, have been socialized in an ambience in which the state has intervened actively. Therefore, although typical tensions exist between the Mexican state and the private sector, acceptable boundaries for state intervention are more generous than in the United States.

Private-sector tolerance of state activity is only one consequence of Mexico's economic history. A second, and perhaps more important, factor is that the state helped to create and strengthen the private sector, by both pursuing an industrialization strategy and forming organizations representing the private sector. In effect, state initiation of national chambers representing business interests insured greater state control than might otherwise have been possible. However resentful the private sector might have been toward this mobilization and control of its interests, generations of Mexican businessmen have passed through an environment of private-sector dependence on government, symbolic and economic.

Within a larger historical framework, self-image and self-definition become important. If we accept the argument that the Mexican state functions as one of many autonomous political actors, then a positive self-image on the part of its most prominent competitor, the private sector, enhances entrepreneurs' potential political power. Yet, although some authors believe economic conditions have been ripe for a positive self-image, Mexican entrepreneurs have not seen themselves positively. Their belief that the average citizen thinks badly of the business community limits their effectiveness in seeking political allies. A negative self-image contributes to a lack of confidence, with the economic consequence of hesitancy to compete in the international market. Even more important is their belief that other political actors exert far more influence than they on the political process. For example, Mexican businessmen genuinely believe that organized labor has carried greater weight than business in the policy process, when all the evidence points to the contrary.

Individual values related to entrepreneurs' definition of the role they should play have a substantial impact on the private sector-state relationship. No single value attracts less consensus than entrepreneurs' views of their social responsibilities. They agree on the basic, traditional functions of the entrepreneur, but disagree on what a businessperson's larger societal role is. Several views exist, including the interpretations that nothing outside of business belongs in the purview of the businessperson; that businesspeople do have a social responsibility, only narrowly defined to include their own employees; and that Mexican society as a whole is the responsibility of the business community.

These differing views explain significant divisions within the business community. Such views are intertwined with entrepreneurs' interpretations of important values—most commonly their personal attitudes toward political participation, individual liberty, and the economic system. Political opponents have been able to exploit these divisions. The fact that businessmen's self-definition is in flux affects the very stability of the political system at a time when its political legitimacy is being challenged on many fronts.

Businessmen who believe that overt political activity is justified and necessary are altering the boundaries of Mexican political behavior. Their participation as allies of opposition parties, as candidates for political office, and as vociferous government critics in the media creates a new private-sector image. This has an educational impact on society's interpretation of the business community vis-à-vis the state. Finally, the degree to which the state accepts this new and antagonistic posture of the private sector may provoke a range of fresh responses from the government to the private sector and other political actors.

4

Entrepreneurial Origins

From the viewpoint of elite theory, one of the most interesting findings emerging from collective biographical materials are differences in the backgrounds of prominent entrepreneurs—compared to the general population and other peer groups—and the importance of their origins in explaining their behavior, achievements, and relationships to other groups.

I found three background variables to be strongly interrelated, together forming an environment through which the typical Mexican passes. Entrpreneurs are also affected by the impact of these three variables: place of birth; socioeconomic background of parents; and location, type, and level of education. Not only is the distribution of certain characteristics among successful entrepreneurs important for identifying some typical Mexican types, but the predominance of various patterns has a long-term impact on entrepreneurial recruitment, suggesting who will continue to dominate the business community.

Place of Birth

Traditionally, research has shown that elites, regardless of occupation, come from urban birthplaces in numbers disproportionate to the general population. Even in the United States, studies find that North American entrepreneurs have come from urban birthplaces in proportions above the national norm. For example, Suzanne Keller found that 26 percent of her 1950 cohort was much higher than the general population, of whom only 15 percent were of urban origin.[1] In Colombia, a predominantly rural society, and a country whose developmental pattern has more in common with Mexico, entrepreneurs were overwhelmingly from urban backgrounds.[2]

Mexican studies of businessmen confirm a similar pattern. For example, Raymond Vernon analyzed individuals comparable in age to the 1950 generation Keller examined and found that 79 percent of his sample claimed to have been born in large towns and cities at a time when three-quarters of the population was rural.[3] Flavia Derossi, who studied only Mexican industrialists in the early 1970s, concluded that 69 percent of her sample were natives of cities.[4]

My data, which cover prominent entrepreneurs from the 1920s through the mid-1980s, suggest two very important findings. First, Mexican entrepreneurs are definitely urban creatures; 85 percent of our total sample are from cities or towns of over 5,000 people. (MEBP) The fact that half of all prominent Mexican entrepreneurs were born before 1910, and the other half after 1910, a date when 71 percent of the population was living in communities with fewer than 2,500 people, suggests the exaggerated numbers of entrepreneurs, in inverse proportions to ordinary Mexicans, who came from urban locales. Second, a constant increase in urban birthplaces is apparent. Even of those born before 1880, 55 percent counted cities as their place of birth, and just a decade later, 72 percent did. These percentages continue to increase, reaching 96 percent among the 1920 and 1930 generations. Since 1940 no entrepreneur in my sample has emerged from a rural birthplace. (MEBP)

One important potential implication of this urbanization is for rural upward social mobility. The same pattern is true of politicians and cultural elites. The point is that regardless of generation, urban birthplaces among elites far exceed those of the general population. More importantly, few positions exist for the rural-born Mexican who desires to reach the pinnacle of private, public, or cultural power. Many Mexican theorists believe that lack of upward mobility in the political bureaucracy was a causal variable in the fall of the prerevolutionary government.

What these data suggest is that individuals from urban centers, per se, have much more access to leadership positions. More opportunities for the rural-born Mexican exist within the officer corps than among politicians, entrepreneurs, and intellectuals, but even this career is rapidly being closed off to younger aspirants. Since rural populations are not participating in the limited leadership positions, their lack of access is likely to distance them from their urban peers and to increase the potential for political instability.

An additional fact revealed in the birthplace data is that the majority of Mexican entrepreneurs in this century have always come from capital or foreign cities. On the average, nearly three-fourths of all entrepreneurs come from the political capitals of their respective states, fom Mexico City, or from a foreign city, generally Spanish. In reality, this specific type of urban background is even less representative of the general population, suggesting the homogeneity of the urban environment among Mexican politicians, intellectuals, and businessmen. The concentration of these groups in capital cities highlights the centralization of economic, intellectual, and political resources in a small number of Mexican urban centers.

Moving from size or type of city to regional location of birth, we find several interesting patterns. In the first place, 27 percent of Mexico's leading businessmen have been born in Mexico City. But this figure does not tell the whole story. Beginning with the group born during the 1890s, Mexico City has accounted for a consistently increasing and disproportionate number of entrepreneurs. Fourteen percent of those born in the 1890s counted Mexico City as their place of birth, 38 percent in the 1920s, and an extraordinary 64 percent of the post-1940s group. (MEBP) Historically, however, an even more significant bias exists among those entrepreneurs born in the North: 40 percent have come from states bordering the United States. This bias is still extreme compared to the general population residing there, but it has declined from 60 percent of all entrepreneurs' birthplaces in the pre-1880 cohort to 27 percent in the post-1940 group.

Finally, these data show that the Gulf, South, West Central and East Central regions are strongly underrepresented in the birthplaces of leading Mexican businessmen, and that the third most important place of birth is outside of Mexico. On average, 8 percent of Mexico's postrevolutionary entrepreneurs have been foreigners, primarily from Spain. Over time, the data clearly illustrate the historic impact of the Spanish influence, which reached its apex among the 1890s generation, when a third were from outside Mexico. Among younger entrepreneurial groups, foreign birthplaces have all but disappeared. Interestingly, whereas foreign origins are a deterrent to a successful career in Mexican politics or the military, they have been important to intellectual and entrepreneurial careers in equal numbers.

Not only is there a substantial bias favoring selected regions as sources of entrepreneurs, but their choice of residence, unlike that of intellectuals and politicians, has a strong minority representation in the North. While nearly 60 percent of leading businessmen have lived in Mexico City, over a third of Mexico's elite entrepreneurs call the North, especially Nuevo León and Coahuila, home. (MEBP) On a regional basis therefore, leading businessmen are not unrepresentative of the population as a whole. They reside naturally where the largest pockets of industry are located (Mexico City—state of México, Monterrey, and Guadalajara). They are sharply divided residentially, a quality uncharacteristic of intellectuals and politicians, who are concentrated exclusively in Mexico City.

Urban birthplaces produce other consequences tied intimately to class background and education. Urban birthplaces have a tendency to become self-perpetuating because they enhance informal credentials affecting the success of entrepreneurs. Urban origin influences parents' occupation. For example, Derossi found that 48 percent of urban-born industrialists were children of industrialists, compared to only 19 percent who had rural origins. My data reveal a similar bias. Among Mexican entrepreneurs who came from middle- and upper-class parents, 91 percent were urban in origin. In contrast, among those whose parents were in working-class occupations, only 45 percent were from urban birthplaces. (MEBP)

The connection between urban birthplace and education is also well established. Throughout Latin America, "a major determinant of whether a Latin American reaches the university is place of residence. Latin Americans who reside in rural zones are less likely to attend a university than their counterparts in the urban areas of the same country."[5] This general statement applies to Mexico. Guy Benveniste demonstrated that as late as 1965, 44 percent of all students in urban areas who started the first grade completed sixth, but only 7 percent of rural children who started first grade reached a comparable level.[6] Among industrialists in the 1970s, Derossi found a similar distortion, with three-quarters of those from urban birthplaces attending college, but fewer than half from rural villages doing so.[7] My data complement these findings, since among those Mexican entrepreneurs who completed a college degree, only 41 percent did so from rural backgrounds compared to 64 percent from urban birthplaces. The bias in urban birthplaces continued as their educational level increased. Only 7 percent of those from rural birthplaces received graduate training and degrees, but 17 percent of those born in cities obtained these credentials.

Social and Family Origins

As I have implied, birthplace, social class, and education are very much interrelated. Whereas types of birthplace correlates with level of education, the critical variable is probably social class, since middle- and upper-class backgrounds are found disproportionately in urban locales. Our data contain very detailed information on class background compared with similar data sets from Mexico or other countries. It is important to mention, nevertheless, that it is easier to determine socioeconomic status if a subject's parents fall into the middle class than if the parent is from a manual occupation, a sign of working-class origin in Mexico.[8] Biographical information is more likely to include references to professional occupations than to blue-collar or peasant activities because of their low prestige in Mexico.

Taking this into account, a clear pattern exists in many societies. Leadership groups generally are from the middle and upper classes. For North American leaders, whether they are political or economic, only 5 percent could be classified as originating from the working class.[9] Among the United States political leadership there has been an increase in the number from the middle class as compared to the upper class, but the fact remains that both historically and in the present, blue-collar families have not produced a proportionate group of leaders.[10] Socialist countries do not have a much better record, especially among the rural working class.[11]

In Mexico, middle- and upper-class social origins are overrepresented among politicians' and intellectuals' backgrounds. For example, two-thirds of all politicians since the 1930s have come from middle-class backgrounds. This figure increases sharply if we confine our sample to younger leaders.[12] Intellectuals' origins are even more biased historically, since nine-tenths of them have come from middle- and upper-class backgrounds. The Mexican leadership group that gives the greatest representation to working-class families, especially from urban locales, is again the officer corps. Among generals, probably only half are from middle- and upper-class backgrounds.[13]

The private sector offers potentially the greatest opportunity to working-class Mexicans because of its size and diversity. Unfortunately, private-sector leadership is no more open to Mexicans from humble origins than political or cultural leadership. In the first known sample of Mexican entrepreneurs, from the late 1950s, nearly three-quarters described their fathers as professionals, white-collar employees, or managers. These data led Raymond Vernon to conclude that leading Mexican entrepreneurs were not Horatio Alger types.[14] Fifteen years later Derossi reconfirmed Vernon's finding for a specific strata of entrepreneurs, noting that their social origins were concentrated among the middle and upper-middle classes.[15]

A more complete sample of leading Mexican entrepreneurs during the entire period from the 1920s through the 1980s suggests the degree to which middle- and upper-class backgrounds are overrepresented. The data from the MEBP reveal that 94 percent of Mexico's top business leaders have come from these social origins. Even as of 1970, generous estimates of Mexico's middle-class population reached only 30 percent.[16] Moreover, if social origins of businessmen are broken down by age, it is clear that their overwhelming middle- and upper-class origin has always been typical, even among those born before the turn of the century.

The social origins of Mexico's business leaders are not unique; studies from other countries suggest similar patterns. In Colombia, where social class divisions are similar to those found in Mexico, one study concluded that 84 percent of the entrepreneurs were recruited from the middle and upper classes.[17] In North America, where social mobility is more fluid than in Mexico, Joslyn concluded in the 1930s that 10 percent of the population produced 70 percent of the business leaders.[18] A comparative study of top management in England and the United States found that only 15 and 20 percent, respectively, were from lower social class origins at a time when nearly 87 percent of the general populations of both countries were in these categories. However, one North American study suggests a single trend that distinguishes Mexico from the United States. Over time, United States business leaders from upper-class backgrounds have declined, while in Mexico their position has been reinforced.[19]

From a historical perspective, a student of Mexico naturally would hypothesize that the Revolution should have opened up economic leadership to a class of self-made entrepreneurs. The generation born in 1900, who would have been of age to take advantage of entrepreneurial opportunities in the 1930s and 1940s, was slightly more open to businessmen from lower social origins than at any time since the Revolution, but the difference from the norm is statistically insignificant. (MEBP)

These data support conclusions of revisionist historians who have examined local or regional leadership groups. For example, in Monterrey, one of the few locales in Mexico where an entrepreneurial class was already in place, the composition of the upper class failed

> to change substantially as a result of the Mexican Revolution. . . . In
> short, 'all of Porfirian society,' as Cosío Villegas claimed, was not 'swept
> away' in the wake of the revolution. To a large extent, the currents of
> the revolution bypassed the Monterrey elite. The sources of the elite's
> economic power, coupled with the nature of the revolution, resulted in
> the survival and continuity of Monterrey's leading capitalists.[20]

The old Porfirian elite in northern Mexico survived through its economic strength and its family ties.[21] Our data make clear that what has
been true regionally for Mexico's economic elite has been true nationally.

Often, the limitation of statistical data is that we do not go
beyond the numbers to examine their content. While businessmen's
social origins have many significant consequences, it is equally important to understand who are these middle- and upper-class parents.
Class origins and place of birth are not the only determinants of
successful careers; occupation is also important.

We often reach major conclusions that do not accurately convey
the meaning of the data in studies of political leadership. One of the
important hypotheses Peter Smith tested in his analysis of Mexican
political leadership was whether or not there was political turnover
among individuals holding national political office. Smith concluded
correctly, on the basis of his data, that turnover was frequent, comparable to rates in other societies.[22] Data limitations did not permit him
to suggest how turnover can be measured not just by who holds an
office and how often an individual repeats, but also by whether family
members have previously held those same offices.

Leadership groups in Mexico already are recruited from a narrow
pool compared to the population at large, on the basis of urban and
middle- or upper-class origins. That pool is further narrowed by the
fact that a disproportionate number of politicians, intellectuals, and
military officers come from parents who themselves were leaders in
these respective fields. The common notion that free enterprise provides an environment conducive to meritorious advancement regardless of other criteria is a myth, because in addition to social origins and
urban birthplace, parents' occupation is critical to success.

In North America, where studies are richer and more varied, a
consensus about the occupational pursuits of leading businessmen's
parents exists. Historically, Reinhard Bendix argues that whether a
United States entrepreneur was born in 1771 or 1891, the portion
whose parents shared this profession has never been lower than

63 percent and increased to nearly three-fourths of all businesspeople's parents by 1920.[23] Joslyn's study, published in the early 1930s, found that 57 percent of his sample were the children of capitalists or top management.[24] The most recent examination, Suzanne Keller's, concluded that 50 percent of the 1900 generation were the children of entrepreneurs, and 57 percent of the 1950 generation.[25] In the United States, in 1900, only 8 percent of the general population were businesspeople.

In Mexico this phenomenon has been largey unappraised. Derossi's examination of industrialists is the only study that provides insights into the occupational backgrounds of one type of Mexican entrepreneur. She found that 43 percent had parents who were industrialists, and an additional 24 percent had merchants, 7 percent had landowners, and 4 percent had bankers or landlords as parents. None of the industrialists in her sample came from parents with peasant or blue-collar occupations.[26] Data from the MEBP are quite comparable to patterns identified in studies of North American businessmen. In Mexico, two-thirds of all leading entrepreneurs are the children of businessmen.

It is equally important to look at the trends in family backgrounds over time. Since the generation born in 1890, when 41 percent of Mexico's leading businessmen had parents in business, there has been a persistent increase in parental business backgrounds. No leading entrepreneurs in the last two generations are known to have been raised by fathers who themselves were not businessmen. North American entrepreneurs share a similar background, but in recent years there is a slight increase among North American businessmen from working-class homes. In fact, one study suggested this pattern was especially true among leaders of large North American businesses.[27] The pool from which North American business leaders are recruited has opened up slightly in recent decades, but Mexico's entrepreneurs have increasingly closed off opportunities to most groups.

To understand more completely the degree to which a business career relies on family business origins, it is worth testing the same pattern among the grandparents of successful Mexican entrepreneurs. Derossi asked this question of her informants, and found that 24 percent of the grandfathers were industrialists, 31 percent were merchants, 19 percent were landowners, and 3 percent were bankers and landlords.[28] The major difference between the two generations is that more grandparents than parents were landowners, because landowning was a more important private-sector occupation in that era.

Although information is difficult to obtain, the MEBP data show that at least 19 percent of the Mexican businessmen in my sample were grandchildren of businessmen. If we control for age, we see the figures nearly double every twenty years, so that among the youngest leading entrepreneurs, half are the grandchildren of businessmen.

Expressed differently, it can be said that leading Mexican businessmen today did not reach their positions in the same way as their grandparents did. They are not self-made, but had family help in climbing to the top. Among Mexican entrepreneurs, only 15 percent were first-generation businessmen, 51 percent were second-generation, 29 percent were third-generation, and 4 percent were known to be fourth-generation. As Keller has suggested in her study of North American businessmen, the sons and grandsons of men who themselves were businessmen had more channels through which they could enter the world of big business than peers without this background.[29]

Family background enhances an individual's ability to pursue successfully a father's career because of the way jobs are obtained. For example, in Turkey, if the father had an elite position, the ability of his son to reach an equally high position was nearly twice that of someone who did not share a similar parent's status.[30] In Mexico, jobs in both the private and public sector are obtained largely through personal contact. Among leading Guadalajara businessmen, 44 percent obtained their first position through a family tie, followed by 29 percent through friendship.[31] The perpetuation of business families in Mexico is not entirely stagnant, since many individuals join established entrepreneurial families through marriage. Nearly a third of Monterrey's entrepreneurs were outsiders who married old-family daughters.[32]

The heavy reliance on family ties for business success is perpetuated also by the value system of the typical Mexican entrepreneur and by the structure of the private sector. Larissa Lomnitz explains this: "*Confianza* is a basic element of economic interaction in the business enterprises which we have described. The entrepreneur requires a circle of persons, each of whom is connected to him through a relationship of trust."[33]

Structurally, the private sector has been dominated until the 1960s by family-owned and operated firms.[34] This fact reinforces Mexican owners' reliance on kinship ties. It is worth noting that the predominance of family ownership contributes to the high level of business careers in parental backgrounds of recent generations of Mexican entrepreneurs. A pattern of family control is being perpetuated at a time when ownership in the private sector should be moving toward corporate control.

The question of the parental origin of Mexico's entrepreneurs should also include parents' national origin. Throughout this century, a fifth of all leading Mexican entrepreneurs have had one or more nonnative parents. Again, the data demonstrate that this was especially true of the generation born in the two decades prior to the Revolution. After the 1930s, only about 10 percent of leading businessmen came from immigrant origins. (MEBP)

In his careful study of Mexican industrialists, Dale Story found a similar pattern. He concluded that 6 percent were born abroad, but that 24 percent had fathers who were immigrants. Although Story's figures approximate mine, he concluded that "a strong immigrant influence is not evident among Mexican industrial elites."[35] In absolute terms, one can understand his conclusion, but in my opinion it is misleading; indeed, the opposite point should be stressed. For example, Derossi's study of industrialists, carried out fifteen years earlier than Story's and therefore sampling an older generation, encountered 20 percent born abroad and 44 percent with parents or grandparents who were immigrants. Both sets of figures are unusual, because Mexico has never attracted large numbers of immigrants, making the extent of the entrepreneurial contribution of the few who have settled there appear all the more remarkable.[36] Whether one examines the 1910 or the 1950 census, the total foreign population figure is less than 1 percent, making the percentage of immigrant backgrounds among entrepreneurs extraordinary.

Immigrant forebears for businesspeople in general is not unusual. In a 1962 study of business leaders from Bogota, 41 percent were immigrants from other countries, and half of those were from European nations affected by World War II.[37] Among North American businessmen, for the 1900 generation, 10 percent were native-born of foreign fathers, and 9 percent were foreign-born.[38] The importance of these figures is not that they are fairly comparable to Mexicans', but rather that the proportion of North American foreign-born executives is lower than the proportion of foreign-born in the United States' general population.[39] Thus, the figures for Mexico are all the more remarkable, because the gap between the immigrant in the general population and in the business leadership is so much larger than in the United States.

Mexicans who have emerged from immigrant backgrounds fit three common models. They are of Spanish, central European, or

Middle Eastern origin. Some insights can be drawn from the experiences of Mexicans who follow these typical patterns. Emilio Goicochea Luna, formerly president of Coparmex, describes his origins:

> My father was a Spaniard who arrived in Mexico City in the late 1930s, a refugee of the Civil War in Spain. He first worked in the Dominican Republic before coming here. He was a businessman and had a CPA degree. My grandfather, on my father's side, was also a businessman who lived in Bilbao, Spain. My father came to Mexico as a salesperson for National Cash Register. He began a distributorship for that company, and later started his own business. I got my own start in business with my father. Later, I established my own industrial firms as well as operated retail companies he originally founded. We now have several family businesses.[40]

An example of the Middle Eastern success story is the career of Carlos Abedrop, an important figure in the banking industry. He describes his father as Palestinian, born in a small town near Bethlehem. According to his account, his father was a typical Arab immigrant who started a small clothing store. He was very successful and was able to educate all of his children, a pattern common to many small businessmen.[41]

Perhaps the most interesting immigrant background told to me by a successful businessman was that of Jacobo Zaidenweber, outspoken leader of the National Chamber of Industries. His story has parallels with those of Goicochea Luna and Abedrop, because in each case the father formed his own enterprise, regardless of how small. Whereas Abedrop used his formal education to manage other individuals' firms, Zeidenweber and Goicochea Luna initiated their careers through their fathers' businesses. More importantly, all three have presided over a major interest-group organization, a position open to entrepreneurs who are not influential capitalists. Zaidenweber's story is particularly insightful because it suggests how a father's career reoriented his son's long after the son had chosen another profession.

> I am a first-generation Mexican, born in Mexico, but my parents were from central Europe. My father was from Germany, and was an immigrant to Mexico in the period after World War I. In that era, immigrants to Mexico had to go into business in order to make a living. There was some industrialization, but not much. My father had a small textile business. He used very old machinery and the business was quite small.
> My childhood was very mixed up with poor Mexican children who lived in the same neighborhood. We also lived through the Cárdenas

era, and in our school, the influence of his regime was very strong. I became strongly nationalistic during my childhood. Later, I became a doctor, and I did my interning in San Francisco and at Columbia University in New York. I spent six years studying cancer in the United States. I returned to Mexico and practiced medicine for many years. One day my father died suddenly. Since I only had one brother, and he too was a doctor, we decided to sell the business. However, because the business had many debts, and because the employees very strongly wanted to remain employed, we could not sell it. So I decided to learn something about the industry, about which I knew nothing, and try to operate the factory.

What I think I did already know was the nature of human beings. So I developed a small group of collaborators around me. Now the business is ten times larger than when my father died. It was through my efforts to make a go of his business that I became involved in the industrial chambers where I am now. Really, the whole process was accidental, I never sought a position of leadership in the private sector. Also, as you might imagine, it is quite rare to reach such a position as a first-generation Mexican. However, I have never encountered any obstacles or prejudice due to that.[42]

An entrepreneur's social background and parents' country of origin are significant determinants of his pursuing a successful business career. Social class background is inextricably tied not only to place of birth, but to level of education.

One of the great myths of North American private initiative is the view of the successful entrepreneur as a self-made person without formal education. As Reinhold Bendix demonstrated in his examination of the North American business elite from 1771 to 1920, more than one-third of each generation received either private schooling or a college education. These figures are at variance "with the common notion that businessmen were not 'in need' of higher education until at least the turn of the century, if not indeed until the 1920s."[43] Suzanne Keller breaks down similar figures for each of three generations. In her study, 30 percent of the businessmen from the 1870 and 1900 generations and 61 percent of the 1950 generation graduated from college. Only 7 percent of the male population in the United States in 1940 had graduated from college, indicating how privileged businessmen have been.[44]

How do Mexican businessmen stack up against their North American counterparts in formal education, especially considering the greater availability of public education to aspiring North American entrepreneurs? The first indication of the connection between education and the privileged class status of Mexican entrepreneurs is revealed in data on their primary schooling. More than three-quarters of the businessmen in our sample attended private elementary schools.

If their level of education is examined, it becomes apparent that Mexican business leaders are, and have been for many decades, extremely well educated. In absolute figures, 61 percent of Mexico's businessmen have achieved a university degree. By the 1900 generation, over half of all businessmen were completing a college degree, at a time (1920s) when only 1 percent of the population was even enrolled in a university program.[45] By the 1930 generation in Mexico, 96 percent of business leaders were college educated, when 2 percent of the population was attending college. The year 1930 also marks the beginning of a trend in which business leaders seek specialized postgraduate training. For the 1940 age cohort, however, the trend is marked; 46 percent actually acquired M.A. degrees, and another 27 percent had education beyond the bachelor's or professional degree. From this generation, none had an education below a university degree.

The tie between class background and educational achievement is all-encompassing, because 94 percent of leading Mexican entrepreneurs are from middle- and upper-class families. If we examine the small group of businessmen who have had only primary education, it is clear that their parents' socioeconomic status was a significant determinant of their limited educational achievement, since 80 percent of them were from working-class families. Stated differently, all Mexican businessmen who have achieved any sort of graduate education or degrees are from middle- and upper-class backgrounds. (MEBP)

Studies of two important regional groups reveal trends comparable to our national data. For Monterrey businessmen, where their education levels were known, fewer than 4 percent had less than a high school education, and 95 percent had some university education or higher level of preparation at a time when only 5 percent of Monterrey's adult male population were college graduates.[46] A study of the owners and managers of large firms in Jalisco found that nearly three-quarters of them had college degrees, and one-fifth had completed M.A. and Ph.D. degrees.[47]

Background characteristics reveal a collective portrait of the Mexican entrepreneur as an urban creature, raised in a middle- or upper-class background, the child and often grandchild of businessmen, and extremely well educated. In addition to these characteristics, the types of degrees businessmen have received suggest skills which the private sector has valued and which are necessary for a successful career in the business world. In Mexico, in the political and intellectual communities, law traditionally has been the dominant professional degree. Therefore, it is not surprising to find that law is one of the two most important degrees businessmen have obtained. But law reached its apex as the first educational choice of entrepreneurs in the 1920s, when one out of four college-educated business leaders pursued this degree.

Engineering, a field unimportant among cultural elites and only secondarily important to politicians, is tied for first place with law as a professional degree sought by business leaders. Sixty-two percent of Mexico's leading entrepreneurs have completed degrees in equal numbers in law and engineering. Among North American businessmen in the 1950s, nearly the same proportion of college-educated business leaders also received their degrees in engineering and law.[48] Whereas law gradually has declined in importance in Mexico since the 1920s, engineering degrees, as a choice of students with business aspirations, took a huge leap from the 1920s to the 1930s, tapering off among business students attending college in the 1940s.

Historically, law is important because it is one of three traditional degrees pursued by educated Mexicans, followed by medicine and engineering. Law plays a very special role because a lateral move from business law to management and investing is one of the career patterns prospective entrepreneurs most commonly choose. This pattern is still common, but the shift from law to engineering as the first choice reflects the private sector's evolution. As the private sector grew, it acquired greater self-definition, reflected in a desire for specialized skills to cope with increasingly sophisticated technology. Engineering became the natural choice of students with private-sector ambitions.

The third choice of college degrees among Mexican businessmen is, not surprisingly, business administration. This curriculum was not really available in Mexico until the 1950s, a fact reflected in the educational data. Whereas 13 percent of all postrevolutionary business leaders with college educations chose this degree, 75 percent of them have graduated since the 1950s. Moreover, of the generations born since 1930, over 40 percent of the college-educated entrepreneurs have chosen business administration. In Mexico today, nearly a third of all students enrolled in higher education are in business administration and economics.[49]

Finally, another 10 percent of the degrees are in accounting. Accounting, like law, is a natural path into the business world. The figures for accounting and the other three fields are not surprising; together they account for 85 percent of the degrees obtained by leading Mexican entrepreneurs. Most surprising is the fact that economics is very low among them.

Economics has not appealed to the private sector because of the way it has been taught in Mexico. The two major institutions graduating private-sector leaders illustrate the contrasting approaches to economics curricula in Mexico. Mexico's most important university for all types of leaders, excluding the military, has been and remains the National Autonomous University (UNAM). For most of its history, economics at UNAM has had a macroeconomic and neo-Marxist orientation. According to one author,

> even in the early 1950s, economics students at UNAM were required to take three full years of Marxist economic theory, with limited or no exposure to neo-classical or Keynesian thought. In 1976 the students take an even longer seven semester sequence, prudently retitled 'political economy,' which centers around labor value theory, dialectical and historical materialism, the theory of surplus value, imperialism, and the economics of socialism. . . . The quantitative area remains light.[50]

Naturally, students seeking business careers would not be attracted to such a curricular emphasis.

Partly in response to this deficiency, the business community in Monterrey decided to create their own educational institution in 1943, the Monterrey Technological Institute of Higher Studies (ITESM). ITESM has been described as thoroughly Western, a staunch supporter of laissez faire economics.[51] It is second only to UNAM as a university producing future business leaders. Regionally, one-third of old Monterrey family members working for the major industrial groups are graduates of this institution or MIT in the United States.[52] MIT looms large in the education of many business leaders because ITESM provided a direct link for its graduates to pursue advanced studies there.[53]

One other aspect of entrepreneurs' educational background that deserves some attention is the preparatory schools and universities they attended. Two criteria affected their choices: income and ideology. As we have seen, parents' socioeconomic background influences businessmen's ability to obtain the highest levels of university education. More importantly, this background also influences whether they attend private or public schools. Leading Mexican businessmen have enrolled overwhelmingly in private schools from the very beginning of their formal education. Only 17 percent reaching the preparatory school level attended the National Preparatory School, compared with nearly half of leading political figures. The single largest group of businessmen, nearly a third, attended private preparatory schools in the United States, and an additional fifth attended private *colegios* in Mexico. Thus, more than half of Mexico's private-sector leadership with a preparatory education attended private schools, the majority of them abroad.

For university-educated entrepreneurs the trends are similar but not quite as exaggerated. Of those who attended college, 44 percent were enrolled at the National University, Mexico's leading public institution. It is only natural that more individuals would attend the leading public university than its preparatory counterpart, the National Preparatory School, since few private alternatives were available. Still, one out of five businessmen attended a private college, the most important of which were ITESM, the Free Law School, and La Salle. Parents of these future leaders could also afford, and placed a high value on, sending their children abroad; 29 percent attended universities outside Mexico, primarily in the United States. In contrast, fewer than 2 percent of Mexico's prominent politicians attended private Mexican universities, and only 3 percent obtained their undergraduate training abroad.

The fact that business leaders attend private schools from primary through university levels can be attributed in part to their class background. Most students who attain a public university degree in Mexico are from middle-class backgrounds.[54] However, many more future business leaders complete a degree than ordinary Mexican college students. (MEBP) For example, in Colombia, one out of three businessmen who attended college received a degree, but among the general population only one out of nine students did.[55] One important reason is that their socioeconomic background facilitates graduating. Whereas a sizable minority of public university students are from working-class backgrounds, recent studies of private schools, such as the University of Monterrey, indicates only 2 percent are children of workers.[56]

The fact that more businessmen attend private schools than intellectuals and politicians affects their ideological orientation, and ultimately their relationship to both groups. Many changes are taking place in the educational patterns of Mexico's leaders in recent decades, as intellectuals, politicians, and entrepreneurs increasingly attend some of the same private institutions. Furthermore, the extraordinary number of businessmen who have studied abroad, in the United States, not only affects their attitudes but, I surmise, separates them in a variety of ways from their political counterparts.

Types of Leaders

These background characteristics, taken as a whole, suggest a rather homogeneous group of Mexicans at the forefront of the private sector. Traditional background variables, however, in combination with other characteristics, are also indicative of multiple types of entrepreneurs. Students of private-sector leadership have found it useful to categorize businessmen by careers, because changes in the proportion of businessmen in each category reflect important alterations in the evolution of business management.

Theorists generally agree that the North American private sector has produced four distinct types of business leaders: self-made, family-made, bureaucratically-made, and professonally-made.[57] The composition of private-sector leaders in these four categories has changed. As might be expected, self-made businessmen initially accounted for 36 percent of the leadership in the late nineteenth century. By 1950 a mere 6 percent fell into this category. The implication of Keller's data is that the growth and institutionalization of the North American private sector into large, publicly owned corporations restricts the ability of self-made individuals to arrive at the very top of the economy.

Keller's findings are not surprising; indeed, the pattern seems only natural. Trends in Mexico, however, are quite contradictory. When I separated Mexican entrepreneurs into two broad groups, self-made and family-made, I found that over the whole of the postrevolutionary period 63 percent can be described as self-made, whether they pursued their careers in interest groups, in the bureaucracies of large corporations, or through corporate law or accounting. If the data are controlled by period, the results are quite different. Since the 1910 generation, the number of self-made business leaders has declined, presently accounting only for 25 percent of prominent entrepreneurs born since 1930. (MEBP) This fact suggests very clearly the increasing importance of inherited opportunity and wealth to the success of prominent businessmen, three-quarters of whom started in well-established family businesses.

Among the Mexican businessmen I interviewed, by far the most interesting story of a self-made corporate president was told by Alejandro J. Dumán Urrea.

> I am a product of the postrevolutionary generation during a period of peace. I was born in Ciudad Obregón, Sonora, what used to be Cajeme, in 1931. It is an agricultural region and my family was very much involved in agriculture. . . . When Cárdenas was president, he expropriated my family's lands and exchanged them for desert in the western part of Sonora. . . . We became one of the first families in this region, an area which is now known to North Americans as Rocky Point. . . . We lived there in our truck, in a tent, before we were able to build a home. Most of the other families in the region lived in caves. Since we

didn't have enough funds after the expropriation to start farming, we began a fishing business. Our home was the first built in the region which was not inside a cave. We eventually sold the truck and bought store goods and food to sell. We supplied the fishermen with many of the canned goods and supplies they needed.

After we established this business, there was a sociopolitical change which was extremely important to this region. During World War II the Mexican government constructed a rail spur from the Pacific railroad. Many of the Braceros came through Rocky Point on their way to Mexicali. . . . When the road and railroad were connected, Rocky Point became a city. Naturally, this produced a tremendous growth in our business. . . . Our population during this time went from 5 (which was our family) to 2,500 persons.

But Rocky Point didn't have schools, and my mother, who had a visionary mind, wanted us to be educated and sent me to Sonoita, which had a school that went through the first three years. I then went to Guaymas for grades four through six. They didn't have a secondary school, so I went to Hermosillo for secondary and preparatory. Then I did my first two years at the University of Sonora, at which time there were only five students for the third year. As a consequence, the University canceled the program in business administration, so I had to go to Mexico City to complete my degree at the National University.[58]

Those who were family-made entrepreneurs in the United States, whom Keller defined as individuals who rose through a family-founded and/or -controlled firm, accounted for a third of all North American businessmen in the 1870 and 1900 generations. By 1950, only 11 percent of United States business leaders were from families like the Fords or Du Ponts. A comparable percentage of Mexican business leaders were products of family-owned businesses, but instead of declining as Mexico's economy grew in the post–World War II boom, their numbers actually grew. In fact, among the top thirty businessmen since the 1960s, two-thirds count inherited wealth in their family backgrounds.

The background of Rómulo O'Farrill, a leading capitalist in the communications industry, typifies the Mexican entrepreneur nurtured within a successful family business:

My father was originally in automobiles in the town of Puebla. We carried various lines and models during those years [the 1930s] and in 1936, I began working for him. In 1940, we had the Packard line for all of Mexico, and the year before, 1939, we established our very own assembly plant. At this plant, I was in charge of the technical aspects of the assembly, and later in my career, I bought a large number of shares in the newspaper *Novedades*. After 1948, I controlled the Novedades Publishing Company. My father was originally the president and director general of the company, but in 1965, I became vice-president and director general of the newspaper.

In 1949, I began my career in the television business by establishing Channel 4. Channel 4 was the first Spanish-language station in all of Latin America. We later added many affiliates and magazines, and presently we have over ninety-two television stations, more than a dozen magazines, including *Vogue*, and the largest TV station in Latin America. . . . Today we are sixty companies.[59]

Unlike the self- or family-made businessman, the only career category used by Keller that has remained consistent over time is that of the professionally-made individual, who accounted for 12–13 percent of all North American business leaders from 1870 to 1950. Among Mexican businessmen, they are a smaller group, since 6 percent of leading entrepreneurs have used their professional careers to achieve prominent positions in the business world.

Today, the most important career group among North American businessmen are what Keller labeled bureaucratically-made leaders, people who move up meritoriously within a corporate hierarchy. According to her data, they accounted for only a fifth of all business leaders in the late nineteenth century but were nearly two-thirds by the 1950s.[60] The social origins of these managerial-type businessmen vary, although in Mexico, with a few exceptions, they are middle-class.

The literature on business leaders in the United States offers the interpretation that publicly owned corporations now are being controlled by corporate managers, who not only are separate from the ruling capitalist class socially, but also have a stronger social consciousness than their capitalist peers.[61] G. William Domhoff goes on to argue, however, that the actual extent of a managerial revolution is difficult to determine because of scanty information on actual North American corporate ownership and the function of boards of directors.[62] The same criticism, with more justification, could be made of Mexican management.

For other reasons, however, it is essential to separate capitalists or capitalist-managers from professional managers. Mexican managers are very proud of the fact that they are professional administrators, not capitalists. Some studies show that these two groups in Mexico can be distinguished educationally, by the fact that managers have higher levels of education than owners and, therefore, differing attitudes—which some feel have a significant structural consequences for entrepreneurial unity.[63] This opinion is bluntly stated by Federico

Ortiz Alvarez, the president of Celanese, one of the largest foreign-affiliated firms in Mexico, who noted, "I want to emphasize that I am an employee, not an owner of the firm, so my opinion is fundamentally different from the capitalist's."[64] Ortiz Alvarez's career is the classic case of a hard-working, urban, middle-class Mexican who rises to the top within the corporate ladder.

> I am a chemical engineer by profession. I was born in Mexico City of Mexican parents. My father was a doctor and my mother was a normal teacher. I am the oldest of seven children. I did all of my schooling in Mexico City from primary through university.
>
> I graduated in 1950 and began working for Mexican Celanese as a quality control inspector. My first promotion was to foreman, the lowest management position in this company. I have worked thirty-six years for Celanese, during most of the development of this firm. I have gone from the very bottom to the top.[65]

Conclusions

An examination of place of origin, parent's socioeconomic background, level and location of education, and type of entrepreneurial career suggest four overriding questions about leading Mexican businessmen worth exploring. First, to what extent are their background characteristics important to their evolution as entrepreneurs? Second, what influence do those factors exert on their homogeneity as a leadership group? Third, do these qualities affect the recruitment of future private-sector leaders? Fourth, and finally, did the Revolution of 1910 alter capitalist leadership after 1920?

Background is clearly important in the formation of leaders, but it is difficult to ascertain what its precise influences are. For example, it seems reasonable to argue that people from an identifiable social class are conditioned by a common experience and are inclined to share a set of similar assumptions.[66] As political scientists have argued, social backgrounds by themselves are insufficient for predicting the outcome of policy decisions.[67] This assertion is true more for methodological reasons—that is, the researcher's inability in the real world to eliminate all other variables—than for its inherent veracity. I learned from Mexican politicians that family background was essential to their formation, and the majority shared certain social characteristics. Moreover, they could identify specific decisions where background experiences were influential.[68] We know that parents' occupations, as well as childhood years, affect a person's views on important economic and political values.[69]

For some reason, research on entrepreneurial elites has not paid much attention to the issue of socialization. One North American study on businessmen argues that a critical element in the complex of attitudes and habits that determine entrepreneurial behavior certainly is social origins.[70] Although it cannot be proven in any quantifiable way, it is significant that a sizable group of Mexican businessmen believe that their family background and environment, and the educational institutions they attended, significantly affected their attitudes, especially toward the government. Ernesto Canales, who grew up in Monterrey, which for many Mexicans symbolizes the private sector and its philosophy, describes the influence of the familial, educational, and regional environment:

> When I grew up my home was surrounded by business, and I was educated in the Christian Brothers School where there is a strong antigovernment attitude. In my professional education I studied law. I was interested in widening my world so I traveled to Mexico City because in those days the schools in Monterrey were not very prestigious. I attended the Free Law School in Mexico City. Most of my companions from the provinces during this time had similar backgrounds. . . . My friends were similar because of the schools they attended and their families. In that generation, we used to think of the public sector as completely corrupt, as dirty.[71]

This statement represents a view shared by many other Mexican entrepreneurs, and it cleary establishes the importance of background variables on the attitudes of this group. In locales like Monterrey, these background variables have an exaggerated importance because family origins and experiences tend to be even more homogeneous than among Mexican entrepreneurs in general. An entrepreneur's background is likely to have a critical long-term impact on the growth of the economy, the resolution of economic problems, and their relationship to the public sector.

Significant on its own merits is the degree of homogeneity background variables bring to business leadership. It does not automatically follow that experience alone is predictive of one set of views. Since Mexican managers distinguish themselves from owners on the basis of shared experiences and backgrounds, it is not illogical to expect similar background characteristics and experiences to contribute to a collective sense of unity. On the basis of certain variables— especially urban origins, middle- and upper-class backgrounds, kinship ties to other businessmen, education in private institutions, and high level of educational attainments—leading Mexican entrepreneurs share important common characteristics, all of which set them apart from the population in general, and many of which set them apart from other leadership groups. The level of cohesion within the Mexican private-sector leadership should not be exaggerated. Entrepreneurs' attitudes toward the state differ in many respects. Taken as a whole, however, entrepreneurs are formed with a shared set of biases not found among politicians and intellectuals. Not only is family environment important, but in regard to their ideology, the influence of private education cannot be overstressed. Whether one speaks to Mexican graduates of private or public schools, universal agreement exists that the orientations of both are different, the ideological ambience of each is unique, and student life outside the classroom is dissimilar.

Finally, certain background characteristics of leading Mexican entrepreneurs perpetuate certain homogenizing experiences. The fact is that without parents from middle and upper socioeconomic backgrounds, these businessmen would not have been able to obtain higher education, now a necessity to be a successful Mexican entrepreneur. As studies of private schools clearly show, their enrollment opportunities are even more restricted to middle- and upper-class Mexican children than public universities.

Economic historians have postulated that the great concentration of wealth in the hands of few Mexicans has taken place in the last three decades. Their argument is that while some capitalists have roots in the period of the postrevolutionary reconstruction during the 1920s, or extend further back to the Porfiriato, most date from World War II.[72] This argument is correct in the sense that major fortunes have been reconstituted during this era. Aguilar Monteverde's interpretation, that the vast majority of Mexico's present large capitalist families are a "new rich" class emerging since 1939, is not, in my opinion, borne out by the data on social class origins.[73] Instead, their parents and grandparents were the tycoons of their age, passing economic and institutional resources on to their children.

The impact of background variables on recruitment is substantial. It is obvious from my data that a Mexican who resides in a rural community, whose parents are blue-collar workers, is not the least bit likely to join Mexico's entrepreneurial leadership for the remainder of this century. Because Mexican businessmen's background characteristics are becoming more, not less, homogeneous, the conditions which perpetuate a restricted pool for entrepreneurial recruitment will continue long into the future. This has already happened among powerful regional groups of entrepreneurs, as in Monterrey, where locally born men, with attendant social and family connections, are overrepresented in the city's elite.[74]

Mexico's private sector, therefore, offers little opportunity for upward mobility at the leadership level, and aspiring leaders must search elsewhere. In my earlier studies of cultural and political leaders, urban and middle-class backgrounds also prevail. As a society modernizes economically and politically, a person's family antecedents normally decline in importance. Mexico offers a counterexample among its political, economic, and intellectual leadership. Whereas it might be argued that Mexico's economy has not reached a level of dynamism to reduce the importance of ascribed characteristics for reaching influential positions, a counterargument is that cultural patterns are stronger in some societies than others, and the consequences of modernization for a similar cultural variable in two countries may not produce the same outcome.

An additional historical interpretation of interest to Mexicanists has been the impact of the Revolution on certain groups, and the consequences for society. Peter Smith argued that Mexico's postrevolutionary leadership was bourgeois, and thus wanted to modernize rather than eliminate the country's capitalist system.[75] According to one scholar, Mexican landed families and incipient entrepreneurs were not exiled nor ruined totally, despite the far-reaching reforms of the 1930s.[76] Data from the MEBP complement these findings, suggesting that a large group of Mexican entrepreneurs trace their familial and economic origins to antecedents in the Porfiriato. Equally important, the Revolution did not, except in a very small way, open up opportunities for working-class families to join the ranks of the nouveaux riches, reaching the apex of economic power in Mexico. What further opening occurred was not nearly comparable to the opening that took place in the 1930s for aspiring politicians from humble origins.

From this fact one can speculate on an additional explanation for why the Mexican state has maintained an interest in populist issues. It is not just because of the nature of the Revolution and the principles encoded in the 1917 Constitution, but because actual leaders in the 1930s, responsible for setting the tone of the state for future decades, had working-class and peasant roots, something *never* true of the private sector. Thus, the ideological conflict between the state and the private sector may be explained in part by a brief historical interlude which allowed a group of public men with popular roots to creep in, even though future generations were quickly enveloped in the middle-class, urban qualities of their private-sector contemporaries.

5

Private-Public Interlocks

The degree of harmony between the private sector and the state is related to many variables. The importance of the state and the private sector's self-image and self-definition of their respective roles vis-à-vis each other has already been demonstrated. However, power elite theorists have always been intrigued by a more concrete characteristic of private-public sector relations, the interchangeability of their respective leaderships.

Interchangeability of leadership has been examined on the assumption that the more numerous the exchanges, the greater the potential for a power elite's existence and cohesiveness. But the degree of various elites' representation among each other's leadership is only a small part of a larger question. This study's focus is the political relationship between the state and the private sector. It can be argued that the extent to which politicians are capitalists and capitalists are politicians facilitates their relationship. Furthermore, the level of interchange may also explain why the public sector has favored private-sector interests without covert influence from the business community in the decisionmaking process. On the other hand, the ways the private sector expresses its demands to the state are affected by the level of access it has to the state.

Historical Interlocks

The common assumption is that throughout the late nineteenth century Mexico had an interlocking economic and political elite. Unfortunately, at the national level, these assertions have not been well documented. However, recent studies at the regional level demonstrate clearly that political and economic leadership were strongly inter-twined. The best evidence of this is William Langston's study of Coahuila. He found that "the political and economic hierarchies inter-locked in a complex web of personal relations, kinship networks, and informal and formal decision-making processes."[1] In other parts of Latin America, similar patterns have been evident on the local and regional level, at comparable periods of time.[2]

Some evidence now exists to support the view that national politicians from the Porfiriato were more likely to have familial con-nections with the private sector than their counterparts in twentieth-century Mexico. For example, among the generations of political leaders in the late nineteenth century, 29 percent were the children of ordinary landowners and businessmen. But if we consider only those parents who were *prominent* landowners and businessmen, equivalent to the elite entrepreneurial group under study in this book, only 6 percent of the politicians had such parents, hardly a significant figure. (MPBP)[3] Furthermore, from 1914 to 1935, such parents all but disappeared from politicians' backgrounds.

For leading politicians since the 1930s, this figure has declined by half to 3 percent, remaining the same to the present. Therefore, while it is correct to say that family ties among prominent entrepreneurial and political figures were more important in the Porfiriato than in the modern political era, they were not particularly significant in either period.

On the other hand, if we look at the careers of prominent politi-cians from the latter part of the nineteenth century and the early decades of the twentieth century, we find that 11 percent were success-ful businessmen before entering politics, more than twice the figure for important politicians since the mid-1930s. During the Porfiriato itself, from 1884 to 1910, one out of every five leading politicians had been an important businessman. Business leaders' participation in politics began a sharp decline with Victoriano Huerta's administration (1913–1914), when only 2 percent came from such occupations. Under Venustiano Carranza (1914–1920) the figure remained a low 3 percent.

The reverse pattern is also true. Ten percent of Mexico's leading politicians from 1884 to 1935 pursued important business careers *after* leaving politics, about twice the figure for politicians after 1935. Again, it was during the Porfiriato that this exchange was most common, where 17 percent of the public figures later turned to busi-ness careers. The interlock between public- and private-sector careers has declined markedly in Mexico since 1935, even though it has never been a very common pattern compared to that in the United States. The 1910 Revolution, however, did have an impact on the level of the exchange. Presidents who served from 1920 to 1934 in the immediate postrevolutionary years surrounded themselves with only a few businessmen (7 percent). The first two administrations after 1935, led by Lázaro Cárdenas and Manuel Ávila Comacho, illustrate how few individuals (2 percent and 1 percent respectively) came from business careers.

The presidential administration of Miguel Alemán (1946–1952) accounts for a noteworthy change in this leadership pattern. The number of collaborators who came from business careers grew from 1 percent in his predecessor's regime to 6 percent in his, a sixfold increase. Nearly all the significant trends in modern Mexican political leadership go back to Alemán. However, the other important pattern to understand is that the level of business careers in the experience of prominent national politicians has remained essentially static through 1988, averaging about 5 percent in each successive administration.

The number of politicians who have turned to business careers after politics, rather than originally coming from the private sector, is smaller—on average only 4 percent since 1935. In the Alemán administration, twice as many politicians as normal later pursued business careers, more than any other administration before or since.

One might conclude from these two different patterns that the concept of recruiting politicians from business management positions evolved well after the 1920s, contradicting an assumption inherited from the postrevolutionary years, that businessmen were not desirable politicians. On the other hand, there seems to be no opposition to politicians entering the private sector *after* their political careers.

These findings contradict arguments presented in neo-Marxist literature that the links between the private sector and the state in the 1920s were quite strong, primarily as a consequence of movement from the public sector to the private sector. These studies cite the names of prominent individuals who clearly represent that pattern, but err in concluding, without empirical evidence, that they are typical.[4] For example, Julio Labastida argued that military officers and government officials were given state subsidies to join the private sector. He suggests that a pattern of recruitment between the state and the private sector was established, and that the state in effect contributed directly and indirectly to the creation of a new capitalist class.[5]

Labastida's assertions are undoubtedly true, but he exaggerates the extent of the state's role in stimulating the private sector by creating entrepreneurs with political origins. This recruitment pattern, as I just demonstrated, existed since the 1880s. Moreover, social background data presented in the previous chapter make clear that "the best statistical chance of becoming a member of the business elite is to be born into it."[6]

The more important issue here is that the postrevolutionary period did not alter the traditional pattern of politicians' involvement in private-sector leadership and some businessmen's involvement in public-sector leadership, other than reducing the overall level. The 1910 Revolution did not reconstruct ties between the leaderships of the two sectors; rather it briefly made it possible for a new social class to achieve prominent private-sector positions.

Access to Mexican private-sector leadership came about through horizontal mobility from the state into the business world. In the 1920s and 1930s an increase of Mexican political leaders with lower-class backgrounds occurred.[7] Some of these individuals had opportunities in the public sector to acquire the necessary economic resources to pursue successful careers in the private sector. Astute businesspeople understood that this period provided extraordinary opportunities for investment and growth. As one author suggests, "friends, relatives and cronies of the political leaders used capital with their government connections to go on to larger and more permanent business establishments. This group was mainly from the small middle class in Mexican society."[8]

Meanwhile, access of individuals from working-class backgrounds to corporate leadership became increasingly restricted, even though the private sector itself set out on an expanded path of development. In the United States, on the other hand, "the son of a wage earner found himself at no substantial disadvantage, as compared with the businessman's son, in entering business and bidding for the favorable consideration of his superiors."[9]

The pattern of exchange with the public sector was also of little help in facilitating lower social group's access to private-sector leadership posts, since Mexico's political leadership quickly moved away from a sizable minority of individuals from lower-class social backgrounds to a leadership that was essentially middle class—often the children of politicians. The public sector did, however, provide a limited channel for people traditionally outside the recruitment process of the private sector to transfer their talents and resources to the business community.

By the 1940s it became clear that Mexican businessmen and politicians had evolved separate recruitment channels. Each set of leaders differed in its source of recruitment, familial background, and education. This situation differs markedly from the extensive interlock between United States political leaders and their counterparts in the private sector. Nearly two-thirds of all cabinet officials in the United States have pursued careers in the private sector before their appointment, and over half have left political office to hold managerial posts in the private sector.[10]

Mexico's private and public sectors do not share this fluid exchange of leaders for historical reasons. In the first place, in the 1920s the Mexican state was quite strong, while the private sector had few resources, and most of those were controlled by a small number of families, many of whom were European immigrants. For cultural as well as economic reasons, the educated Mexican pursued a career with the state, or as an independent, practicing professional. Few opportunities for talented individuals without familial connections existed in the private sector.

Second, the contradictory rhetoric that emerged after the 1910 Revolution made it difficult for Mexican politicians to pursue private-sector careers openly. Publicly, politicians are proponents of populist values that deprecate the importance of the private sector. It therefore behooves a professional person with political ambitions to avoid strong ties with the private sector, including career experiences.

Mexico's political stability permitted political leadership to institutionalize its political recruitment patterns. Whereas these patterns were more haphazard and less predictable in the past, they became increasingly structured after the 1940s. As I have shown elsewhere, higher education became the key variable in the recruitment process, because politician-professors were the teachers and recruiters of successive generations of politicians. (MPBP) A prospective politician who initially entered the private sector usually participated less than his peers did in the teaching of future politicians. By the 1950s, entrepreneurs themselves had become so concerned with the educational ambience offered in Mexican public universities that they either opted to send their children to the United States or created private institutions to form their own leadership cadres. Thus, in a few short generations, the private sector emulated the public sector, institutionalizing selected educational environments as required experiences for their leaders.

Contemporary Interlocks

Numerous assertions have been made about the level of Mexican private-public sector interlocks in recent years. Most studies, with the exception of those by Dale Story, have not been based on empirical evidence, have not examined movements from the private sector to public life as well as the reverse, and have not analyzed data over time. Empirical data over the last sixty years provide definite evidence of significant trends in the exchange between private and public leaderships.

The one other study that used empirical data to test some assumptions about the exchange was Peter Smith's. Smith (as I explained earlier) had comprehensive data on politicians through 1970, although his family-background data were severely limited, and his comparative data on entrepreneurs are, as he readily admits, confined to Derossi's study of industrialists at one point in time. He concluded that entrepreneurs and politicians, although sharing certain similarities, were separate, and that these two groups did not form a power elite.[11] In many respects, his qualified conclusions are supported strongly by the following analysis. On the other hand, I suggest changes in their relationship, and many other significant patterns, untouched in earlier studies.

Having examined the entrepreneurial activities of national politicians, let us now turn to the political careers of leading entrepreneurs. Fifteen percent of the entrepreneurs studied have held national political office. This figure says something quite different from the figures cited earlier on the small number of prominent politicians who have transferred from careers in the private sector, or who have followed business careers after leaving political office. It is commonly accepted among businessmen themselves that essentially no exchange between the two exists. The data bear out this view, showing that only 10 percent of Mexico's cabinet have private-sector career experiences at the management level, whereas at the cabinet level in the United States, more people have such careers than not. (MPBP)

The fact that 15 percent of Mexico's leading entrepreneurs were prominent politicians implies two very important conditions. First, Mexican politicians, at least at the highest level, are twice as active in top private-sector positions as are businessmen in top national political leadership. Moreover, the interchange between the two sectors is twice as frequent at the cabinet level as among all leading politicians. Second, 15 percent is not a very large figure, but I would argue that whatever influence prominent politicians exert on the private sector, the frequency of their presence in top business leadership positions is likely to be much higher than the frequency of politicians in lower-level private management posts, and therefore their influence is more keenly felt.

The Mexican scholar Alonso Aguilar Monteverde believes, however, that former politicians are found at lower levels more commonly than at high levels in the private sector. Numerically this may be true, but in percentage terms it is doubtful. He argues that generally the politician is not an entrepreneur in the active sense of the word; he is more likely to be an investor or landlord. Pointing out that the investor may be wealthier than the entrepreneur, he maintains that politicians use this investment approach to protect their image of not being businessmen.[12] In this sense, the activities of the Mexican entrepreneur are more open to public scrutiny than those of the investor, which may have some interesting economic consequences. This is why individuals from both the private sector and public life succeeded in opposing the government's efforts in 1972 to pass a reform law that would require stockholders' identities to be made public.[13]

Another recently offered assertion is that executives with careers in some of the leading business organizations are leaving to follow highly placed public careers.[14] To what extent is this true, why does it take place, and has it changed over time? If we examine the presidents of the leading organizations, the following figures emerge: The National Federation of Chambers of Industry (Concamin) between 1918 and 1984 has had only four presidents who pursued careers in the public sector, 12 percent of all its presidents. These four men held office in the 1960s and early 1970s, giving the impression that a trend had begun. However, all succeeding presidents have remained in the private sector.

The single most important organization of the private sector is the Mexican Council of Businessmen, and no member of it has held public office since its formation in 1962. The National Chamber of Commerce (Concanaco), founded in 1917, like Concamin has had only four presidents (12 percent) who became or had been national political figures. These entrepreneurs represented the organization during four different decades of its history, most recently during the mid-1960s. The National Chamber of Industries (Canacintra), founded in 1941, has had only two presidents (8 percent) who served in prominent political posts.

The private-sector interest group with the largest representation of entrepreneurs who entered politics is the Mexican Bankers Association, in existence as an independent organization from 1928 to 1982. Of its forty-eight presidents seven, or 15 percent, were men who mixed politics with banking, most of them before the 1950s. Of the fifty-five leading entrepreneurs in our sample who held national political office, one out of eight was president of this organization. On the other hand, in the leadership of the leading regional chamber, the Monterrey Chamber of Commerce, no politicians are represented.

These figures reveal some important characteristics about the interchange between Mexican entrepreneurs and politicians. In the first place, more entrepreneurs who have become politicians have held important interest-group offices than have held management positions. Thirty-one percent of all leading entrepreneurs with political offices were national interest-group presidents. This is not surprising, since the two positions require similar skills. It would be more natural for someone who had been an interest-group leader to move over to the public sector than to become a leading capitalist, investor, or chief executive officer. The second pattern apparent from these figures is that absolutely no chronological trend toward an increased exchange from private- to public-sector posts, or the reverse, is or has been taking place among interest-group leaders.

The most notable finding from these figures is that the banking industry interest organization is best represented by entrepreneurs who have circulated in public offices. This finding is all the more significant because the Mexican Bankers Association is a "free organization," that is, its membership is voluntary, not required by law. The heavier representation of political types in banking-sector leadership further documents my hypothesis that the banking industry has historically been an important channel linking the public and private sectors.

Interest-group-organization leadership provides only one means for examining the private-public interlock. Another way to examine it is to look at the entrepreneur's economic activity. It is difficult to assign entrepreneurs a single activity since many are represented in multiple areas. Nevertheless, when we are forced to make a choice on the basis of their largest holdings, we could classify the leading entrepreneurs in our sample as follows: 59 percent industrialists, 20 percent bankers, 9 percent interest-group leaders, 6 percent professionals (law and CPA firms), 3 percent retailers, 2 percent real estate, 1 percent insurance, and less than 1 percent in industrialized agriculture.

If we return to those leading entrepreneurs who previously were prominent *political* figures (15 percent of the total sample), we find the industrial sector, the heart of the business community, very much underrepresented, since only 30 percent have been industrialists. On the other hand, politician-entrepreneurs are greatly overrepresented in two marginal fields—professional firms, which account for 17 percent of the politician-entrepreneurs, and real estate, where 6 percent of them have invested their resources. The only basic economic activity in which politician-entrepreneurs are overrepresented is banking, where compared with entrepreneurs who have never left the private sector, twice as many politician-entrepreneurs have found it attractive.

These findings are very important because they suggest occupational differences in entrepreneurial leadership and important differences in the proclivities of politicians who turn to business compared with orthodox entrepreneurs. In the first place, banking has been an attractive niche for politicians, an indication of why bankers often have been represented by ex-politicians in the Mexican Bankers Association. Historically, banking was attractive to politicians because of efforts by leading bankers to work with the public sector. Their positive attitude conveyed an attractive environment to ex-politicians, and over time, became self-perpetuating.

The reason why professional firms (law and public accounting) have been overrepresented among politician-entrepreneurs is that most politicians themselves have been lifelong bureaucrats or professionals. These firms often serve as brokers between businesses and the public sector, and therefore those individuals with ties to the private sector who are most likely to pursue a temporary career in the public sector come from this background. A classic example of this pattern is the career of Roberto Casas Alatriste, a prominent Puebla native who represented the Mexican government as a financial agent in the United States, becoming one of the first Mexicans to have an independent certified public accounting firm in Mexico. A federal deputy in the 1920s, he used his accounting knowledge to invest in a number of Mexican firms, including La Provincial Insurance.

Real estate also is overrepresented in the backgrounds of entrepreneurs who have been politicians because property values have been most dynamic in the Mexico City area, where many politicians retire, and where they see investment opportunities firsthand. Moreover, privy information can be translated more easily into personal fortunes in real estate, and some public officials have not been averse to using their knowledge for personal gain. Finally, as suggested earlier, most politicians want to hide their business connections, and real estate provides a haven for investors.

Certain economic sectors, as a result of a higher representation of politicians in their leadership, are more open to Mexicans of lower social-class origins. Entrepreneurs who are self-made have much greater opportunities for success in real estate, professional firms, interest-group organizations, and banking. A disproportionate number of these self-made entrepreneurs are politicians from middle-class backgrounds with no previous connection to the private sector. The industrial sector has few individuals who have succeeded in political careers, and self-made men are less commonly found there than in other economic sectors.

The private-public interlock also can be examined at different levels among leading entrepreneurs through looking at the board membership or officers of major Mexican corporations and banks. The figures are very clear. If we examine an elite group of major company presidents, the representation of politicians declines. For example, 39 percent of the politician-entrepreneurs were presidents of the top 200 companies since 1920, compared to 51 percent of the entrepreneurs without political careers in our sample. However, of all the board presidents in our sample, only 12 percent were men with political careers. If we look at board membership of the most powerful fifty companies in Mexico during the same period, the figures decline further. Twenty-four percent of all politician-entrepreneurs were on these boards, compared to 49 percent of all entrepreneurs. More importantly, only 8 percent of all the board positions were held by politicians. Finally, among the wealthiest thirty families in Mexico, only 8 percent were politicians.

Place of Birth and Residence in Interlock Patterns

The patterns in the exchange between politicians and entrepreneurs have been well established and consistent over time. Two characteristics that may, or are likely to, influence this exchange are place of residence and, most important, location of school.

One of the characteristics revealed in recruitment literature is that various leadership groups, whether political, cultural, or economic, generally choose like disciples. For example, in Keller's examination of United States businessmen, she found managers wanted subordinates with similar traits.[15] Many of those traits are learned by businesspeople in a familial and educational atmosphere reinforced by living in close proximity to one another. In other words, growing up in an environment where one's peers have the same values and goals encourages a repetition of those qualities from one generation to the next. In his study of Monterrey entrepreneurs, Andrews concluded that "the families prefer candidates whose life experiences have been as similar to those of family members as possible."[16]

An important determinant of similar life experiences is place of residence. Probably the best example of a distinct nurturing environment for businessmen is Monterrey, Mexico's fourth largest city. The ordinary Mexican views Monterrey as an industrial center and, more importantly, the seedbed of private initiative in Mexico—an ambience that reinforces the pursuit of business careers. As one prominent figure from the Alfa Group explained, "there is a natural tendency among the families in Monterrey to pursue careers in the private sector. Of course there are some important exceptions, but they are just that, exceptions."[17]

Place of residence is important to private and public leadership in two respects. In the first place, it is a significant determinant of each group's characteristics. For example, people who live together not only "come to share a mode of life, they participate in the same social activities, live in the same residential areas, send their children to the same schools and last but not least, they intermarry."[18] In Monterrey, where the potential for middle- and upper-class families with similar values to live together is higher than in the more cosmopolitan and diversified Mexico City, intermarriage is common. In her study of industrialists, Derossi found that a much higher percentage of industrialists with relatives in business were from Monterrey (80 percent) than Mexico City (48 percent).[19]

According to many Mexican businessmen, even businessmen who live in Mexico City are perceived differently from those who live elsewhere. One view is that "the businessmen in Mexico City are like strangers, they are not well respected by people in the provinces. The provincials don't trust them, and because they think Mexico City businessmen are untrustworthy, they lack faith in Mexico City."[20] Alejandro J. Dumán Urrea goes on to argue that a difference in business mentality exists between the provincial and the Mexico City businessman. Indeed, one's very business culture is affected by geographic location.

Geographic location appears to affect the behavior of entrepreneurs in several ways. The typical Mexico City businessman's commercial sophistication is different from the provincial's. Moreover, some businessmen argue that business size is affected by location. For

example, Monterrey tends to have larger industrial enterprises than
Mexico City; one explanation is geographic proximity to the United
States. Finally, the general perception among all business leaders is
that family-owned enterprises are much more typical in the provinces
than Mexico City.

The most important potential influence of residence is on the
present relationship between the public and private sectors. An important argument offered by Monterrey entrepreneurs is that in general
they are more independent of government than their peers in Mexico
City. The explanation for their relative independence is that "in Mexico City the influence of the government is so much stronger that it has
an effect on the relationship."[21] Likewise, it can be argued that the
physical distance between Monterrey and Mexico City creates an
insular environment in Monterrey conducive to a distinctive and identifiable culture. If an individual is raised in Monterrey in an environment more suspicious and independent of government influence, he is
less likely not only to have much in common with a politician but also
to make a lateral move into public life at any point in his career. This
assertion can be tested by examining birthplace and place of residence
of businessmen who entered political life.

The data from the MEBP support the view that place of birth and
residence are conducive to entrepreneurs having political careers.
Nuevo León, the state where Monterrey is located, supplied only
8 percent of the fifty-five leading businessmen who held national
political office, although 29 percent of all entrepreneurs were born
there. On the other hand, one would expect a higher proportion of
entrepreneurs born in Mexico City to enter political life. This is the
case. Although Mexico City supplied 26 percent of all leading businessmen, slightly less than Monterrey, it accounts for 72 percent or
three times as many, of those who entered politics. One's place of birth
and early childhood affect individual inclinations to politics, but so
does adult place of residence. Whereas slightly fewer than two-thirds
of all entrepreneurs reside in Mexico City, nine out of ten who enter
politics live there. In contrast, in the entire Northern region, where a
third of Mexico's entrepreneurs live, only 7 percent enter politics.

Chapter 4 noted how concentrated Mexican leadership groups
are in several major urban centers, led by Mexico City. Most elite
studies have focused on political leadership and generally concluded
that certain regions and cities have a preponderant representation in
the backgrounds of such individuals, as is the case of Madrid for
Spain, Istanbul for Turkey, or Tokyo for Japan.[22] Thus Mexico City is

not unusual. However, if the assertions concerning the influence of place of residence on increased cohesiveness of cultural values and homogeneity of a population are correct, then changes in the proportion of entrepreneurial and political leadership living in special locales become significant. Two figures from Chapter 4 are quite revealing of the trends. Among leading entrepreneurs born since 1940, 64 percent were born in Mexico City. Simultaneously, Monterrey declined as the birthplace of leading entrepreneurs in the oldest age group, from 60 percent to only 27 percent in the post-1940 generation. These data suggest that the potential for contact among future leading politicians and entrepreneurs at a young age has increased steadily since the 1920s, as both groups are born and raised in Mexico City. The potential for intermarriage, shared social activities, and similar educational experiences has increased, facilitating closer ties and improved relations.

One of the most important vehicles for creating a smoother path for exchanges between the private and public sectors is school location. In part, one's choice of a university is determined by residence. Mexico City has been, as noted earlier, a dominant force in higher education. As Charles N. Myers suggests, "Between the end of the Revolution and 1940, the District maintained and probably increased its dominance of the manpower resources of the nation. . . . It is unlikely that a large percentage of the graduates settled elsewhere."[23] Therefore, as the percentage of potential leaders living in Mexico City increases, so does the potential for their attending a select number of institutions. Furthermore, the comparatively advanced level of economic development characterizing Mexico City influences children's attitudes toward politics. In Mexico, children raised in the capital know more about politics than in any other place. The more knowledgeable children are about political life, the more likely it is they will ultimately participate in politics.[24] This finding offers not only an additional reason why an increasing number of politicians come from Mexico City, but also an interpretation of why more Mexico City entrepreneurs might also be inclined toward political careers.

These findings can be transferred to children who might pursue other occupational interests. In the past Monterrey, because of its high level of economic development and its private-initiative orientation, cultivated youngsters with substantial knowledge about Mexico's private sector, compared with their peers elsewhere. Thus, an additional explanation for the disproportionate number of leading entrepreneurs from Monterrey in the early years might be attributed to their initial socialization. As the decades have gone by, and more individuals have moved to Mexico City, the artificial separation between Monterrey and Mexico City decreases, and the potential for increased knowledge about both private initiative and politics occurs.

Educational Trends and the Interlock: Private versus Public Institutions

Historically, as my data have shown previously, the education of entrepreneurs and politicians is divided along two important lines. Politicians have been overwhelmingly educated in public institutions, primarily located in Mexico City, and only 2 percent attended private universities. (MPBP) In contrast, one-fifth of Mexico's entrepreneurs attended private universities. Second, whereas an equally small number (3 percent) of politicians attended undergraduate programs abroad, nearly a third of entrepreneurs received foreign undergraduate degrees.

Differences in educational patterns are important for several reasons. In the first place, the educational credentials of each respective leadership group influence the socioeconomic backgrounds of its members. Education should be a democratizing influence, but if only a small minority of Mexicans actually completes a degree, and that minority is from the middle and upper classes, it institutionalizes the means for reproducing certain class dominance.[25] In the North American business world, higher education has been linked directly to social mobility.

> The rapid expansion of great state universities especially, and of higher education in general, has for some decades had an accelerating effect on mobility in America, compensating for many factors that work towards status rigidity. It may well prove to be that a continued high level of social mobility in American business will depend on the degree to which the colleges and the private ones especially, continue to recruit students from all strata of our society.[26]

However, Mexico's record on degree completion among students from lower social strata is poor at best. Even at large, public universities, students are predominantly from upper socioeconomic family backgrounds.[27]

One of the consequences of the exchange between the private and public sector is that it may provide a channel for introducing atypical leaders into each group, thus altering to some degree their respective recruitment processes. Politicians, who, compared to entrepreneurs, provide somewhat more potential for individuals from lower classes to join their numbers, have closed off these opportunities because of the high levels of education required. As politicians begin to move away from public to private and foreign colleges, they reinforce the limitations on upward social mobility already present in the private sector's leadership.

Education has been shown to be an influential variable also in the views of potential leaders. For example, in a study of Mexican students, one author found that those from lower socioeconomic backgrounds were more decisively against the political system, and for the need to change, than their middle-class peers.[28] An Italian study also found that as education increased, traditional political concepts received more support.[29] Thus, educating both politicians and entrepreneurs screens out dissenting or innovative views inherited with class origins. As their education becomes more homogeneous, entrepreneurs who become politicians will be less able to offer perceptions that differ from public officials, and politicians who turn to private initiative will offer few ideas foreign to the private sector.

Some long-term trends now taking place in Mexican education ultimately may affect the relationship between the public and private sectors, especially their potential for interlocking leadership. The most significant change is that public leadership is emulating the private sector by moving away from state-supported institutions to private and foreign universities. This has led to a situation in the public sector in which two sets of leaders exist side by side. One set of leaders, generally trained in public institutions or selected European colleges, maintains a set of values sympathetic to populist economic policies. Another set of leaders, who in the past were also trained in public universities, espouse a neoliberal economic philosophy. However, those neoliberals are increasingly attending private or United States institutions.

The effect of this educational pattern is twofold. It is quite possible that the more important consequence is an emerging division between political leadership and the masses. The population is being socialized through the public school system to favor a populist view of the Mexican state. Simultaneously, the leadership is being trained in increasingly elitist institutions supportive of private-sector values. Thus, as politicians and entrepreneurs move closer together in educational experiences, the general population and Mexico's leadership move further apart. The second consequence is that the state's leadership is becoming more divided between populist and antipopulist groups who in the past have spoken the same language learned through a shared public university experience, if not sharing the same methods for achieving development.

The state's leadership will have to work constantly at creating a compromise between those two major groups of Mexican public leaders in the 1980s and 1990s. Differences have always existed since the 1920s, but will be sharper than in the past. At the same time it can be argued that the private sector is obtaining new allies within the state because of shared educational experiences. From the previous discussion, it is obvious that the Mexican private sector is as heterogeneous as the state, but that recent educational trends have far more negative implications for state cohesiveness and more positive implications for private-sector homogeneity.

Scholarly evidence confirms political figures' and others' perception of the ideological orientation of private institutions and their ties to the business community. Daniel Levy, in his recent book on private education in Latin America, concluded that ITESM, which could be considered the prototype private university established by the private sector, is "strongly laissez-faire and United States oriented, geared to serve the desires of Mexican business," and that the "rector, hand-picked by the business leaders, has a major role in setting general academic policy."[30]

Some groups have begun to recognize the importance of education in the battle for the minds of the population in general, as well as for the minds of the leadership. Coparmex, the private-sector interest group most strongly supporting an activist political role for Mexican business leaders, has "also committed itself to take on a greater role in influencing university curriculum since it is university graduates who will determine the future of free enterprise in Mexico."[31] By the mid-1980s the PRI and the leftist parties had become so concerned with the use of foreign theories and religious creeds, and the neglect of free government textbooks in the primary schools, that the Chamber of Deputies established high fines for private schools ignoring the government's curriculum.[32]

Similar criticisms can be applied to the public institutions. To Mexican entrepreneurs, too many graduates of public institutions have Marxist ideas—especially in economics. Their view is that such graduates have little to offer the public sector, and even less to the business community. Their attitude is concisely summed up by Emilio Goicochea Luna, former Coparmex leader:

> The trouble with education here in Mexico today is that it tends to have an ideological orientation or content. This is important because it produces or creates a certain point of view among its graduates. There are many Marxist graduates who can't work in Mexico because they can't do the job, that is, they were never trained to do the work necessary in their profession. Unfortunately, in my opinion, many of these end up in the government.[33]

Private-sector leaders are critical of this ideological orientation, not only because it opposes their values but because they believe many economics graduates receive only theoretical Marxist teaching. As one younger entrepreneur on the board of a leading private institution frankly stated, "the economics they have learned is pure bullshit when it comes to working in a private company," whereas the typical graduate of Autonomous Technological Institute of Mexico can use his degree in concrete circumstances.[34]

Entrepreneurs, therefore, do not give first priority to applicants for entry-level management posts to graduates of public universities, even though the majority of businessmen in Mexico today probably are graduates of public institutions. For example, in the early 1970s, Guadalajara businessmen preferred graduates of ITESM and the Ibero-American University to those of the National University.[35] On the other hand, Mexican politicians have indicated in recent interviews that they too now prefer private over public school graduates. This has led one observer to conclude that the privatization of public power is occurring much more rapidly through politicians' education than through entrepreneurs taking public posts.[36]

An important source of state power in any society is its ability to attract or even monopolize human resources. In Mexico, the government always has been the institution most attractive to educated professionals. That attraction explains in part why the state has had better-educated leadership than the private sector. The state needs to retain a wide array of skills, and one of the best means of accomplishing that goal is to maintain a regular flow of elite university graduates into high-status positions.[37] In effect, the state must now compete for graduates from private institutions because the best students presently are attending these schools. "Someone who could actually work for the Bank of Mexico now, and had an offer from the Bank of Commerce (a private institution at that time), would probably work for the Bank of Commerce."[38] However, the Mexican state is not in any immediate danger of suffering a brain drain, especially because it has shown flexibility in coopting good private school graduates.

A second reason why the state continues to attract capable graduates, even individuals with private-sector aspirations, is its real and perceived dominance over Mexican social interests. For Mexicans with strong social concerns, the state is enticing. Ernesto Canales raises this point:

> I have come to learn that it [the state] has many capabilities for the goals that most Mexicans want to achieve. No matter how large your company, you can have more influence through the government in Mexico than with any firm in the private sector. I think that an imbalance exists between the two in the sense that young people with social interests now think of the public sector as the only alternative rather than also entering the private sector.[39]

Canales' observation implies that politically active businessmen will be slow to emerge in Mexico since those Mexicans most aware of social issues will choose to follow public, not private, careers.

Ideological differences between public and private institutions traditionally have helped to maintain an artificial separation between entrepreneurs and politicians. Entrepreneurs also have recognized that attending a public university may give them certain advantages in their relationship to politicians. Carlos Eduardo Represas, whose father founded Nestlé in Mexico, considers his background unique. He attended the economics department of the National University in the 1960s at a time when its orientation was Marxist. He believes his experience at UNAM was critical for three reasons. First, he came in contact with many future politicians, a number of whom are now in cabinet-level positions. Second, and perhaps more important, his education at the university made it possible for him to speak the same language as politicians. In his words, "they understand each other." Finally, he believes this experience broadened his knowledge of the Mexican government and its relationship to the private sector.[40] Represas' experiences are echoed by older generations in the private sector, individuals who also attended the National University, but in the 1930s and 1940s.[41]

There is a definite relationship between the location of an entrepreneur's education and the likelihood of his entering politics. Of those entrepreneurs born in Mexico City who entered public life, 93 percent graduated from the National University. Of those who remained strictly in the private sector, only 39 percent attended UNAM. Among entrepreneurs born in the North who did *not* enter politics, only 9 percent attended UNAM, but among those who held high political office, 46 percent were UNAM alumni. (MEBP) Regardless of where a prospective entrepreneur is born, public university education, especially at UNAM, provides certain values which make an exchange between private and public careers more feasible. What holds true for entrepreneurs with public university educations has been the case of politicians with private school educations. As noted, however, most politicians would not have made contact with entrepreneurs in private universities because so few actually attended such schools. However, a much larger group, although still a minority of politicians, went to private preparatory schools. Hugo B. Margáin, secretary of the treasury in the Echeverría administration, argues that he had plenty of contact with the private sector because he graduated from the Morelos Preparatory School, whose students were mostly from the upper middle class. He believes his educational experience gave him an advantage with social contacts unshared by colleagues who attended public schools.[42]

Education takes on even added importance to the private-public sector relationship and the potential for an interlocking leadership, if one believes that the culture of the institution influences the culture of the elite graduate. Such a point has been made about an elite preparatory school in Turkey, where "students were effectively socialized into an acceptance of the values, attitudes, and patterns of behavior that were necessary for success within the administration. For this reason any assessment of the performance of the Turkish bureaucracy, or at least of those ministries where Mulkiye graduates are concentrated, must take into account the culture of the school."[43] In Turkey, Japan, and Egypt, future politicians learned a pro-statist ideological orientation at their schools.[44]

As Mexican public universities continue to decrease in influence, graduates with a strong statist orientation will have to learn pro-state views elsewhere. Concomitantly, as the private university increases in importance, graduates who enter the public sector will share more clearly some of the values of their private-sector counterparts from these institutions, one of which is an antistate view. Because of increasing contact between private- and public-sector leaders in higher education, and because they may share more experiences and consequently values, it is only logical that younger entrepreneurs might find public service increasingly attractive, and younger politicians, at the culmination of their careers, might find private initiative a more welcome career alternative.

The public-private educational split has one additional consequence, confined only to politicians. I have argued for some time that

educational experiences are helping to create another split within
Mexican public-sector leadership—between the political technocrat
and the traditional politician. One of the few places where the political
technocrat has had hands-on political experience is in the public
university environment. As politicians move away from public institutions, they graduate without those skills or experiences.[45] The Mexican public figure who best articulates this change is Antonio Ortiz
Mena, the treasury minister most responsible for Mexico's years of
stabilizing economic development in the 1960s.

> The concept of a political career is changing. Let me explain. These
> students don't study, but try to initiate a political career at the univer-
> sity, thus the public system has deteriorated rapidly. So, the students
> who really want to study go to private schools. The importance then, is
> the division taking place between the politically motivated student and
> the academically motivated student. . . . In earlier generations, students
> combined both qualities. Now, we have many people in public service
> who are well prepared academically, but without any political expe-
> rience.[46]

Foreign Education in the Private-Public Interlock

Mexico is also witnessing an increase in foreign-trained leaders. As the
data on entrepreneur origins demonstrate, numerous businessmen at
all levels since the 1920s have been educated abroad. Studies clearly
demonstrate the ideological impact of those foreign experiences.[47] It is
fair to say that an individual who studies in the West cannot completely reject that experience—to do so would be to deny part of
oneself.[48]

An additional experience that might facilitate the exchange between politicians and entrepreneurs is their increasing tendency to study
at similar institutions abroad. For example, the Mexican Yale University alumni group is proud of the assertion that Yale has educated more
executives and directors of American corporations in Mexico than any
other university. Among its members, six have been important figures in
the public finance sector, including Jesús Silva Herzog and Gustavo
Petricioli, secretaries of the treasury in the 1980s.[49] It can be argued that
this shared educational experience, like the shared undergraduate education at private Mexican universities, increases the homogeneity of the
two groups. At minimum, it is likely to increase their common language
and culture, prompting greater possibilities for future exchanges.

Some private-sector leaders who have studied abroad agree with this interpretation. Jacobo Zaidenweber, who studied medicine before taking over his father's company, observed:

> There is no doubt that the public sector has people who come from private universities, who are cultured, well prepared, and sensitive to the position of the private sector. Of course, there would be a shared experience if these individuals came from the same university, and some communication would result. This would be good for both sectors. . . . What you learn in the United States may not have very much application in Mexico because of our very different circumstances economically and socially. But it does plant a seed, and this seed will have an effect on the minds of Mexicans. Whether that effect is good or bad, we don't really know at this point.[50]

One point is clear, however, and accepted by both the private and public sectors. Foreign education adds diversity to leadership values. One of my research hypotheses is that the changing educational patterns of Mexican public figures who attend school abroad and private schools in Mexico increases the range of their political and economic views. With the financial crises of the 1980s, hundreds of students have returned from their studies abroad, unable to finance them. Some of these same types of students will also be unable for financial reasons to attend private preparatory and university programs in Mexico. The generation entering public life in the next decade will simultaneously contain both the private or foreign university graduate and the public school graduate. As long as the economy misbehaves, the trend toward private education will be limited.

Many public figures, in spite of these economic limitations, are deeply concerned about the trend toward foreign university degrees, more than about the increased number of politicians coming from private Mexican institutions. For example, Hugo B. Margáin indicated that numerous labor leaders have told him they are worried about Mexico's leaders being educated in North America. These Mexicans believe that such an education will not accurately serve the needs of their country.[51] Other observers believe North American education will have a beneficial long-run impact, suggesting that management techniques will be improved.[52] Representatives of North American businesses believe so strongly in the latter view that the American Chamber of Commerce sponsors the Desarrollo Empresarial Mexicano program, "designed to transmit the private enterprise philosophy and give adolescents training in running companies."[53]

Many individuals in both the public and private sectors, however, remain unconvinced that increased foreign and private education among Mexico's public figures will alter their basic views or make them more compatible with the private sector. Their reasons for rejecting this hypothesis fall into several categories. The most convincing argument, shared by representatives of both groups, is that family upbringing is much more influential than education. As Antonio Armendáriz argues, "athough the school has an important impact on the knowledge or the type of knowledge an individual receives, the family socialization is much more significant and strong in producing the moral qualities of the individual."[54]

Data from the MEBP support the importance of family environment to future career choices. Of the entrepreneurs who served in high political office, only 35 percent came from parents who were in the business world, compared with 75 percent who remained in business careers alone. Stated differently, four times as many entrepreneurs who entered politics were first-generation business leaders as were entrepreneurs who remained nonpolitical. The same impact can be seen in businessmen's extended families. The greater the involvement of family and spouse in business backgrounds, the more likely is the entrepreneur to stick to a business career.

The argument has been made not only that socializing influences of family and education are unequal, but that family upbringing may be critical in predetermining an educational institution. Ernesto Canales explains why: "The reason why someone goes to the Wharton School of Economics, or on the other hand to Harvard, is because of family influence and conditioning of that individual to pursue a career in the private or public sector. I believe you have these values even before you attend the university, so that they may be there during your educational experience and its influence is much less than it otherwise might be."[55]

Another argument offered by Mexicans who dismiss the potential influence of changing educational patterns is that each sector's values are so strong that contradictory personal values would not survive a trip inside either sector's culture. For example, José María Basagoiti's view of government is that "it tends to force graduates, whether they are from the private or public universities, to conform to its views once they become part of public life. In my own company, we have many graduates from both types of universities, so it would be very hard for me to say whether or not the majority of graduates actually come from private universities."[56]

Finally, another group of Mexican respondents believe that experience influences one's values more than other factors. As one politician bluntly remarked, "politics is something you learn from experience, not from the university."[57] Experience alone does not convert someone from a private to a public career, or vice versa. However, according to many Mexican leaders, experience—or the lack of it—does explain why the division between the two sectors is so sharp, and why each group lacks sympathy for the problems of the other. Some entrepreneurs felt that because so few politicians had ever been businessmen, in any sense of the word, they could not understand entrepreneurs. Even prominent politicians agreed with their interpretation. Antonio Martínez Báez, former secretary of industry and commerce after World War II, argued that

> to become a better politician, you need to have more experience in the private sector. It would be very useful for all public servants to have some basic experience in the private sector. I also believe it would serve both sectors because the private sector would have some contact with government officials. The conflict between the two is partly the fault of the lack of reciprocal or mutual experiences. The public officials I know who have had private-sector experience are often better for it.[58]

On the other hand, one of Mexico's top businessmen, who had worked for the government as a student, repeatedly emphasized how valuable that experience was to his understanding of the Mexican public-sector culture and the language of politicians.[59]

Conclusions

Social scientists are intrigued by the level of exchange between the private sector and the state for two primary reasons. First, power elite theorists believe that the higher the level of interchange between the two leadership groups, the greater the private sector's potential for influencing government decisionmaking, either because entrepreneurs are holding positions of political power, or because former business-people are using their contacts to facilitate the business community's interests. Second, the level of exchange between the two groups suggests the tone of their actual relationship.

The characteristics of the Mexican interlock between private- and public-sector leaders suggest several important findings about and consequences for the relationship between the state and entrepreneurs.

The exchange itself has historical roots in Mexico extending back at least to the latter part of the nineteenth century. The exchange is not, as some authors have implied, a product of the Revolution. Furthermore, historians have suggested that the relationship between the state and Mexico's undeveloped private sector was closer and more integrated before the Revolution. If one accepts that leadership exchanges improve private-public sector relations, then the higher figures for their exchange in the prerevolutionary era help explain this closer relationship.

Data presented in this chapter also make clear that the Revolution of 1910 altered leadership sufficiently for the exchange between the private and public sectors to decline briefly but precipitously, almost disappearing during and immediately after the civil violence. However, the traditional exchange between the two groups was quickly restored. On the other hand, postrevolutionary governments have never exhibited the level of exchange between political and economic leadership found in the pre-1910 period, nor has the level of exchange at any time in the twentieth century been large compared to that found in the United States. Finally, contrary to popular assertions, there has not been a subsequent increase in the level of exchange in recent administrations.

Whatever the explanation of the difference in the exchange pattern between Mexico and the United States, it is longstanding. One possible explanation is cultural. A set of values evolved during the national era that nurtured a private, Catholic culture on one hand, and a public, secular culture on the other.[60] Structurally, this cultural bias was complemented by two conditions. First, entrepreneurship was a family affair, so ambitious young men tended to pursue careers in the professions or the public sector rather than business. Because the private sector offered few opportunities for the self-made entrepreneur, and because many Mexicans did not receive values conducive to private initiative, a stronger demarcation between the private and public worlds emerged. Second, compared to its counterpart in the United States, the private sector was relatively undeveloped, and foreign entrepreneurs controlled many of the resources.

In the United States, the nature of the business community changed significantly from the nineteenth to the twentieth centuries. Oscar Handlin notes that the power to make economically significant decisions was associated with the possession of capital. However, he maintains that the traits that formerly aided entrepreneurs in the drive toward the accumulation of wealth are not the same as those now associated with managerial ability. His argument is that the changing function of entrepreneurs from capitalists to managers significantly altered recruitment patterns.[61] One of those changes in the United States was increased upward social mobility for individuals desiring successful careers in the private sector.[62]

Mexico is moving in the direction of corporate ownership, but so slowly that patterns found in the United States have not yet taken hold. In fact upward social mobility in the private sector has been inhibited in Mexico. Therefore, corporate ownership in Mexico has not brought public- and private-sector leadership closer together.

Interlocking leadership always has been tested and conceptualized on the basis of leaders holding decisionmaking positions in both institutions. Holding powerful offices is really only the culmination of what elite interlocks imply and in that sense is an incomplete measure. In societies that are more stratified socially and less integrated culturally and geographically, other variables play a significant role long before occupational exchanges occur.

In Mexico, the importance of place of birth and educational location to the relationship between private- and public-sector leaders is clear. Power elite studies in the United States suggest very few differences in educational location between leaders in the business world and the government, partly because the integration of their educational experience corresponds with the integration of the leaderships: the former perpetuates the latter. North American analysts have sought to make a case for certain elite schools producing a disproportionate number of leaders. Whereas these studies suggest the differences between masses and leaders, they do not identify differences, if any, between private- and public-sector leadership.

Mexico's case is quite different. The entire concept of interlock can and should be examined at an earlier chronological point in the individual leader's life, beginning with place of birth, educational location, and adult residence. These variables are intertwined, but in United States studies they have never been examined in relation to the concept of interlocking leadership. Early environment, whether familial, geographic, or educational, affects the proclivity of an individual in the private sector to transfer personal skills to a state setting. Thus, those entrepreneurs who have lived in Mexico City, which has its own version of Washington's "Potomac fever," are much more likely to enter public careers than their peers who grew up in Monterrey, an urban environment mirroring private initiative and antistate values. Furthermore, entrepreneurs from both places who chose to attend

Mexico's most prestigious public university were disproportionately represented among businessmen who moved into national political life.

Since place of birth and place of education facilitate the exchange between private- and public-sector leaders, major alterations in the place of birth and education of entrepreneurs or politicians will influence the extent of their occupational interchange. Mexican businessmen have confirmed that their attendance at schools frequented by public figures has improved their contact with the state.

Two recent trends are important to this relationship. Educationally, politicians and entrepreneurs are becoming more homogeneous as more public officials attend private Mexican universities and travel abroad. However, private university education is still not fully acceptable in Mexican political culture by politicians or ordinary citizens. This equivocal posture is nicely illustrated by Genaro Borrego Estrada, who as PRI's 1986 gubernatorial candidate for Zacatecas, defended his education at the Ibero-American University as "circumstantial" and the "product of his own labor."[63] In terms of birthplace and residence, increasing numbers of entrepreneurs are born and raised in the capital, where they not only come in contact with future and incumbent public officials, but are raised in an environment pervaded by the statist rhetoric of the postrevolutionary era.

Traditionally, all these background differences have reinforced the separation between the two groups. According to some entrepreneurs, because the interchange between the two sectors is so limited, when a well-known private-sector leader goes into public life, Mexican entrepreneurs are severely critical of him.[64] One of the leading figures from Monterrey, Eugenio Clariond Reyes, director general of Industrias Monterrey (IMSA), explained his frustration with these boundaries between the two sectors:

> I envy the Japanese because they have such a constant interchange between both sectors, without any negative repercussions for either group. Here the attitude is very different. It is very difficult to go from one sector to the next. When people from the private sector join the public sector, they seem to become our worst enemies, and I would identify two such examples as Campillo Sáinz and Alessio Robles. Maybe the reason for this is they're trying to show they're as independent of the private sector as the typical career bureaucrat.[65]

The state, however, seems more sensitive to these differences, and intuitively understands the environmental conditions separating the two groups. When President López Portillo nationalized the banks, he placed politicians who claimed special ties with the private sector in the directorships of the leading banking chains. For example, these designations included José Juan de Olloqui, son of a Monterrey banker, who took charge of the Serafin chain, Mexico's third largest.

Increases in the exchange of Mexican leaders from one sector to the other are not likely in the immediate future. But changes taking place that affect the proclivity toward such an exchange, and affect relationships between the two groups, are already in place. Some of their consequences are predictable; other changes, such as increasing foreign educations on the part of both leadership pools, are not. It is definite, however, that alterations in the behavior of both groups are on the horizon.

6

Entrepreneurs and Decisionmaking

Because the state is an autonomous actor, it can and does make policy decisions not attributable to specific group interests. However, political leaders' interests do not always conicide, especially concerning the state's own role. Therefore, although the state has generally favored private-sector goals, the private sector must constantly pressure the state to do so.

The nature of group influence on politics can be divided into two broad categories: passive and active. Up to this point I have analyzed a variety of ways Mexico's business community acts as a passive influence on the state and vice versa. For example, familial, geographic, educational, and occupational experiences shared between future entrepreneurs and politicians have a socializing effect on both leadership groups. A belief in private initiative is reinforced through a variety of experiences. The more these experiences are shared with the political community, the greater the potential for a more positive relationship between the private and public sectors.

Of these passive influences, the occupational linkage between politicians and entrepreneurs has attracted the greatest scholarly attention. The assumption in determining the level and degree of exchange between the two sectors is that the greater the number of leaders with backgrounds in the sister sector, the more compatible the interests of both the state and the private sector. Critics of this approach, however, have suggested appropriately that business studies tend to assume that an exchange of leadership is evidence of entrepreneurial influence on political decisionmaking.[1]

Scholars have accepted without much evidence the conviction that entrepreneurs have an active influence on Mexican decisionmaking. This chapter examines the extent to which entrepreneurs perceive themselves as influencing the outcome of policy decisions, and the extent to which they *do* have influence, compared with their most important domestic opponent, organized labor. Second, because Mexico's private sector includes both state-controlled and foreign-dominated firms, is an analysis of the perceptual and actual impact of multinational corporations on the Mexican entrepreneur's relationship to the state.

The Decisionmaking Context

The level of state and outside actors' impact on decisionmaking cannot be easily determined without understanding who makes decisions in the Mexican state. Whereas it is easy to assume that all national political officeholders at a certain level exercise influence over policy, characteristics of the Mexican political system shift greater power to selected individuals and agencies. It is important to remember that decisionmakers are really a minority of political and other leaders who participate in the allocation of resources, and that their influence can be measured by decisions taken or not taken.[2]

Without belaboring the point, most actual decisionmaking in Mexico takes place in the executive branch. In no realm of the decisionmaking process do the judicial and legislative bodies exert an equivalent influence. Within the executive branch, individual agencies exert considerable influence. Because of extensive state involvement in the economy, certain parastate enterprises, known as decentralized agencies, often are more influential than traditional cabinet agencies.

Most students of Mexican bureaucracy agree that historically, little coordination has occurred among various agencies.[3] This lack of coordination is important because it affects access to decisionmaking and mutes the lines of responsibility between agencies for various programs. From one administration to the next there is little policy continuity. The lack of continuity in policy and personnel makes it possible for firms to improve access denied them earlier, and removes any guarantee that firms with access will continue receiving a favorable hearing of their demands.[4]

The president delegates considerable power to cabinet secretaries and agency directors.[5] The most important power he delegates is budgetary. Presidential control has decreased so substantially that individuals operate almost autonomously over indirect expenditures.[6] For example, Cárdenas' secretary of public works reduced or withheld funding to governors whose projects the secretary opposed.[7] Presidents even have been known to give their treasury secretaries authority to review presidential allocations, allowing their secretaries to veto them. Such a relationship existed between Ruiz Cortines and his treasury secretary.[8]

Students of the Mexican decisionmaking process generally agree that agencies operate largely independently of one another, agency heads are given tremendous authority, very little continuity exists between presidential administrations, and only a small number of individuals actually are involved in the decisionmaking process. The small numbers who influence the process affects the access of interest groups.[9]

Most Mexicans believe that the president retains power, rather than delegating it. In one sense, their perception is quite true—the president can withhold or dispense authority to a greater or lesser degree.[10] Naturally, the degree to which a president can now manage the responsibility for decisionmaking is limited by the government's enormous size and complexity.

The popular view of the omnipotent president is important for two reasons. First, though educated Mexicans should know better, the president is blamed personally when something goes wrong. For example, when López Portillo promised not to devalue the peso, and then was forced to do so, most Mexicans felt a sense of personal betrayal.[11] The president himself understood this.[12]

Mexican presidential power is substantial, and has led to a degree of deference toward the president that has significant consequences for the policy process. The level of deference Mexicans pay to executive authorities is so institutionalized that it exists at the state as well as the national level. An aura of deference surrounds governors and presidents.

Deference to the president reduces the range of available information essential to Mexico's decisionmaking process. The most outspoken leaders of the private and public sector agree on this. Ernesto Robles Levi, former member of the elite Mexican Council of Businessmen, has this to say:

> We suffer from an excessive emphasis on the president. Many people are willing to accept a decision uncritically without informing the president of their views. We have this concept that the president of Mexico

orders everything. . . . We have this myth that all things are done in the name of the president of Mexico.[13]

Presidential deference is ingrained in Mexico's political culture. The problem with it is that it is widespread not only among the population but among the president's political collaborators. Individuals who represent interest groups also find it difficult to speak frankly to the president. In 1984, during an interview with Carlos Mireles, then president of Canacintra, one of the most important business chambers in Mexico, we were interrupted by a call from a cabinet secretary. Mireles explained that earlier in the day he had met with President de la Madrid, cabinet members, and union leaders. The cabinet member had called, among other reasons, to scold Mireles for speaking too frankly to the president. Mireles argued that he did not agree with his friend's interpretation, and that the president himself had complimented Mireles, "saying he appreciated my identification of all the problems and the frankness with which I spoke."[14]

Individuals like Carlos Mireles are unusual, though on the increase in Mexico. This anecdote reveals how unique it is for interest-group leaders to speak candidly to the president, and the pressure a president's collaborators exert to prevent open expression of dissenting views.

The president must actively seek out contradictory interpretations, so as not to receive an incomplete view. Mexico's president has three sources of information: collaborators, groups or individuals, and the media. The most important of these three are collaborators.

Very few individuals and groups see the president personally, through business has as much or more access to him as any actor in Mexico. Most entrepreneurs and their interest group leaders deal with lower-level figures or, at best, cabinet members. Evelyn Stevens suggests why the lack of varied opinion is so critical to the president and other decisionmakers:

> Lower echelon decision makers define each new situation to conform with the stereotyped images which have shaped their political world. In effect, they have decided a priori to confine their responses to an extremely narrow range of actions, which present protest groups with a reduced range of choice as to their subsequent behavior. Decision makers at higher levels lack, or are deprived of, information which might enable them to reevaluate the situation and search for alternative methods of dealing with it.[15]

The nature of successful Mexican political careers is not conducive to the sharing of public information. This has two consequences for decisionmaking. In a negative way, information is used as a primary resource for political power. Those who have knowledge can manipulate the system to benefit their own interests and careers.[16] However, there are cases where individuals withhold information. The two most notable examples in recent years were: Pemex officials kept the true figures for oil reserves out of President Echeverría's hands because they opposed his economic policies, and Bank of Mexico officials kept the figures for Mexico's international reserves hidden from treasury personnel.[17] The positive side of restricting information within the Mexican political system is that it encourages politicians to cultivate a broad range of contacts among various important actors in the political arena, including the private sector, so they will have independent and diverse sources of information.

The president might find some useful interpretations in the media, but as I have suggested in my examination of the relationship between intellectual life and the state, Mexico's media lacks serious investigative reporting. Much of what the media publishes is fed to it by government news agencies.[18] Even presidents in societies where media is more independent have difficulty finding time to read those views. Interest-group advertisements in leading Mexican national newspapers, however, do provide a prime means for "taking the political pulse of the country."[19] Private-sector groups frequently use this approach with individual cabinet members and the president himself.

Presidentialism—and the qualities that characterize it—is not about to disappear rapidly from the Mexican scene. Mexican politicians lack an organizational base of power. Instead, they rely on their standing with the president. As long as politicians are indebted to the president for their careers, presidential deference among politicians will persist; and as long as the president retains considerable influence over economic resources, outside groups will defer as well.

Peer pressure among entrepreneurs and politicians helps this deference remain part of Mexican political culture. The independent behavior on the part of a certain segment of entrepreneurs, when they openly state their complaints directly, challenges politicians' ability to manipulate information reaching their superiors.

The Mexican state channels access to decisionmakers and the decisionmaking process along certain paths. Other than testing entrepreneurial influences in concrete policy decisions, probably the most important element to examine in the private-public sector relationship is business leaders' access to the government. On this issue Mexico's private sector expresses a consensus: most businessmen claim ready access to the state.

Leaders in the state of México, the country's most industrialized region, closest geographically to Mexico City, believe they have excellent channels of communication with state government. Guillermo Sánchez Fábela, president of the Chamber of Commerce of Toluca, México's capital, noted that businessmen have very few problems with state and local officials. "The higher you go, however, the less contact we have because of the local nature of my particular organization. We do have frequent dialogues with the government and with national chambers to exchange our views."[20] He went on to say, however, that de la Madrid listened to representatives of his organization as a presidential candidate and, when he became president, initiated formal contact with local business groups in the state of México for the first time.

Most Mexican business leaders were in agreement that at the national level they too had access to government officials.[21] Interestingly, in a political culture which thrives on personal contact, most businessmen believed that the institutional channels were sufficient for access. Although friendship makes it easier to make an initial contact with a government official, most businessmen found government officials willing to hear their views.[22]

Trends in the private sector's access to the state in the 1980s appear favorable. Most entrepreneurs agree that the de la Madrid administration has improved communications between the business community and the state. The source of the improvement was not confined to the posture of the president, but included a change in the personnel in recent governments. Mario Segura Quiroc, president of the Mexican Stock Exchange, explains why:

> High- and middle-level positions today, in my opinion, are being increasingly occupied by very capable individuals. . . . I think this is partly due to the fact that students from the private universities now can pursue public careers.[23]

Previously I argued the importance of educational trends for the entrepreneur's values and for the exchange between individuals in the private sector and the government. Segura Quiroc's comment suggests that many businessmen find it easier to deal with political office-holders trained in an environment they themselves share. Education affects the long-run relationship between the state and the private sector as it alters leadership values, and in the short run it may actually enhance the level of communication.

Older entrepreneurs don't see the same benefits stemming from a newly educated political leadership. Ernesto Robles Levi claims that in an earlier era, if he wanted to speak to someone, he could easily talk to a cabinet secretary. He believes that in the 1980s access is more difficult. He argues that cabinet secretaries, well trained technically, are much less politically prepared than during his era. In part, he attributes this to their foreign education and their incomplete understanding of the Mexican reality.[24]

The point that can be drawn from Robles Levi's interpretation is that a technically competent politician is attractive to businessmen because, as noted earlier, they can speak the same language. However, if technical ability supplants political sensitivity in Mexico's leadership, politicians will not know when to speak to entrepreneurs, and may be less sensitive to granting them immediate access. Therefore, the issue of effective dialogue must be separated from effective access.

Access, of course, does not guarantee any actual influence on Mexico's decisionmaking process. Proof of access, amply demonstrated in my interviews, is important for several reasons. The state improves its own image and enhances its political legitimacy by facilitating communication with the private sector. Further, no group, including the business community, can influence the outcome of decisions without reaching the threshold of influential government leaders, especially the president. The private sector, structurally speaking, is in a position to affect the Mexican policy process.

Private-Sector Influence and Self-Image

Examining the role of the Mexican private sector in concrete policy decisions is one means of testing its political influence. As I argued earlier, self-image is a key element in the private sector-state relationship. One aspect of self-image that contributes to the overall quality of this relationship is the degree to which entrepreneurs believe they are politically influential, whether or not it corresponds with reality. To what extent do businessmen believe they affect policy decisions?

If the opinions of leading Mexican businessmen actually could have been ascertained, they would probably have ranked their influence in the 1920s and 1930s as negligible. This response would have resulted as much from their lack of economic strength and their disorganization as from the public-sector leadership's perception of entrepreneurs' proper role. That is, public figures in the postrevolutionary era did not encourage the private sector's active involvement in decisionmaking.[25]

Naturally that historic posture on the part of both the private and public sectors has evolved, yet for Mexican politicians and entrepreneurs today, a consensus within and between the two groups on the nature and extent of business influence does not exist. What is important at this juncture is how entrepreneurs *perceive* their own influence. If Mexican businessmen believed their influence to be nonexistent in the decades immediately preceding the 1940s, then something contributed to changing that attitude dramatically by the 1960s.

When asked which interest group exerts the most influence on economic policies, Mexican industrialists in Derossi's study in the 1960s ranked their own associations as most influential, followed by bankers and labor unions. Foreign investors ranked a poor fourth.[26] According to these industrialists, only these three actors were really important to economic policymaking. Eighty-eight percent of the industrialists responding also believed they *could* counteract unfavorable government policies, and only 12 percent believed alternatives were not available to them.[27] According to two historical case studies of López Mateos' presidency (1958–1964), the administration immediately preceding the date of the survey, business did exert a significant influence over two decisions, the railroad strike and profit sharing.[28] Both cases are important because the major protagonist in each was organized labor.

The most notable group Mexican industrialists left out of their answer was politicians (perhaps because of the way the researcher worded the question). In other words, at that time industrialists did not perceive the state, or sections of it, as autonomous political actors. However, a few years later in 1972, in a questionnaire administered by the National Confederation of Manufacturing Industries (Conacintra), 168 firms were asked who was most influential in economic policy decisions. This time the respondents, again all industrialists, ranked public officials first, politicians second, bankers third, and large industrialists fourth.[29]

By the end of the 1970s the picture from the late 1960s had changed dramatically. Dale Story again interviewed a group of leading industrialists in 1979 and 1980, asking them to rank the most influential political actors. Although he did not specify economic policy, the answers are quite revealing. According to Mexican industrialists in this period, the most influential were politicians, bankers, large industrialists, and workers.[30]

The differences between what Story and Derossi found are extremely significant. In the first place, over the last fifteen years those groups with little or negligible influence have remained constant. Contrary to the view most Marxist economic historians take, industrialists are in agreement that multinational corporations play only a minimal role in Mexican economic policymaking—an issue we will return to in the next section. More importantly, whereas the private sector as a whole went from a minimal role in the postrevolutionary decades to their most important role in the 1960s, when Mexico's economic model was at its apex, it saw itself decline in influence during the 1970s and 1980s.

One explanation for this changed perception lies with the events of 1968. They produced a chain reaction in the 1970s, during which public figures, intellectuals, and entrepreneurs themselves questioned the efficacy of Mexico's political and economic model. Derossi completed her interviews in 1969, immediately following the events of 1968, but too soon for the impact to be felt. The fact that industrialists in the latter two surveys included politicians and/or public officials in their answer suggests an increased sophistication on the part of the respondents, and an understanding that the state acts to defend its own interests, not just those of various social groups. Politically, if 1968 did anything, it widened the gap between two major factions within the state. The fact that the pro-statist groups were exerting increased influence during or immediately preceding the second and third sets of questionnaires may explain why industrialists saw public officials' influence displacing their own.

When Dale Story asked industrialists in the late 1970s if they had actually achieved much success in affecting postwar economic policies, only half responded affirmatively. The other half believed that industrialists' interests were not well represented in government policy. Instead, when he asked them who actually benefits most from government policies, they ranked politicians, bankers, large industrialists, and merchants as most important.[31]

The data in the three surveys substantiate another point, offered by Susan and John Purcell during the same period, that "there are very few, if any, nongovernmental groups to provide a countervailing force to business interests."[32] On this point the three different surveys are in agreement. If the state as an actor is excluded from the responses, the banking sector and the industrialists are the most influential, followed by labor unions in two out of three surveys. In all three surveys bankers are at the top.

Bankers, as I argue frequently in this book, have served as a key channel for private-sector influence. When the government nationalized the banks in 1982, they removed instantaneously one of the two most important political actors in the eyes of Mexican industrialists. The removal of financiers from the private sector propelled industrialists into a more prominent position, since they now speak with a somewhat more unified voice for the whole sector. The position of organized labor is also strengthened, since the removal of bankers leaves only one, rather than two, strong competitors, each with greater influence on the state.

Story's findings indicated a trend that has since worsened. The general reaction of private-sector leaders since 1982 is that they have a limited influence on government policy, less than that of organized labor, although a range of views exists as to their level of influence.

Those Mexican businessmen who are willing to admit that the private sector is the most influential interest group are definitely a minority. However, even those who support this interpretation suggest their influence is limited. Ernesto Robles Levi bluntly states this position.

> The only group with any real influence in Mexico is the private sector. But our influence can be measured by the degree to which we can limit the activities of the state. We can't achieve what we want in a positive direction. What I mean to say is that we can limit its action in terms of the resources we control, and in this we are very strong, but we can't achieve new and constructive policies on the part of the government. In a sense, we are only consulted, but we are not an obligatory influence.[33]

Prominent business organization leaders who have spent their lives negotiating with the private sector suggest their influence is not actively positive. Pedro Sánchez Mejorado, who was president of the Coordinating Council of Businessmen (CCE), believes that whereas contact with the government has been considerable, during his lifetime the private sector has exerted very little influence. He argues, "We do not have lobbying in Mexico the way you do in the United States. We do take the initiative, but our initiative from the CCE is one of preventive measures, rather than having any significant impact in changing policy."[34] Other individuals used the word "consulting," implying that whereas the government respects their organizations, it rarely consults them, and it was up to the private sector to take the initiative.[35]

When Mexican entrepreneurs are asked to explain why they believe their influence has been minimal, they suggest several reasons. The most antagonistic of these, which sees the government as purposely conspiring to limit the private sector's impact, stems from the interpretation that entrepreneurial interests are incorporated beneath the wing of the state as part of a larger, corporatist political structure. This view suggests that Mexico's private sector cannot be influential because the state tries to control and dominate business chambers.[36] Moreover, the state has done everything in its power, as I argued in Chapter 3, to delegitimize the private sector in the eyes of the public.

The private sector's unfavorable image is a key variable in decisionmaking. Sophisticated businessmen suggest that many politicians accept the public's negative view of the business community. They believe business would be in a much stronger position to exert influence on the state if it could achieve a better public image. Andrés Marcelo Sada Zambrano, a leading figure of the Monterrey Group, believes the real battle for private-sector political influence will be won in the minds of the Mexican people.

> I think the real battle in the next few years is not at all in politics. Those entrepreneurs who are participating in politics will gain us some time. The real contest is for the minds of the people. Our situation today is the result of what people think about us, not corruption, or other causes. Really, I believe that society is a reflection of what people think. There is a change in the climate of what people think, and that is why political participation among other groups including businessmen, has increased.[37]

The other explanation for the private sector's limited influence is structural. Mexican business organizations have a limited effect on government policy because they have been automatically excluded from the government party. This structural exclusion puts them at a disadvantage compared to other groups and reduces their prestige in the public's eyes.

The most remarkable change in businessmen's attitude toward their political influence since the 1980s is their view of union power compared to their own. According to three groups of industrialists, union influence after the 1960s was well behind their own and that of bankers and public officials. Recently, nearly all leading Mexican entrepreneurs, industrialists included, believe unions are far more influential on the decisionmaking process. This view was stated most blatantly by José María Basagoiti: "I definitely believe that unions have much more influence than we do. They are allied with the state, and they are the ones who make the most important decisions in this country. In a democratic country, this wouldn't be possible, would it? All interests should be represented, but they are allied with the state against the private sector."[38]

No scholar of Mexican politics has ever suggested that organized labor is the most influential interest group. Furthermore, political economists have demonstrated clearly that government policies favor the interests of the private sector over the long run. Therefore, how is it that Mexican entrepreneurs see their influence as far less than organized labor's? Business leaders provide several explanations. One interpretation says that the private sector-government and the labor-government relationships differ in nature, implying that the private sector only influences government on a narrow range of economic issues. Businessmen see labor exerting more political influence over a broad range of issues. Consequently, they believe government officials fear union more than private-sector influence.[39]

A final view is that neither unions nor any other group are important because the Mexican state makes its own decisions. It does not favor private interests consistently, but a policy favoring private-sector and labor interests. This complex explanation is offered by a leading political activist in the Monterrey Group:

> In the first place, the state has favored the interests of the private sector, not because the private sector has forced them to pursue this goal, but because the interests of the private sector happen to correspond to the interests of the state. Secondly, I don't believe that it can be said that in all administrations the private sector has been a greater beneficiary than the workers. Third, I would also consider that the workers . . . are really part of the private sector. By this I mean that when the private sector is favored by the state and grows, then so are the workers. When the state become stronger, both of us suffer. In the last three administrations what has happened is that the intervention of the state has made both of us worse off. Therefore, what I am trying to say is that the real problem exists within the state, and not with groups outside the state and their relationship to it.[40]

Government officials in a position to know the level of influence exerted by the private sector find these explanations for minimal private-sector influence, especially compared to the unions, unconvincing. Hugo B. Margáin—who served in the secretariat of industry and commerce, played a key role in the profit-sharing decision in the early 1960s, and functioned as Echeverría's first secretary of the treasury—was incredulous at the view that the private sector has been uninfluential. He counters the typical entrepreneurial interpretation, simultaneously offering an explanation of why Mexican businessmen believe in what they say.

> It is ridiculous to say that the private sector has not had an influence on the state. It has always had an influence in this country. In all of my positions during the many years I have been in public life, they have always been active and I have always listened to their opinions. Politically, it may seem as though the unions always influence the government because they help us in an open manner in the political aspect of the government, and we also assist them. From that point of view, it does seem like the unions together with the government are against the private sector.[41]

Margáin's interpretation emphasizes visibility as a determinant of political influence. Behind-the-scenes maneuvering does not produce the same image as open political participation. Unions, even in the eyes of their opponents, appear to benefit from more influence than they actually have. In this sense, structural decisions excluding and including interest groups have a long-term impact on their perceived role.

Antonio Ortiz Mena, architect of Mexico's "stabilizing development" and highly respected by the private sector, supports Margáin's view. "Our contact with the private-sector leaders was constant when I was in government. We would call them, give them our ideas about a policy, wait for their reaction, and then we would analyze these reactions, take them into account, and incorporate them in our final policies."[42]

Multinational Influences and the Private-Public Relationship

Much has been written about the extent of multinational corporations' influence, economically and politically, in Latin America. The purpose of this book, however, is to examine the relationship between the *domestic* private sector and the Mexican state. Within that focus it is to be expected that the foreign private sector plays an important role. Most studies imply that multinationals, when present in large numbers, exert considerable economic influence over political decisionmaking.

Economic statistics have been used to document the extent of multinational corporations' growth in Mexico during the 1960s and

1970s. A reasonable argument is offered that foreigners' control over certain vital industries gives them considerable influence in the Mexican economy. Their conduct is so crucial to the economy that the Mexican government has sought to regulate them and foster the development of Mexican-owned industries.[43] It has been argued further that foreign domination of certain industrial sectors weakens the government's political control over the economy.[44] Regardless of how true these assertions are, the dynamics surrounding the relationship between the domestic private sector and the state are altered. However, most Mexican entrepreneurs do not see a connection to their relationship with the government.

As economists have pointed out, for many years, the overall foreign investment in Mexican manufacturing has represented less than 10 percent of the total national investment.[45] On the other hand, foreign influence in certain sectors, such as automobiles and pharmaceuticals, is substantial. For example, a study of the automobile industry indicates that the government is affected by the needs or demands of foreign groups, and that affects its relationship to the private sector.[46] Moreover, there are two types of foreign companies: those who are coinvestors and do not seek influence because they depend on Mexicans to deal with their problems; and those who retain principal control and play a more direct role in the policy process. The presence of foreign-operated companies tends to further separate the economy into heterogeneous groups.

The important role the state has had in the Mexican economy also complicates this relationship. When foreign capital cannot find a partner in the Mexican private sector, it seeks out the state. This means that certain economic activities are being controlled by the state and foreign investors, without domestic private-sector participation. Moreover, the state itself is being financed by increased international foreign capital as it expands its own role in the economy.[47] The National Finance Bank, one of the most important state-controlled industrial financial institutions before 1982, obtains half its resources from foreign sources.[48] It seems likely that government policies might be affected in an economic structural sense by the source of investment credit, although it would be difficult to ascertain how this effect might occur.

Moving from the economic to the political realm, the real concern of this book—several authors have intimated that multinationals exert influence independently. Foreign entrepreneurial groups, like domestic groups, have access to cabinet and other leaders and use it to influence the formulation of domestic economic policy. However, they rarely have direct contact with the president, and when such an interview occurs, it is generally because a persistent problem has remained unresolved.[49] It also has been suggested that since the early 1970s, chief executives from some of the major multinational corporations have infiltrated the leadership of several important chambers, including Canacintra and Concamin.[50]

A more direct political role of multinationals appears to be very limited. One of their most important influences on the political relationship between the domestic private sector and the state is cultural. As with the influence of foreign education on individual businessmen, very little analysis of this impact is available. Derossi's work, the earliest serious study, concluded that Monterrey businessmen came closest to being acculturated to the North American model, but that in general Mexican entrepreneurs only imitate the United States management style, not their goals.[51] Her interpretation, correct as far as it goes, underestimates the tremendous impact subtle cultural values are having on Mexican entrepreneurs, not just in their economic behavior, but politically as well.

In an excellent study of the attitudes of Mexicans working for multinational corporations, James Dull found several significant beliefs that would affect the private-public sector relationship. Multinationals' most important effect is on Mexican managers' nationalism. He concluded that "the evidence reveals that for most of the executives, the needs, goals, and welfare of the firms often take precedence over national policy and that the managers will promote corporate objectives through direct challenges to or through manipulation of national law and policy."[52] The firm's importance creates hostile and suspicious attitudes on the part of the Mexican multinational corporate officer toward the state. These attitudes compound domestic entrepreneurs' already antagonist views toward the state.

Mexicans who work for multinational corporations have not only mixed loyalties to company and state but also an altered view of political freedom. Dull argues that many executives question the efficacy of the present Mexican political model. Moreover, he found indications that their experiences with foreign corporations reinforced their desire for expanded political freedom.[53] Dull's findings are borne out more concretely by evidence that Mexicans affiliated with multinationals were extensively represented on the board of one of the first organized interest groups which sought to educate the public and influence government policy.[54] Expanded political freedom, as I argue in Chapter 9, supports the posture of organizations like Coparmex, which advocates a more aggressive policy favoring state political reforms. Increased political activism further divides the private-sector community and complicates the private-public sector relationship. Numerous Mexicans affiliated with multinationals regard national economic practices and values as inferior to the foreigners' and incapable of achieving economic progress.[55] In addition to the complications in the private-public sector relationship brought on by regionalism, size of firm, and education of the two sets of leaders, an inferiority complex about private-sector practices further divides the private sector.

One of the most interesting values multinationals may encourage Mexican entrepreneurs to uphold is the concept of social responsibility, discussed in the section in Chapter 3 on entrepreneurial self-image. The definition of social responsibility becomes a noteworthy variable because it has broad political implications, and because a newer breed of multinational chief executive officers see themselves as mentors in a country of disciples. An aggressive posture is taken by Bernardo Galei, director of a highly successful complex of cement manufacturing plants, who believes that his company offers a model of private entrepreneurship for Mexico. His firm combines their primary economic activity with agriculture in the surrounding community where they are located. They have invested considerable capital beyond that of the primary firm to bring employment and production to the community. He believes this approach is a part of a larger definition of social responsibility and hopes to convince Mexican business leaders of its applicability. This is how he described his model:

> We are doing this not for a medal, but to inspire better conditions for the world's population and to demonstrate that we understand how the benefits of capitalism can be used to improve those conditions. We are attempting to convey that philosophy to the people we are helping. I believe we are the only company in Mexico that has done this, and believe it or not, we have actually been able to return profits from this social responsibility aspect back to the community in which we are located. . . . Furthermore, it protects our main investment, it improves the condition of the worker, and it creates a new set of activities for those individuals who cannot be employed in our regular firm. . . . We have done this now with two companies. We cannot wait for the government to make the changes necessary in Mexico—if we did, it would be too late. I have tried to interest other companies in Mexico in this because it doesn't really cost anything to accomplish.[56]

If Galei's concept of social capitalism becomes more widespread, it not only means a different economic attitude among Mexican businessmen, but also indicates that businesses can alter the community's view toward them and their role in society. The larger and more positive their role, the more it flavors their societal image, giving them political ammunition with which to confront the state. With stronger support from the citizenry, the private sector can become a more powerful political actor. Such changing views are already occurring. If multinationals play a leadership role, because of the existing sense in Mexico of national inferiority to foreign economic models, the attraction of increased social responsibility and political activism will be stronger.

These are some of the ways the foreign private sector has had and can have an impact on Mexico, specifically on the relationship between the domestic private sector and the state. Very few Mexican entrepreneurs, however, believe that multinational corporations affect, in any way, their relationship to the state. Maybe one of the reasons Mexicans do not perceive foreigners as important to their relationship is because they do not view foreign companies as having much influence on the state.

According to Ernesto Robles Levi, who as a former member of the Mexican Council of Businessmen would be in a position to know their impact, foreign companies do have an influence on government. He believes the Mexican government takes multinationals into account, although they cannot admit politically that foreigners have this type of influence. The state often makes public statements to the contrary, but their relationship with the foreign private sector is very good. Although the foreign private sector is not joined together in any organic way, they are represented by the American Chamber of Commerce in Mexico.[57] It has been suggested by another chamber leader that good relations between the Mexican government and foreign entrepreneurs have a positive impact on the relationship between the domestic sector and the state.[58]

A minority of Mexican businessmen believe foreigners do have an impact on their domestic relationship. They believe multinationals' influence stems from their association with the government rather than with domestic businessmen, in recent years. This argument asserts that the Mexican government has not applied certain laws consistently, that it has made exceptions because of its desire for foreign investment.[59] Government flexibility with foreigners provides an object lesson for domestic entrepreneurs, who can use it as a bargaining chip in their own negotiations with the state.

Overwhelmingly, though, the view among leading Mexican entrepreneurs is that multinationals have no influence whatsoever on their ties to the state. This view reflects a strong consensus by age and sector. When asked to explain why they believe this, they give several answers. One interpretation is tied to history—to the rhetoric of the Mexican Revolution and to postrevolutionary nationalism. As one important figure in the construction industry argued, if foreign entrepreneurs tried to directly influence government policy, it would have disastrous results. Mexican entrepreneurs and politicians can talk privately with each other, and examine mistakes and achievements, because both are Mexicans. Foreign investors are excluded from this type of relationship because of their less-than-equal position before nationals of either stripe. Consequently, they exert no influence on Mexican domestic economic policy.[60] Not only does the Mexican government view foreign businessmen differently from domestic entrepreneurs, but multinationals themselves behave differently from their Mexican counterparts.

Why do Mexican entrepreneurs feel that foreigners have no impact on their relationship to the state? Carlos E. Represas, director general of Nestlé, one of Mexico's largest multinational corporations, stressed the importance of history and suggested that at least since World War II, foreigners have had a knowledge of Mexico's history and the difficult relationship between foreign investors and Mexico in the past. Therefore, they maintain an extremely low visibility in Mexico. Because they want to maintain a low-key posture, they would never think of participating in politics. Instead, they try to maintain a good relationship to and contacts with the government through traditional informal channels, never through political activities. Top-ranked government officials, subject to such influence, agree with this interpretation.[61]

Another set of views coalesce around the interpretation that whereas foreign companies are important to the economy, they operate separately from the domestic private sector. This explanation suggests that while there is no formal division between foreign and domestic entrepreneurial groups, close communication between the two does not occur, nor do they articulate their views very well to each other. The reason each group remains distant from the other is that their problems are different, their resources are dissimilar, and their methods are unique. As one entrepreneur suggests, "the American Chamber of Commerce maintains a very low profile, it is there and it has some influence, but it has a very moderate attitude and is discreet and never attacks any of the other groups in the private sector."[62] Another economist with more than fifty years of experience in the public sector agreed, adding his view that the two private-sector groups have rarely formed an alliance against the state.[63]

Finally, public-sector leaders are in agreement with the private sector that multinationals do not affect the relationship between Mexican entrepreneurs and the state. Both believe this is true because multinationals have been invited to Mexico under special legal provisions. They argue that the only time foreigners interfere is when they believe one of the laws which governs their presence in Mexico has been violated or will be altered by the government or some other group.[64] Government officials believe that one of the most powerful resources foreign businesspeople bring to bear on their relationship to the state is their effect on Mexico's image abroad. This leverage with the Mexican government does not directly affect the government's relationship with the private sector.[65] Officials also agree that foreigners understand Mexico's environment, and therefore, in their governmental relations, act like Mexicans.[66]

However, multinational corporations that follow the traditional Mexican pattern of remaining outside the political arena have an indirect impact on domestic entrepreneurs in two ways. In the first place, as an independent interest group whose prestige carries some weight with entrepreneurs and politicians, they reinforce the traditional actions of Mexican businessmen. On the other hand, as the domestic business community further divides on the issue of political participation, foreigners, who generally participate politically in their own societies, may opt to take a more visible role in the policy process, claiming that they are emulating their indigenous peers.

Labor's Influence—Fantasy and Reality

Mexican businessmen see the influence of multinationals as unimportant; their view of organized labor could not be more opposed. The range of attitudes entrepreneurs have about labor as a powerful political force may stem from their view that it has been a detrimental force in Mexico's economic development. In general, they distrust labor leadership.[67] When Derossi surveyed industrialists in the late 1960s, she found organized labor ranked well behind bankers and industrialists in influence. However, her findings appear to have been based on their definition of an interest group; that is, they tended to think of labor unions as merely an extension of government influence, rather than as independent interest organizations.[68]

By itself, it is valuable to know that Mexican businessmen do not see themselves as particularly influential in the decisionmaking process. It is equally important to understand that they see organized labor as far more influential. This is particularly noteworthy since Marxian economists have argued that organized labor sees itself as having to fight both the state and the Mexican entrepreneurs because their interests are intertwined.[69] Mexican businessmen, on the other hand, see themselves as having to fight both the state and organized labor.

Fantasy or perception is just as real to the individual as reality, and the consequences of fantasy can be more important than those of reality. There are two ways to test the reality of organized labor's influence on economic decisionmaking. The first method is to examine the results and direction of government decisions over the long run.

To my knowledge, no economic historian has ever suggested or provided evidence that the Mexican government since 1920 has pursued a long-term policy beneficial to organized labor, especially vis-à-vis the private sector. The best way to test this assumption is to examine organized labor's benefits as a consequence of economic policies.

Real *family* income of the industrial work force has stayed the same or increased slightly from 1939 to 1955.[70] The only period when real income has increased significantly since 1939 is after 1958, the high point of stabilizing development. Antonio Ortiz Mena, the public figure most responsible for implementing that economic policy, argues that the private sector's perception of labor influence is incorrect. In his opinion, "the only period when real salaries rose in Mexico was from 1959 to 1970. In all other periods, they have remained stagnant or declined. This means that organized labor has been sacrificed to serve the interests of the state and its goals, and the state has been incapable of defending these workers' interests. From 1970 to the present, the loss in real income has even been greater than before 1959."[71]

Another measure of the working class's influence is distribution of income. Even during the period when income increased, from 1958 to 1970, its distribution favored higher-income groups, including private-sector leadership. The income share of the poorest 40 percent of the population declined from 15 percent to 12 percent while the wealthiest increased their share from 36 percent to 39 percent.[72]

Nor has labor fared well in social welfare. Government expenditures in social services, where organized labor has worked to increase the federal budget, remains behind Chile, Venezuela, and Brazil, and only slightly ahead of Somoza's Nicaragua. According to one analyst, these figures are explained by a stagnant tax base and government appropriations to subsidize services to private industry.[73]

The other means of testing the private sector's assertions about the influence of organized labor on specific decisions is to examine concrete cases of policymaking. Detailed evidence over a long period is not available, but a small number of case studies suggest several important patterns. First, even beginning in the 1920s when labor and the private sector were both involved in the evolution of labor laws, the state, not either interest group, was in command of the decision-making process. Labor expressed its views, but did not alter the decision.[74] Thirty years later, when the National Teachers' Union went on strike, the government was forced to compromise in meeting their demands. This suggests that in individual cases, if numbers are sufficiently large (teachers have the largest occupational union), if the union is urban based, and if its members are middle class, the state will compromise.[75]

The most-studied case in the 1960s is the profit-sharing plan, another decision heavily involving the private sector and organized labor. Again, certain patterns from the late 1920s are reconfirmed. First, the president provided the initiative for the reforms. Second, organized labor played a very passive role. Third, labor lacked unity. Fourth, labor's role was reactive. Fifth, compared with the private sector's, labor's efforts to influence the outcome were unimpressive.[76]

There is no doubt that in the 1970s and 1980s labor has exerted an increasingly important influence in supporting the regime's political legitimacy. On the other hand, the serious economic situation, the lack of unity within the labor movement, and the small number of Mexicans who are actually union members limit organized labor's influence on the decisionmaking process. Whatever occasional concessions labor receives, it has never been a crucial actor in the broad sweep of government economic policy.[77]

The scholarly view and the economic facts themselves suggest at best a minor role for unions. That is the reality. What about their image? Businesspeople believe they are extremely influential, much more so than the private sector. A confusion between politics and policy is the most important reason for this entrepreneurial view. Emilio Goicochea Luna, who favors an aggressive political role for the private sector, observed that "we are not in politics, but in the field of policy. On the other hand, the labor unions definitely are involved with politics."[78] Mexican entrepreneurs believe that unions are more influential because they are politically active and involved, whereas entrepreneurs participate only in the policy process.

Entrepreneurs have a fixation on the original exclusion of the private sector and inclusion of labor in the semicorporatist architecture of the Mexican polity. As I noted in Chapter 2, the important distinction is that while both belong to state-initiated interest organizations, entrepreneurs collectively are excluded from the official party—in effect, politically from the state. This has led entrepreneurs for the last five decades to see themselves as "nonpolitical," as though a sheltered role in the policy process is nonpolitical.

There seem to be three sets of overlapping concepts that Mexican entrepreneurs confuse. In the first place, they do not clearly understand that influencing policy is political, that the ultimate purpose of political behavior is to affect policy. They have confused method with purpose. In one sense, their perception is accurate. They believe they are in a disadvantaged position because the state has formal relations with groups. The only excluded groups are entrepreneurs and clergy. (It might be argued that Cárdenas seriously erred in his decision to exclude business, and that a fully coopted interest like labor is more effectively pacified through its proximity to and identity with the state than a group delegitimized by its exclusion from the state.)

Secondly, entrepreneurs believe that being part of the state gives an interest organization more rather than less influence. In this sense they confuse proximity and legitimacy with influence. For example, René Becerra states that "you shouldn't forget that it [labor] is a pillar of the official party and that it has made use of the rhetoric of the Mexican Revolution."[79] There is considerable logic to this argument. Theorists have long assumed that the larger the exchange between private- and public-sector leadership, the greater the influence exerted by the private sector over the public sector. The same view can be applied to the exchange between labor union leaders and government officials. The fact that union leaders are incorporated automatically in the state apparatus, especially participatory organizations such as the party, increases their actual exchange. The entrepreneurial view can be tested simply by examining the extent of union labor's control over important government offices. It is true that in the past, union leaders have been well represented in political offices, much more so than entrepreneurs at any time since the 1920s. Even one Mexican president could be said to have been briefly a union leader. On the other hand, it is also true that union officials rarely direct cabinet posts, specifically agencies determining economic policies. Moreover, politicians from union backgrounds have all but disappeared from executive agency leadership. (MPBP)

Finally, entrepreneurs have concluded that the more visible the process of achieving influence, the more extensive the influence. Thus not only have they confused method with purpose, but they believe method determines policy. The very nature of the Mexican political system, in terms of its policy process, is to operate in a closed manner, away from public view. Entrepreneurs seem to visualize the Mexican system in a North American light, accepting the notion that the more visible actors are the most influential. A former treasury secretary explains how this view came about: "I think one of the most important elements in the private sector's perception is the press. The press exaggerates this whole relationship between the unions and the government. The way I would describe it is that the unoins are politically influential while the private sector has always been influential in economic policy."[80] Margáin is saying that to the uneducated public eye it seems as though unions are always politically involved with the government while the private sector is not. In reality, the private sector has had much more influence on economic policy even if its influence is less obvious.

The Mexican government's relationship to groups parallels personal social relationships. The cliché that people judge you by the friends you keep offers much insight into the private sector's perception of union influence. Historically, the state has tried to befriend organized labor, not only by incorporating unions into itself—thus suggesting that their interests were shared—but by purposefully publicizing this relationship as intimate. The state made this choice for ideological reasons—organized labor fits in more closely with the public rhetoric of the Mexican Revolution.

The state also chose organized labor as a bosom political friend because of its size. As Ortiz Mena admits, organized labor is one of the mass interest groups, and therefore the government "gives the impression that it is defending at a level of 100 percent the interests of labor, even if in reality it may be responding at a 40–50 percent level. Politics is what you can accomplish in reality. . . . The private sector believes what it is telling you because the government gives the impression of supporting the workers, not because it actually fulfills policies which necessarily benefit workers."[81]

One of the characteristics that emerged from the earlier analysis of entrepreneurs' self-image is their general lack of political sophistication. This deficiency could explain, in part, why they confuse politics with policy, and public visibility with powerful influence. The more sophisticated businessmen, however, concede that the private sector is more influential in the economic realm than unions. Yet they, too, separate policy influence into two distinct categories.

In the back of the sophisticated entrepreneur's mind is the idea that the Mexican state has made itself indispensable to entrepreneurs because its control over labor is critical to the viability of any economic policy in Mexico. Stated differently, government control of labor is a tool for government control of business. The state can encourage or discourage strikes as a means of exerting pressure on a recalcitrant business community.[82] Many businessmen see union influence on the increase in recent years, corresponding to the decrease in the state's political legitimacy. Union influence on business may also wane. If union leaders cannot control their workers, and the state cannot control union leaders, then business might find it more advantageous to bargain with workers independently rather than through the state.

Businessmen also attribute union influence on policy to the continuity and cohesiveness of union leadership.[83] Furthermore, businessmen are threatened by the state's encouraging unions to buy their own companies, thus alloting them an economic resource that previously has been only in the hands of business.[84]

Two Case Studies of Private-Sector Influence

In the few available case studies of important decisions involving private-sector interests versus the interests of organized labor, Mexican entrepreneurs always come out on top. Businessmen are easily the most important and influential of outside political actors, whatever their self-image. Studies of Mexico's 1960 decision to join the Latin American Free Trade Association (LAFTA), the 1963 implementation of a profit-sharing plan, and the 1979 decision to remain outside the General Agreement on Trade and Tariffs, demonstrate that the ultimate heavy among political actors is the state, not traditional interest groups.[85] My analysis of the LAFTA decision almost two decades ago revealed that groups within the bureaucracy itself can play a role more typically assigned to special interests, and given the nature of the Mexican political system, that role might be increasingly common.[86]

In two major decisions since 1982, the bank nationalization and the rectorship of the economy, both of which affect the structure of the private sector, its relationship to other actors, and its ties to the state, the private sector was not even consulted. As I implied in the Introduction, the theoretical view that the state is an autonomous actor is very much borne out by recent actions. In his interpretation of business influence, Kane suggests that entrepreneurs usually affect government policymakers in three ways: they can try to influence the government to adopt a policy beneficial to them; policymakers may try to persuade the private sector to undertake a task they conceive of as vital to the nation's interests (such as José López Portillo's Alliance for Production); and the objectives of both groups may be sufficiently congruent that neither has to exert pressure over the other.[87] A fourth scenario that does not involve the private sector in the decisionmaking process is for the state, or a faction within it, to make a decision without consulting the affected groups.

No better example of the fourth alternative exists than the nationalization of the banks. When President López Portillo announced the decision in his State of the Union address in 1982, he caught the country by surprise. Many speculations have been offered as to why he made the decision, and until he gives his own version, no one can know for sure. They range from a president desirous of a distinguished place in Mexican history to pure revenge against the private sector.[88] One of the few individuals involved in making the decision, Carlos Tello, makes it clear that the initiative came from the president, and that Tello and one other cabinet secretary outlined nationalization as a possible alternative in a report commissioned personally by the president.[89] The secretive manner in which the decision was reached, and the small number of individuals consulted, suggest several characteristics of the decisionmaking process and the private sector's role in it.

In the first place, in spite of the literature correctly indicating the declining pattern of presidential decisionmaking authority in Mexico in recent years, the bank nationalization reveals that a Mexican president, without consultation, can make a decision of earthshaking consequences to the political system. That a single individual can alter a historic relationship some fifty years in the making suggests a serious weakness of the Mexican system. The president exercises sufficient political authority, if misused, to bring down the entire governmental apparatus.

The decision also elucidates the validity of the autonomous state as a critical actor in the decisionmaking process. In this case, as Sylvia Maxfield argues, the bank nationalization was the result of a temporary ideological domination by a small group of left-wing economic advisers within López Portillo's circle of consultants.[90] In short, the state's impact as an autonomous actor is not dependent on a consensus among influential state actors or large numbers of political sympathizers.

The president made the decision in such a manner precisely because no consensus existed to support it, and because the private sector and sympathetic interests within the government could be expected to oppose it strongly. The disadvantage of making the decision this way is that the lack of consensus dilutes its long-term influence.[91] The president's advisers chose to nationalize the most effective target within the private sector, with the possible exception of the foreign-controlled drug industry. Banks were an easy target because two major chains controlled 50 percent to 60 percent of all banking, and therefore the businesses of five or six families could be nationalized without a ripple effect on large numbers of entrepreneurs. Moreover, bankers were the most unpopular economic group in the private sector.[92]

It is not clear from insiders in the decisionmaking process, or from analysts who examined the decision, whether the president actually understood that bankers were unpopular. It is obvious, however, that Mexico's political leadership questioned the increasing power of the banking community. According to William Glade, the advent of large banking chains in the 1960s and 1970s "brought on stage formidable new private sector actors who, with their foreign partners, seemed capable of challenging the primacy of the state and the domination of the PRI. The political class and the intelligentsia were especially discomforted, and the allegation was widely made that business groups had gained control of Mexico."[93]

The state's original conception of the banking community was quite different. Historically, bankers have had an especially close relationship to the Mexican state. The data on leadership exchanges clearly point to the government having stronger ties between the banks than with the private sector generally.

Public officials responsible for building the contemporary relationship between the state and the private sector viewed bank resources as politically neutral, that is, they were not part of the private sector's arsenal. Antonio Ortiz Mena explains this significant state interpretation:

> The nationalization of the banks is very important indirectly, in the sense that in 1960, when we began the concept of 51 percent Mexican control over foreign investment, we used the banking system to make this possible. Domestic capital was insufficient or was not available to expand Mexican industry. We thought of domestic banking capital as neutral, that is, it wasn't foreign nor was it private-sector capital, rather it belonged to everyone since all Mexicans contributed their savings to form that capital. . . . In this way, banks indirectly became extremely important in controlling the private sector, but it is important to remember that this control occurred as a result of government implementation of the 51 percent law.[94]

The irony is that the nationalization decision converted a resource the Mexican state initially considered neutral into a politicized weapon the state itself could use. The state never conveyed its perception of capital as a neutral resource to the private sector, to opposing political actors, or to politicians in general.

There is considerable evidence that a large amount of latent support for the nationalization of the banks existed in Mexican society, even among entrepreneurs themselves. In a national poll conducted by PRI, flawed because it disproportionately samples higher-income and educated groups, more people supported than opposed nationalization.[95] Entrepreneurs' dislike for bankers had practical reasons. Gabriel Zaid, a leading Mexican intellectual, noted that many entrepreneurs perceived bankers as authoritarian. The greatest cost to any Mexican business in the 1970s and 1980s has been interest on loans. Many companies and bankers formed a special economic relationship. For example, an individual bank might control 10 percent of a corporation's assets. The bank would guarantee further credit to protect their original investment, but if a bank did not have an initial investment in a specific company it might not be willing to provide the necessary credit.[96]

Mexico's banking chains exaggerated the tendency Zaid describes, for not only did banks give preference to customers with whom they had previous investments, but certain firms received preferred treatment. These firms were large enterprises formally associated with the holding companies to which all major banking chains were tied. As one leading entrepreneur concludes, "it is logical that the big banks gave preference to their stockholders and to the holding companies with which they were affiliated."[97] Public officials also found these great chains difficult to work with, and there is a hint of arrogance in bankers' behavior. Hugo Margáin notes that when he served "as secretary of the treasury (1970–1973), we had a difficult time with the large banking firms and groups. Generally, they tended to act like clans, and were very difficult to penetrate and develop a sense of social responsibility."[98]

The Mexican government has capitalized on the dissension within the private sector toward the banking community by putting an end to the preferential financing that major industrial enterprises counted on in the past.[99] The government can use the implementation of the nationalization decision to capitalize on a real or perceived complaint on the part of medium-sized and small businesspeople who believe they lacked competitive access to credit. This tactic not only mollifies opposition to the nationalization decision, but also helps the state to recement relations with the private sector, notably firms other than the leading industrial groups.

Some entrepreneurs remain unconvinced that credit preference was a source of dissatisfaction within the private sector. As one entrepreneur argued, "Everyone that I know was very much opposed to the nationalization of the banks. They objected both to the decision and to its results. . . . I never detected . . . favoritism among the banks toward giving out credit before 1982."[100] Derossi's 1969 study lends support to this interpretation, since industrialists claimed that criteria for bank loans was 73 percent economic and only 8 percent friendship.[101] However, credit preference to a firm because of its holding-company affiliation might be seen as economic rather than personal. True or not, many Mexicans outside and inside the private sector perceived the banking establishment as a powerful monopoly favoring the interests of a small minority of families.[102]

The state can also be blamed for the perception small and medium-sized entrepreneurs had of the banking community. The main issue in the late 1970s and the 1980s was the availability and price of credit. Entrepreneurs' perception of preferential loan criteria was probably second to the lack of available credit. Whereas bankers may have received the blame, the state was often the culprit. Glade explains why: "the difficulties smaller firms have had in getting bank credit have been only partly attributable to the superior borrowing claims of bank-related firms (those *de la casa*); there was also significant 'crowding out' effect from the 'governmentalization' of loanable funds. According to some estimates the public sector absorbed 60 percent of bank credit in 1981 and 77 percent in 1982."[103]

The nationalization decision is the single most important cause, structurally and psychologically, of the rupture of the relationship between the Mexican private sector and the state. It is more significant than the consequences of 1968 because it was directed at the private sector and, more importantly, changed the rules of the game between the private sector and the state. Whereas 1968 caused the political leadership, entrepreneurs, intellectuals, and the middle class to examine the efficacy and legitimacy of Mexico's economic model, the nationalization decision specifically altered the relationship by redefining the model and the balance of power of the actors. The chief architect of the decision, Carlos Tello, summarizes the consequences of his recommendations:

> If one can distinguish between an administrative policy versus a state policy, nationalization has in effect become part of state policy. That is, the possibility of nationalization has now become a permanent part of the public sector's policy, not something tied to an individual administration. Therefore, the psychological impact is still present, and will be so for a long time, regardless of how far any single administration goes to reverse the implications of the original decision to nationalize the banks.
>
> The private sector has learned the enormous power the executive branch can bring to bear, and especially the power the president himself controls in making such decisions. Moreover, the realization both by the private sector and society at large of the support the president will have when he makes a decision in the nation's interest has become a concept which is part of the larger philosophy of our postrevolutionary heritage.
>
> The decision to nationalize the banks has definitely affected, in an essential way, the relationship between the private and public sectors, in spite of the fact that the present administration has done everything to minimize this impact. It is a cornerstone change, in the same way the 1938 petroleum expropriation affected Mexico. It now means that the government in fact is willing to consider national interests above the specific interests of any group. When the government perceives its independence, and the base of its power as being in danger, it can fall back on that consideration. This is clearly perceived by the private sector since 1982, in the same way that this same perception took place among the foreign entrepreneurs after 1938.[104]

Tello is suggesting that the government may use the threat of an economic decision involving national sovereignty to control powerful interest groups. A significant change in the relationship with the private sector is that now entrepreneurs, having been treated to the bank nationalization of 1982, are aware that such an option is more than just a threat; it exists as a very real future policy. The political consequences can be seen from several perspectives. One interpretation is that the nationalization helped polarize important actors in both sectors. Confrontation between political activists in the private sector and propopulists in the public sector makes it increasingly difficult for moderates in both groups to retain their dominance without seeming defeatists in their own sector's interests.[105]

Another point of view, not necessarily contradictory, is that the state redressed the political balance by destroying the power of the new economic class. According to this interpretation, the nationalization decision can be seen as conservative rather than radical, because it restores the traditional hegemony of the state, giving it the power to pursue its own goals.[106] A publicly controlled banking sector can take a more relaxed view in the repayment of loans, widening its basis of political support among hard-pressed businessmen.[107]

If the state perceived itself as losing control over the traditional political balance and used the nationalization of the banks to regain its position, in the eyes of the private sector the decision had radical implications. Mexican entrepreneurs see nationalization as radical because they perceive the decision, tied with the de la Madrid administration's constitutional amendments regarding the state as rector of the economy, as going beyond an individual administration. They also believe the balance of power is too skewed in favor of the state. The relationship cannot return to a pre-1940 condition. All the actors, their relationship with each other, and their positions in society have changed. For entrepreneurs, therefore, the future is in doubt, and their confidence in the state is at a low ebb.

A second post-1982 decision that countered private-sector interests was the state's institutionalization of its role as "rector" of the economy. President de la Madrid introduced constitutional changes that very clearly spell out the authority of the state as director of the Mexican economy. This provision has not been inherently upsetting to entrepreneurs. What most upsets Mexican businessmen is the institutionalization of the so-called social sector. A social sector has always existed in Mexico, but its constitutional legitimation has created many doubts in the private sector about where the state is going. Worse, the social-sector provision is seen by some observers as a concession to labor for its support during the crisis of 1981–1982.[108] The constitutional reforms identify three sectors: private, public, and social. The government can only intervene in those areas of the private sector permitted by the constitution. This regulation provides a certain sense of security to the private sector, yet gives status to a sector that previously had no constitutional standing. Economic cooperatives, such as the *ejido*, are part of the social sector. The private sector is afraid cooperatives might take over economic activities traditionally performed by the private sector, and cooperatives have certain tax privileges not granted to the private sector.[109]

Coming on the heels of the bank nationalization, and implemented by a succeeding administration trying to convince entrepreneurs that it has tried to nullify the economic impact of nationalization, short of returning the banks to their original owners, the rectorship of the economy is critical. One leading entrepreneurial figure expressed this concern. "It isn't the laws that bothered me in particular, and many of my colleagues, what bothers me is the intent of the regulations themselves. What I am worried about is that in the future someone who is not responsible is going to use the power present in those regulations to come down hard on the private sector."[110]

Interestingly, even those entrepreneurs who believe that the rectorship of the economy should be in the hands of the private sector are upset by the other provisions in the constitutional amendments. What concerns them is that the state should not have the privilege to judge what falls into public, private, and social categories.[111] Additionally, the social sector is confusing because it encourages unions to engage in entrepreneurial activity. In fact, unions are beginning to buy their own firms. If unions are capitalists, then why does Mexico need a separate sector in the constitution?[112] This question further confuses private-sector perceptions of their present and future relationship to the state.

Early in this book I noted the importance of constitutionalism as a legitimating force in entrepreneurs' self-image and interpretation of their relationship to the state. Reactions to the "rectorship of the economy" in the 1980s reconfirm the importance of the constitution as a symbol of societal norms and relationships in Mexican life. The state has been able to use the constitution to its advantage, but it may also find that codifying antagonistic and unclear provisions with direct implications for its relation to the private sector will, in the long run, destroy their working relationship. In the past, it made the same mistake prior to the formulation and implementation of a specific profit-sharing law. In that case the constitutional amendment, which both angered and frightened the private sector, was narrow enough to be identified only with the regime of President López Mateos, and only for the short term.[113] In contrast, the codification of a social sector is permanent, long-term, and a threat to all aspects of the private-public sector relationship.

Conclusions

The ultimate goal of any interest group in society is to influence the outcome of policy. Each society, and Mexico is no exception, evolves a set of rules by which groups traditionally play the political game. In Mexico, special characteristics apply historically to the decisionmaking process, both to the relationship between the private sector and the state, and to how decisions are reached within the state.

Many characteristics of the Mexican decisionmaking process are apparent, but one of the most significant is the degree to which deference is paid to the president, both by his collaborators and by individuals seeking state favors. The level of deference toward the president flavors many other qualities of Mexican politics and is deeply embedded in the Mexican political culture. In this sense, stronger parallels can be drawn to the British system than to the United States.

Conclusions from a small number of case studies and from interviews with leading entrepreneurs demonstrate an alteration in the private sector's traditional behavior and posture toward the state, the decisionmaking apparatus, and its societal role. The fact that many younger entrepreneurs favor an aggressive, open stance in presenting their demands to the state not only exhibits the level of dissension between interest groups and the state, but also changes the tone of the deference previously accorded Mexican presidents.

Politicians have difficulty in changing the very essence of their political behavior. Their own culture has internalized certain rules of behavior, one of which is deference to presidential authority. The degree to which Mexican leaders have fashioned deferential behavior as part of their political process is threatened by outsiders, who shatter a false calm surrounding the president with contradictory truths. Politicians find it awkward to adjust to these changes because they have not initiated them, and because their consequences are broad. Private-sector behavior alters the rules of the game for organized groups vis-à-vis the state. Entrepreneurial rudeness, as many politicians would label it, creates dissension within the state.

As seen earlier, the state has created its own rules, many of which extend back to the prerevolutionary era, and expects the players to follow its lead. And it has gone beyond designing the rules of the political game in that it has actually created and strengthened the players. Consequently, several of them—including the private sector and organized labor—are in a position for the first time since the 1920s to take the initiative. Their potential for independence is short-lived, since the 1982 bank nationalization removed the overwhelming economic power an aggressive private sector could bring to bear on the state, and the economic crisis, with its accompanying high unemployment, weakens organized labor. Yet the state itself, its legitimacy in decline since 1968, remains weak. In its own self-interest, it cannot continue as a viable entity without the cooperation of both entrepreneurs and workers.

Prior to 1980, at least among the industrial sector, entrepreneurs had considerable self-confidence as to their political influence on the policy process. In their eyes, either they or the state exerted the greatest control over economic policy. Since 1980, that positive view has changed. They now see organized labor wielding much more influence on government policy. The 1982 bank nationalization has had a tremendous impact on entrepreneurs' vision of their own role in the Mexican polity. Bankers, second only to industrialists, were seen by the private sector as a critical force in Mexican decisionmaking. Mexican politicians always have seen bankers as an important link to the private sector. Their removal from the private sector and incorporation into the public sector not only transformed the balance of economic power but tremendously modified the balance of political power, especially as perceived by leading Mexican entrepreneurs.

Their own confusion about Mexican politics and policymaking explains in part why Mexican entrepreneurs perceive their influence as inferior to that of their major opponent, organized labor. The fact that most entrepreneurs are confused about the distinction between political participation and policymaking further suggests the importance of perceived roles in Mexican politics, and the relationship between interest groups and the state. Entrepreneurs dislike the Mexican state, but have always felt discriminated against because of their exclusion from the official party, the most visible means of state participation.

Most experts who understand the subtleties of the Mexican policy process realize that an important role in party affairs has little, if any, impact on decisionmaking. In fact, one might argue that the state created a nicely balanced trade-off between labor and the private sector, incorporating labor very visibly in the party and emphasizing its public support in various holiday parades. Whereas the public image created by the state and labor is one of collaboration and support, they share a symbiotic relationship that is not translated into strong labor influence on economic policy. On the other hand, the private sector believes labor is more influential because its political role is visible and officially condoned, whereas in the policy realm the private sector has more influence than labor.

The Mexican private sector cannot be blamed for its perception, and subsequent conclusion, that public visibility means political influence. What is significant to emphasize is that this perception, however erroneous, is causing the private sector to follow a course that will increase its political activity, believing that this choice will enhance its decisionmaking power. Entrepreneurs' belief in one sense is justified. If they can exert more influence in the political arena, they gain a resource other than economic, one they have never employed. Because the PRI and the state both refuse to allow formal incorporation of the private sector into the party, they have opted to join the opposition, notably the Right. Andrés Marcelo Sada Zambrano, a leading member of the Monterrey Group, explains:

> Those that are actually doing this are doing it because of their strong feelings that the citizen in Mexico has an obligation to change the political control of the government. They support PAN because there is an overlapping of basic values between the two groups. Yes, the activities of the entrepreneurs in politics can indeed change the relationship between the two sectors in the sense of putting more pressure on government decisionmaking, similar to the pressure used by the unions.[114]

In a fully democratic system such a political strategy would be viable. In the Mexican political system, however, the only way entrepreneurs can increase their influence through political participation is to change the rules of the game altogether. The state seems to have sent a message in the 1985 and 1986 congressional and gubernatorial elections that electoral participation is not an acceptable vehicle for private-sector influence, and the state will risk its own legitimacy to block that path. Entrepreneurs believe that "the government isn't disposed to give the opposition a fair piece of the pie."[115] This has led certain business leaders, including the head of Vitro, a major Monterrey corporation, to prohibit their managements from participating in political campaigns.[116] The government has created an environment for politically active businessmen similar to what exists in the publishing world for intellectuals. Most of the censorship in Mexico is self-initiated, by publishers. Likewise, many entrepreneurs, afraid of repercussions from the state if they support opposition parties, have anticipated what they thought the state would do and initiated their own policy.[117] Thus, as the private sector seeks to open new channels for political influence, the tensions between entrepreneurs and the state are exacerbated.

Finally, the state's own aggressive moves to crimp private-sector resources through the nationalization of the banks, and the constitutional reforms institutionalizing the social sector, have reshaped their relationship with entrepreneurs permanently. The consequences are not just economic, but psychological. The psychological impact may very well be long-term. According to Mexican entrepreneurs, the behavior of the foreign private sector toward the state has been affected deeply by the state's historic behavior toward multinational companies, especially the 1938 petroleum decision. The 1982 bank decision is bound to have similar consequences for succeeding generations of domestic Mexican businessmen. It is possible that the aggressive posture of a minority of entrepreneurs is a temporary phenomenon similar to the behavior of the North American and Canadian oil companies in 1938. On the other hand, other entrepreneurs may come to terms with this new state posture, and a gradual redefinition of the relationship with the state will evolve.

7

Private-Sector Interest Groups

Mexican entrepreneurs, like citizens in other capitalist cultures, avail themselves of a variety of methods and channels for communicating their interests to the state. Some methods are especially culture-bound. Others are more universal. Among the most important variable that exert an influence on the relationship between the private sector and the state are: the historical role of the private sector, the legitimacy of private versus public interests, the values learned through family and educational socialization, the origins of public- and private-sector leaders, the career experiences of both groups, the monopoly of powerful economic interests by a small number of extended kinship groups, and finally, organized interest groups.

General Characteristics

Organized interest groups in Mexico generally have a unique position, especially compared with their role in the United States, because of two structural features of the Mexican political system. The first feature is that the government created most of the powerful interest organizations. In the general pattern between the Mexican state and interest groups—including labor, agriculture, and business—demands to the state are channeled through formal interest organizations.

As a result of government intervention, two types of private-sector interest organizations evolved. The first type, government-initiated, are semiofficial. The second type, developed solely through

private-sector initiative, are autonomous of the state and termed independent. The semiofficial organizations include Concamin, Canacintra (CNIT), and Concanaco; the independent organizations include
Coparmex, the Mexican Bankers Association (ABM), and the Mexican Insurance Association (AMIS).

The second feature of the Mexican polity's influence on interest-
group activity is the power of the presidency vis-à-vis the legislative
branch, and the expansion of the executive branch's influence. The
fact that the legislative branch plays at best a minimal role in the
decisionmaking process means interest-group communications are
aimed toward agency heads and the president.

Keeping in mind these two features of Mexico's political system,
an analysis of private-sector interest organizations reveals the extent
to which private-public relations are institutionalized along formal
lines, and the extent to which these organizations serve as useful
channels in the decisionmaking process.

When the Mexican state made the decision to organize groups
along occupational lines, it followed a pattern established immediately
after independence. Agustín de Iturbide, Mexico's independence leader,
formed a legislature that included strong occupational representation
from bureaucrats, clergy, workers, intellectuals, and merchants. The
extent to which bureaucrats, intellectuals, and clergy were overrepresented is significant.[1] The state worker, even in 1824, exercised more
influence than any occupational group, indicating how Mexican political figures early on perceived the state as a dominant force.

Mexico's historical predisposition toward organizing political interests through groups rather than individual actions has led various
authors, including Karl Schmitt, to attribute corporate characteristics
to Mexico's present political system. He suggests that corporatism
"postulates a harmonious, organized society of smoothly functioning
parts, each performing a necessary and useful task for the general
welfare, and regulated by an all-powerful state."[2] Indeed, Schmitt is
accurate in suggesting that Mexico's governmental relations with various groups have taken on corporatist features; yet Mexico does not
easily fit this model.

The Mexican state-private sector relationship cannot be said to be
ideally corporatist for two reasons. First, as I will demonstrate in the
following analysis of leading private-sector organizations, not all
groups fall into the category of quasi-state institutions. Second, despite extensvie institutionalization of political processes, individual
demands play a preeminent role in the political process.

Originally the Mexican government included the private sector in its semicorporatist design because the private sector required a shot in the arm. As Vernon explains, "To leave the growing business class out of the system would have been at deviance with the strategy of giving a stake in the continuance of the system to every major source of power, in order to reduce the threat of subversion and revolt. Besides, once in the system, business could act as a useful counterfoil to labor and agriculture."³

As I emphasized in Chapter 2, the state did not treat labor, farmers, and businessmen equally. It categorized business as the black sheep, formally excluding it from the official party. A natural consequence of this second-class treatment is that business groups are perceived prejudicially. The exclusion of business groups causes entrepreneurs to view their role in an entirely different light, believing their interest groups play a nonpolitical role compared to that of major labor unions.

An equally important consequence of state-initiated interest organizations was that the government emphatically identified semiofficial organizations or federations (groups of chambers) as the channels through which businessmen should conduct their affairs. Frank Brandenburg believes that the state wanted businessmen to act in concert in presenting their demands, rather than as individual entrepreneurs.⁴ From the private sector's point of view, the formation of these organizations provided them with a logical vehicle through which to make their perspectives known to the government. Obviously, they acquired strength through numbers.⁵ Brandenburg even claims that these organizations are consulted by the government every time a bill affecting their interests is passed.⁶ Whereas in general that may be true, noteworthy exceptions have occurred.

The role of semiofficial organizations in the decisionmaking process, the direction their approach takes, and the entrepreneur's perception of the federations' (commonly called chambers) relationship to the government is aptly conveyed in this businessman's assessment:

> Sometimes it is the business groups which approach the government concerning policy questions, and in other situations it is the government which takes the initiative with the private sector through the individual chambers. It is really what you might call a corporatist situation in which the government and the private sector are tied together as far as interest representation. The difference between our system and that in your country is that here we try to influence directly the minister of the appropriate secretariat rather than going through the legislative branch.

Normally, even though we try to directly influence the minister in charge, we first go through the chamber before approaching the individual personally.[7]

It can be assumed that the state acted out of self-interest in creating the semiofficial business organizations, not out of an unselfish desire to see the private sector strengthened. In doing that, the state not only legitimized semiofficial organizations but delegitimized the development of independently supported interest groups modeled after North America. It discouraged semiofficial and voluntary types of business groups from taking an aggressive political posture.[8]

Historically, Mexican entrepreneurs have not always found their semiofficial, second-class status acceptable. As early as 1957, a National Unification Center, composed of members from the National Chamber of Commerce (Concanaco), proposed that an industrial-commercial sector be added to the official party. The government never responded to their suggestion.[9] It is not known why the business community was excluded from the official party as a separate sector. Newell and Rubio speculate that President Cárdenas decided to use the party as a vehicle for popular interests, and the private sector as a counterbalance to the entire party.[10] The other possible explanation is that to incorporate businessmen into the party would tarnish the populist image the party wished to convey to the electorate.

As decades passed the party performed crucial functions in the political process, but a strong voice in policymaking was not one of them. The electoral arena was devalued as a channel for communicating interest-group demands. Instead, business chambers have funneled their wishes through the bureaucracy to the president personally.

The weak role of the party and of elections in decisionmaking have a twofold effect on business interest groups and their relationship to the Mexican state. First, semiofficial organizations have increased in importance since they are the primary vehicle of conveying political demands to the state. The second consequence, despite ups and downs in the relationship between the private sector and the state, is that entrepreneurial organizations have been largely successful in conveying their demands through bureaucratic channels. Not only did they not need to use elections for political influence, but to do so appeared unseemly. Politics, in the sense of electoral participation and party politics, became a dirty word to most Mexican entrepreneurs. When Story examined industrialists at the end of the 1970s, most admitted to political participation, but only within their organized interest chambers. He noted that 80 percent of his sample said they turned to their industrial association whenever they wanted to influence public policy.[11]

The major semiofficial business organizations—Concamin, Concanaco, and the National Chamber of Manufacturing Industries (Canacintra or CNIT)—by virtue of legal statutes, are restricted in their political behavior. Direct political action is prohibited.[12] By the 1970s some private-sector groups, disenchanted with the outcome of various policy decisions affecting entrepreneurial interests, decided to behave like North American interest organizations. This decision led to divisions in the private sector and a new level of divisiveness within state-private sector relations.

In the 1980s, signals emanating from the private-sector leadership are unclear. The impact of their increasing participation in electoral politics is thoroughly analyzed elsewhere. Far from moving toward the extreme of establishing their own political party, business leaders still act as if they do not want to politicize their organizations. They believe forming a political party is not the answer to their problems.[13] Even their self-definition as a pressure group is ambiguous. Emilio Goicochea Luna, outspoken leader of Concanaco, has stated that "business organizations are not pressure groups, rather groups of expression, in which they speak the truth, without shunning responsibility."[14] His statement, juxtaposed to his repeated quotes in this book, suggests that he wants political activism without a nasty label.

Interest organizations have not been involved directly in the electoral arena, although leaders of independent organizations have advocated political involvement. Electoral activity among entrepreneurial organizations, especially local and regional groups, is likely to increase. Even an increase in the number of major interest organizations poses added difficulties for the state in keeping entrepreneurs in line.

Businessmen recognize the value of collective representation, even in special situations. In 1984, after the de la Madrid administration made clear its intent to return certain state-owned enterprises to the private sector, a group of entrepreneurs formed an organization to negotiate the acquisition of state-owned companies outside of those acquired through the bank nationalization.[15]

The effectiveness of business organizations in Mexico is restricted not only by their origins and acceptability in the political culture, but by their internal characteristics and beliefs. One of the frequent self-criticisms the activist private-sector faction has offered refers to their lack of combativeness in confronting the public sector. Jorge Arrambide, director of the Chamber of Industries of Nuevo León, the most important regional manufacturing group outside the Mexico City area, lamented the cautiousness of local chambers in their negotiations with the government.[16] One explanation for this lack of combativeness has been offered by a former secretary of commerce and industry who actually discussed eliminating the semiofficial federations with President Alemán. He believes that if the state eliminated these organizations altogether, it would, in the short term, remove their collective resources and weaken the private sector. On the other hand, he argued that if membership were not required "they would have become more independent and combative."[17]

The other reason the organizations have not been combative is their officials' belief that traditional channels are effective. When Dale Story interviewed industrial chamber officials, he found without exception that they believed their semiofficial status enhanced their influence.[18] In my interviews with independent organization leaders, however, they were convinced that their independence made them influential. Interestingly, the same argument appears among labor union leaders and in the literature on independent versus semiofficial unions. The evidence, up to this point, suggests that independent unions have not obtained better contracts for their members than government-affiliated ones.[19]

One can argue that the behaviors of independent unions and independent business organizations are not comparable. Whereas both are much less under the thumb of the government than semiofficial unions or organizations, independent unions essentially use the same approach, the legal strike, as their semiofficial counterparts to obtain their demands. Independent private-sector leadership, however, is suggesting that businesspeople focus on government weaknesses in the electoral arena, supporting opposition candidates as a method of pressuring the government on policy issues. This strategy might give voluntary business groups more influence than the traditional approaches taken by the large chambers.

Interest-Group Leadership

Business interest organizations may not exert the same leverage as union organizations in the Mexican political process because of the separation between interest-group leadership and capital. In Mexican union organizations, the individuals who usually call the shots (with the exception of the petroleum union) have always been the actual power brokers in the unions. For example, Fidel Velázquez, the single most powerful leader in Mexican labor for the last three decades, actually directs the leading union. In business interest groups, the most important entrepreneurial families rarely are represented in leadership positions.

Business organizations and chambers are led by four types of individuals: owners (capitalists), professional managers, interest-group careerists, and politician-entrepreneurs. Eduardo Bustamante, who had many dealings with prominent Mexican entrepreneurs when he was in the cabinet in the late 1950s and early 1960s, and who is a stockholder and board member of many firms, suggests that most business organizations in Mexico have never been directed by the captains of industry, but rather always by capitalist hired guns.[20] His assertion can be tested by examining the leadership of Mexico's most important national and regional organizations.

An analysis of the leaders of these national organizations suggests several patterns concerning control by Mexico's leading capitalists and their families. From 1918 to 1985, of the thirty-two businessmen who presided over Concamin, Mexico's most important organization, only two were from prominent capitalist families (Table 7-1). One of those men, Juan Sánchez Navarro y Peón, is the grandson of Carlos Sánchez Navarro y Beraín, the largest landholder in Latin America. The extent of Sánchez Navarro's own holdings are unknown, and it may well be that he does not belong properly in the capitalist class. However, he is the model example of a professional interest-group leader, having been the only Mexican to preside over Concamin, Concanaco, and the Coordinating Council of Businessmen (CCE) as well as serve on the Mexican Council of Businessmen (CMHN). The other individual is Antonio Ruiz Galindo, head of the Ruiz Galindo family, the controlling interest in the Desc Group.

The data in Table 7-2, which lists the presidents of Concanaco, Mexico's leading manufacturing organization, reveals a pattern similar to that of Concamin. With the exception of Enrique Sada Muguerza, scion of the Monterrey Sada Muguerza clan, who served as the founding president of Concanaco, only Juan Sánchez Navarro and Ernesto J. Amezcua, a stockholder in the banking and insurance fields, including La Provincial Insurance, might qualify as truly important capitalists. Other owners appear among the presidents, as is true of the Concamin presidencies, but are not representative of leading entrepreneurial families.

Table 7-1.   National Federation of Chamber of Industries (Concamin), 1918–85

Presidents	Tenure
Adolfo Prieto	1918–19
Carlos B. Zetina	1919–20
Carlos Robles	1920–21
Jesús Rivero Quijana	1921–22
Carlos B. Zetina	1922–25
Robert D. Hutchison	1925–26
Federico T. Lachica	1926–27
Hilarion N. Branch	1927–32
Evaristo Araiza	1932–36
Genaro P. García	1936–38
Lorenzo Pérez Castro	1938–41
José Cruz y Celis	1941–42
Agustín García López	1942–42
José Cruz y Celis	1942–46
Pedro A. Chapa	1946–48
Guillermo Guajardo Davis	1948–50
Edmundo J. Phelan	1950–53
Licio Lagos	1953–54
Guillermo Barroso	1954–56
Eduardo Prieto López	1956–58
Jacobo Pérez Barroso	1958–60
Manuel Fernández Landero	1960–62
Juan Sánchez Navarro	1962–64
Antonio Ruiz Galindo	1964–66
José Campillo Saínz	1966–68
Prudencio López	1968–70
Miguel Alessio Robles	1970–71
Alejandro Alvarez Guerrero	1971–73
Carlos Yarza Ochoa	1973–75
Jorge Sánchez Mejorada	1975–77
Luis Guzmán de Alba	1977–79
Ernesto Rubio del Cueto	1979–81
Alfonso Pandal Graf	1981–83
Jacobo Zaidenweber	1983–85

Table 7-2. National Chamber of Commerce (Concanaco), 1917-84

Presidents	Tenure
Enrique Sada Muguerza	1917–18
Carlos Arellano	1918–19
Fernando Leal Novelo	1919–21
Pafnucio Padilla	1921–24
Manuel E. Izaguirre	1924–25
Lamberto Hernández	1925–27
Federico T. Lachica	1927–28
José Cruz y Celis	1928–33
Manuel Muñoz Castillo	1933–35
Ernesto J. Amezcua	1935–37
Leopoldo H. Palazuelos	1937–44
Alejandro Noye	1944–45
Ernesto J. Amezcua	1945–46
Eustaquio Escandón	1946–48
Mariano R. Suárez	1948–50
José Rivera R.	1950–51
Carlos E. Mendiola	1951–52
Ernesto Ayala	1952–54
Clemente Serna Martínez	1954–56
Juan Sánchez Navarro	1957–58
Juan Martínez del Campo	1958–60
Heriberto Vidales Ibarra	1960–62
José Gómez Gordoa	1962–64
Jorge Orvañanos	1964–65
Armando Fernández	1965–66
Francisco Cano Escalante	1966–68
Alfredo Santos M.	1968–71
Miguel M. Blásquez	1971–73
Jesús Vidales Aparicio	1973–74
Víctor Manuel Guadiano	1974–78
Guillermo de Zamacona Félix	1978–80
Jorge A. Chapa	1980–82
Emilio Goicochea Luna	1982–84

The third major organization, numerically quite large, is Canacintra (Table 7-3). Since its founding none of its presidents has come from a leading capitalist family. The only major federation even bordering on having strong representation among capitalist families is the Mexican Bankers Association (ABM), an independent organization founded in 1928. A comparison between Mexico's leading entrepreneurial families (Table 8-4) and the presidents of the ABM (Table 7-4) reveals the presence of five leading families, including Bailleres, de Iturbide, Espinosa Iglesias, Legorreta and Saénz, three of whom are synonymous with Mexican banking. Also among the presidents is Mario Domínguez, an important investor and original member of the Buda Group.

Before nationalization, the Mexican Bankers Association was the major independent private-sector organization in the economic sector. While the majority of its leadership has not come from prominent capitalist families, it is important to know why prominent entrepreneurial families are better represented in banking than any other private-sector organization.

Throughout this book I have suggested the special role bankers played in the relationship between the Mexican state and the private sector. Compared to industrialists and manufacturers, the attitude of bankers has been one of compromise toward the government and a belief in dealing directly with it. Bankers, more than other types of entrepreneurs, have negotiated with politicians as equals rather than from a position of arrogance. The Legorreta family provides an ideal example (with two generations appearing as presidents of the ABM). Nora Hamilton notes that the family dealt effectively with the post-revolutionary governments in the 1920s despite those administrations' animosity toward the banks, and since that period realized, as a personal leitmotif, the importance of close contacts with public figures.[21]

The assertion that capitalist families do not control major interest organizations also applies to the other significant independent organization, Coparmex, even though the Monterrey Group very much dominates the source of its leadership. In its early years Coparmex benefited from leadership continuity, with only eleven presidents from 1929 to 1985 (Table 7-5). Of those, only two are from major entrepreneurial families, both related to the original Monterrey Sada family. Luis G. Sada García founded the organization in 1929, serving briefly as its first president, and Andrés Marcelo Sada Zambrano, his nephew and director of the Cydsa Group, served as president in the 1970s.

An examination of two major local organizations, the National Chamber of Commerce of Mexico City (Canco) and the National Chamber of Commerce of Monterrey, reveal the same pattern found in the national organizations. Even the Monterrey organization has not been led by notable capitalists, but rather by smaller businessmen, some of whom are related to the original northern families.

Table 7-3. National Chamber of Industries (Canacintra or CNIT), 1941-85

Presidents	Tenure
José Cruz y Celis	1941–42
Guillermo García Colín	1943
José Rivera R.	1944
José Domingo Lavin	1945
José R. Colín	1946
Joaquín de la Peña	1947
Jorge M. Heyser	1948
Agustín Fouque	1949–50
Alfonso Cardoso	1951–52
José Crowly	1953–54
Guillermo Castro Ulloa	1955–56
Santos Amaro	1957–58
Joaquín de la Peña	1959
Guillermo Briones	1960
Emilio Vera Blanco	1961–62
Alfonso Cardoso	1963–64
Raúl A. Ollervides	1965–66
Nazario Ortiz Garza	1967–68
Agustín Fouque	1969–70
José Terrones Langone	1971–72
Ernesto Barroso Gutiérrez	1973–74
Amilcar Ranero García	1975
Joaquín Pría Olavarrieta	1976–77
Juan Manuel Martínez Gómez	1978–79
José Porrero Lichtle	1980–81
Ignacio Barragán de Palacio	1982–83
Carlos Mireles	1984–85

Table 7-4. Mexican Bankers Association (ABM), 1928–1982

Presidents	Tenure
Alberto Mascareñas	1928–1932
Agustín Rodríguez	1932–1935
Gonzalo Robles	1935
Salvador Ugarte	1935–1936
Luis G. Legorreta García	1936–1937
Epigmenio Ibarra	1937–1938
Mario Domínguez	1938–1940
Adolfo Desentis	1940–1941
Raúl Bailleres	1941–1942
Aaron Sáenz	1942–1943
Luis G. Legorreta García	1943–1944
Salvador Ugarte	1944–1945
Mario Domínguez	1945–1946
Carlos Novoa	1946–1947
Luis Montes de Oca	1947–1948
Anibal de Iturbide Preciat	1948–1949
Alfonso Díaz García	1949–1950
Gustavo R. Velasco	1950–1951
Pablo Latapi	1951–1952
Arturo Bueno y Urquidi	1952–1953
Alfonso Díaz García	1953–1954
Agustín Legorreta	1954–1955
Anibal de Iturbide Preciat	1955–1956
Augusto Domínguez Amezcua	1956–1957

Roberto G. Sada García was the only major capitalist figure to hold the presidency of the local Monterrey chamber from 1918 to 1971, and the Mexico City chamber never had such a figure in its six-decade history.

Nationally, two other independent organizations exist to represent business interests. These two institutions see themselves, and are seen by other entrepreneurs, as "the" apex organizations. The Coordinating Council of Businessmen (CCE), allegedly designed in the mid-

Table 7-4. Mexican Bankers Association (ABM),
1928-1982

Presidents	Tenure
Salvador Ugarte	1957-1958
Augustín Legorreta	1959-1960
Francisco F. Maldonado	1960-1961
Rolando Vega Iñiguez	1961-1962
Jesús Rodríguez Gómez	1962-1963
Manuel Flores	1963-1964
Carlos Mendiola	1964-1965
Manuel Espinosa Yglesias	1965-1966
José Antonio César	1966-1967
Ladislao López Negrete	1967-1968
Héctor Flores	1968-1969
Rolando Vega Iñiguez	1969-1970
Manuel Cortina Portilla	1970-1971
Manuel Espinosa Yglesias	1971-1972
José María Cuarón	1972-1973
Manuel Cortina Portilla	1975-1976
Agustín F. Legorreta	1973-1974
José Pintado Rivero	1974-1975
Ruben Aguilar Monteverde	1976-1977
Eugenio Eraña García	1977-1978
Carlos Abedrop Dávila	1978-1979
Rolando Vega Iñiguez	1979-1980
Arcadio Valenzuela	1980-1981
Víctor Manuel Herrera	1981-1982
Carlos Abedrop Dávila	1982

1970s to coordinate the private sector's opinion on major policy issues, has had seven presidents from 1975 through 1985, none of whom are from important entrepreneurial families, with the possible exception of Juan Sánchez Navarro.

The second of these organizations, and the most elitist private sector group in Mexico, is the Mexican Council of Businessmen (CMHN), founded in 1962 with a limited membership never exceeding

Table 7-5. Mexican Employers Federation (Coparmex), 1929–1985

Presidents	Tenure
Luis G. Sada García	1929–30
Leopoldo H. Palazuelos	1930–45
Mariano R. Suárez	1945–59
Roberto Guajardo Suárez	1960–73
Jorge Orvaños Zúniga Lascuraín	1973–75
Armando Fernández Velasco	1975–76
Andrés Marcelo Sada Zambrano	1976–78
Manuel J. Clouthier	1978–80
José Luis Coindreau	1980–82
José María Basagoiti Noriega	1982–84
Alfredo Sandoval González	1984–85

thirty individuals. Originally constituted to represent Mexico's most prominent business leaders and capitalist families, its actual distribution of membership by individual status mirrors the rationale behind the group's formation. (Table 7-6) Nearly half its members to date (44 percent) have been members of Mexico's prominent capitalist families. Of the elite families in our data, a fourth have had direct representation on the CMHN. Among the leading entrepreneurial families (Table 8-4) represented on the CMHN are: Arango, Azcárraga, Bailleres, Ballesteros, Cortina, Espinosa, Garza, Larrea, Legorreta, Pagliali, Quintana, Ruiz Galindo, Senderos, and Vallina.

Except for the CMHN, major entrepreneurial families do not play a direct role in interest-group leadership. In fact, if the presidencies of all the major chambers, national and regional, are lumped together, only 35 percent of leading family entrepreneurs in my sample have held a top interest-group post, precisely the same percentage for all important businessmen. (MEBP)

Most leadership positions in the private-sector organizations have been held by lesser capitalists or by professional interest-group leaders who have used their experience to join the ranks of self-made Mexican entrepreneurs. The professional interest-group leader is a remarkable figure among leading entrepreneurs. His role as a representative of the chambers is important for several reasons. In the first place, some

Table 7-6. Mexican Council of Businessmen (CMHN), 1962–1983

Members	Tenure
Arango Arias, Jr., Jerónimo	1962–1983
Aranguren Castiello, Ignacio	–1983
Azcárraga Tamayo, Gastón	1962–1983
Bailleres, Alberto	1962–1983
Balsa, César	1962–
Ballesteros Ibarra, Cresencio	1962–1983
Cortina Portilla, Juan	1962–1983
De Iturbide, Anibal	1962–
Escandón, Eustaquio	1962–
Espinosa Yglesias, Manuel	1962–
Fernández, Justo F.	1962–1983
Garciarce Ramírez, Abelardo	1962–1983
Garza Laguera, Eugenio	1962–1983
Garza de la Mora, Santiago A.	–1983
Garza Sada, Bernardo	–1983
Garza Sada, Camilo	1962–
Larrea, Jorge	1962–1983
Legorreta, Augustín F.	1962–1983
Longoría, Octaviano L.	1962–
López, Isidro	1962–1983
López, Prudencio	1962–1983
O'Farrill, Jr., Rómulo	1962–1983
Pagliali, Bruno	1962–1983
Quintana Arioja, Bernardo	1962–1983
Represas, José	1962–1983
Robles Levi, Ernesto	1962–
Rojas Guadarrama, Enrique	1962–1983
Ruiz Galindo, Jr., Antonio	1962–1983
Sánchez Navarro, Juan	1962–1983
Senderos, Manuel	1962–1983
Valenzuela Valenzuela, Arcadio	1962–1983
Vallina, Eloy	1962–1983
Vega Iñiguez, Rolando	1962–1983

leading Mexican entrepreneurs argue that any individual who functions in a leadership capacity within the private-sector chambers has unique qualities. This argument implies that a dichotomy exists between those who lead organizations, or are members of the CMHN, and those who have never served in any interest-group capacity. The implication is that interest-group positions attract one specific type of entrepreneur, one who understands and is interested in the political relationship between the private and public sectors. An erroneous view of Mexico's private sector would be obtained from conversations solely with interest-group leaders, or only with entrepreneurs who have never filled such posts.

The professional manager who functions as an interest-group leader is inclined to become an ally of the state. Eduardo Bustamante believes this tendency is very dangerous to the private sector. He suggests that after holding these offices professionals often find the state more attractive than before.[22] He implies that their underlying sympathy for the state may make them carry out their defense of private-sector interests with less ardor. A goodly percentage of the few businessmen who move horizontally into public posts comes from interest groups. (MEBP)

Their movement has led to some fallacious assumptions about the interlocking leadership between the private and public sectors. James Cockcroft best expresses this notion when he concludes that "these capitalist organizations are not 'pressure groups,' but form an integral part of the governing bloc. They are connected to the state through their members' circulation in and out of government."[23] As I demonstrated in Chapter 5, very few capitalists ever hold decisionmaking posts in Mexico's government or in private-sector interest organizations.

An analysis of the major organizations shows that no politician-entrepreneurs have ever been invited to join the CMHN, although Antonio Ruiz Galindo, Jr.'s father was in Alemán's cabinet. None has served as president of the CCE, although Jorge Sánchez Mejorada through his uncle is distantly related to a Porfirian political family in Hidalgo. Two individuals in the presidency of Concamin in the 1960s had political connections: Antonio Ruiz Galindo, a businessman who went into politics and left it abruptly in 1948; and José Campillo Saínz, an example of an interest-group leader who became enamored of political life, who became Echeverría's secretary of industry and commerce in 1974. Another president, Miguel Alessio Robles, the son of a 1920s cabinet member, also served as director of Sidermex, the government steel complex, for de la Madrid. Concanaco has never had a president involved in high-level political office. Canacintra has had only two: Nazario Ortiz Garza, who long before his presidency was a prominent figure in the Alemán cabinet as secretary of agriculture; and José Terrones Langone, son of a former senator and constitutional deputy, who served briefly as assistant director of the National Finance Bank after leaving Canacintra's presidency in 1972. Finally, no presidents of Coparmex, the most aggressive of the independent private groups, has entered politics.

The only organization of the private sector that can claim a healthy representation among businessmen who followed careers in public life, or public figures who became entrepreneurs, is again the Mexican Bankers Asociation (Table 7-4). From one perspective this is not surprising, since banking was so well represented in the choices of politicians who have turned to entrepreneurial careers since the 1920s, despite the fact that five politician-entrepreneurs—Alberto Mascareñas, Gonzalo Robles, Aaron Sáenz, Carlos Novoa, and Luis Montes de Oca—served as presidents of the ABM, all before 1948. Mascareñas was assistant secretary of the treasury before his post in the ABM, and directed the Bank of Mexico after his presidency; Aaron Sáenz and Luis Montes de Oca were cabinet members in the 1920s, and Carlos Novoa became director of the Bank of Mexico at the same time he assumed the presidency of the ABM, after having served as a general manager of the association for many years.

Mexico's leading interest groups, on the whole, are led by company managers and owners who are neither members of the most important entrepreneurial families nor the national political caste. The extent of direct leadership by certain types of entrepreneurs suggests capitalists do not believe strongly in interest groups. Obviously, entrepreneurs with political connections are not sufficiently represented to alter the role of formal interest groups.

Interest-Group Representatives

Indirect control over the leadership of the interest organizations is as important as direct control; observers disagree on the characteristics of this control. Typically, according to scholars, a small group of entrepreneurs has determined the actual leadership. This pattern began at the birth of these organizations. By the 1970s little had changed, and two analysts of the major interest organizations again found great economic groups (or families), sometimes in association with foreign capital, dominating the selection process of interest-group directors.[24]

The question of who controls prominent interest organizations raises a larger and theoretically more significant issue: how representative are Mexican business interest groups of their constituencies? Critics of the major federations, which include thousands of members, suggest that quantitatively the member firms are not fairly represented in federation policy positions. They further argue that the leaders, whom scholars have found to be controlled by large capital, do not represent their memberships' interests.

These criticisms have importance for the private-public sector relationship for at least two reasons. The state can ignore interest-group arguments when small and medium-sized member firms are believed to hold a view different from the large capitalist members. Second, if the small and medium-sized firms believe themselves to be unrepresented by an organization's position on important issues, their resentment divides the private sector on other concerns.

Entrepreneurs themselves give two opposing points of view about leadership selection in the interest organizations. Alfonso Pasquel believes that the leaders of the federations do not represent the views of large firms only because they themselves are not large-scale capitalists and are chosen by the more numerous medium-sized and smaller companies. He notes that each member firm votes on the leader, with one vote going to each firm, regardless of size. Then each member chamber casts a vote.[25] Alejandro J. Dumán Urrea, himself an owner of medium-sized firms, argues that the process is supposed to work this way, but actually does not. His view is that

> influence in the chamber is determined by the size of the company, not an individual vote. . . . Let's take an example, the one of the Chamber of Commerce of Mexico City [Canaco]. There are essentially five companies which dominate this organization. They are: Sears, the Palace of Iron, Aurrera, which is actually a mixed foreign and privately owned company, Comercial Mexicana, and Gigante. There are actually over one hundred thousand other members . . . but the chamber does what these five companies want. The representation today is backward.[26]

It is difficult to ascertain which view is correct, but the majority of entrepreneurs interviewed and the most detailed studies agree that the leaders, and therefore the views of the chambers, often do not represent the whole membership. Ricardo Tirado found in the early 1970s that of the 321 interest groups represented in the six major organizations and the CCE, just 12 percent controlled half of the leadership positions.[27] The difficulty with Tirado's data, however empirically sound, is that over time we do not know if control is fluid. What can be said with certainty is that many leading entrepreneurs and public figures believe the federations are undemocratic.

When I gave major interest-organization leaders of the 1980s an opportunity to respond to this criticism, they did not deny the charge precisely, but instead explained why this perception may have come about. The most complete response was provided by Emilio Goicochea Luna, head of Concanaco from 1983–1984:

> Remember that the membership of both Concamin and Concanaco are such that everyone must belong by law whether they want to or not. Secondly, total consensus is always impossible to achieve regardless of the type of organization that you are in. Third, our organization is governed by statutes and a set of principles that I, as a leader of the organization, am supposed to defend. Fourth, the membership of the organization is served by an executive council which represents all interests of the members of the chamber. I am in this position because of my own ability to evaluate the alternatives that are available to us as an organization, and because national leaders of the chambers usually are the best informed about their own sectors. Now, what happens when the rest of the sector doesn't have the information I or my colleagues have in the chambers? They don't understand what we have done, and that's why they often criticize our position. We always consult the executive council before making any decision affecting the interests of the chamber membership.
>
> There are cases of misunderstanding between interests represented by the chamber and the leadership. I don't think this is true most of the time, it is really a question of maintaining good communication. The chambers are supposed to contact all the individual members, not the confederation, which is what I am president of. In other words, the chambers are subdivisions of the confederation itself, and it is their responsibility. Naturally, we can't please everyone. What is important is that the president of this confederation visits several states each week and has considerable personal contact with various members all over the republic in order to learn their sentiments about the issue.[28]

Goicochea's comments are revealing because they illustrate the management style of the larger interest organizations. The key variables, as in the relationship between the state and the private sector, are communication and consultation. The accusation that these organizations are undemocratic or unrepresentative is significant for several reasons. Earlier I noted that geographic differences and jealousies between the periphery and Mexico City were a general weakness among entrepreneurs. The same charge is brought against interest groups. They do not give fair representation to the provinces or to small and medium-sized firms.

If chamber leaders are categorized by geographic affiliation, the vast majority of the semiofficial organization presidents have been from Mexico City. The same is true for the ABM, where more than 90 percent of the presidents have been capital natives. The only groups with strong geographic diversity in their top leadership, which therefore might better represent the interests of the provinces, are Coparmex—which is identified correctly with the Monterrey Group—and the CMHN. Coparmex's presidents have been divided half-and-half between Monterrey and Mexico City, which of course gives Monterrey a strong voice but ignores other regions such as Guadalajara. CMHN also ignores Guadalajara but gives some representation to the Northwest (Chihuahua Group) and some to Monterrey, although well over half come from Mexico City. (MEBP)

A gradual change in the geographic distribution of leadership in these organizations may be afoot. Tirado's study indicated that from 1970 to 1976 provincial industries increased their leadership from 13 percent to 27 percent, while Mexico City entrepreneurs declined from 79 percent to 65 percent.[29] If the Monterrey and other provincial groups are actually increasing in power, there may be a trend toward expanded representativeness and geographic decentralization. If decentralization has continued in the 1980s, it would be important because it would be in opposition to the increasing centralization of intellectual and political leadership.

The lack of fair representation in the leadership of private-interest organizations contradicts the ideology businesspeople are fighting for in the political arena. Jorge Arrambide—an interest-group leader who admits that they are run by a few major firms—laments, "Mexico does not have a concept of democracy, which is why they put up with this in the chambers. . . . If the private sector wants the government to democratize, then it has to be democratic itself." Arrambide goes on to argue that a "closed elite," analagous "to a big tree without roots," runs these chambers, and consequently, they cannot speak with the authority of a group having a large, cohesive base.[30] For example, the president of the ABM was chosen by an informal group of bankers.[31]

The contradiction between the way interest organizations are operated and the way many entrepreneurs want their society to function suggests a paradox in the private-sector value system. Businessmen have not made the jump from theory to reality in their own behavior. This gap between theory and reality leads to a vicious cycle, because democratic behavior has not been institutionalized anywhere in society—in the home, politics, or business. Consequently, we return full circle to the importance of personal channels of communication in Mexican private and public life. Mexican business organizations may well be more democratic than political institutions, but they are not close to the model businessmen themselves demand of their government. A public figure with many ties to the private sector suggested, using examples from his own family, that many medium-sized and small businessmen continue to use personal channels because they are unsatisfied with their representation in the interest organizations.[32] In other words, satisfactory institutionalization will never take place until businessmen see themselves fairly represented in their organizations and rely on them rather than on individual channels to present their demands.

Comparison of Major Interest Organizations

Internal relationships within major organizations affect their ability to represent entrepreneurial demands to the public sector, perpetuate weaknesses within the private sector, and mirror problems found generally in the business community. In practice, however, how do the major organizations differ from one another and what is their impact on Mexico's policy process?

The three most important semiofficial organizations are Cancanaco, Concamin, and Canacintra (sometimes referred to as CNIT). They have in common that they were formed by the state, membership in them is required by law (on the basis of type and size of firm), and they use a one-firm, one-vote principle. In the case of Concanaco and Concamin especially, most members are not actively involved because they resent required affiliation; small industrialists have played an important role in Concanaco's leadership.[33]

Concamin and Concanaco are also similar in their posture toward the government. Both have executive committees representing their various member chambers, which (as Goicochea Luna explained) act as advisory councils.[34] They differ from several of their counterparts ideologically because of their membership and their structural relationship to the state. Structurally, the semiofficial status of these organizations goes back not only to the state's role in their creation, but to the fact that a representative of the ministry of industry and commerce may attend executive meetings with a voice but no vote, as illustrated by Concamin.[35] The leaders of these two organizations are primarily from the Federal District and its environs. Because of their proximity to the center of political power, businessmen from the capital area traditionally have had a more reasonable view of the state than their provincial counterparts. These two organizations "have a realistic policy because their national leaders, generally from the Federal District and the state of México, adopt moderate positions which reflect their realistic view of the relations between the state and the means of influencing decisions."[36]

In addition to their ideological posture toward the state, they tend to share a similar view of foreign investment and state intervention. Because more of their membership is made up of enterprises which generate their own credit, or borrow from private sources, they are not as disposed as Canacintra to allow the state to intervene in the economy. Canacintra prefers government intervention to protect its interests because it has smaller firms fearful of foreign competition.[37]

Canacintra's history was controversial from the very beginning. The youngest of the semiofficial organizations, it was established in 1941 under the government of Manuel Ávila Camacho. Although formed formally as part of the umbrella chambers under Concamin, Canacintra quickly exerted its independence. It was made up of newer industrialists, primarily small and medium-sized, who needed the support of the state to expand. Because of their need, they began their state relationship with a degree of closeness and mutual support not found between the other semiofficial organizations and the government. Analysts have suggested that Canacintra went beyond economic relations to support the government in other arenas, thus emulating a relationship to the government similar to that of the Mexican Federation of Labor.[38]

Canacintra's fledgling industrialists became known as the New Group, since most of their firms were created during World War II. They relied almost entirely on Mexican capital and, very importantly, they did not have good relations with the principal financial institutions in Mexico.[39] Their size, youth, and strained relationship with established private-sector banks led them to take on ideological positions quite distinct from their well-established counterparts. In the first place, they advocated a purposeful policy of continuous and intimate contact with government agencies. Secondly, they defined the scope of public intervention much more broadly than larger, older firms in Mexico. Third, they sought out the cooperation of organized labor to promote Mexico's industrialization, advocating a philosophy of shared benefits for workers and owners. Most importantly, they were aggressive, vigorous, and bold in their actions.[40]

Stylistically, an analogy can be drawn between Canacintra in the 1950s and Coparmex in the 1980s. Both represent the interests of younger entrepreneurs. Both advocate a posture different from their predecessors. And both believe aggressiveness could be translated into an increased role in the policy process. The major difference between the two, of course, is ideological. Canacintra wants certain types of state intervention, while Coparmex wants to narrow vastly the state's economic influence. Regardless of opposing ideologies, their approaches demonstrate that businesspeople in general, and business interest groups specifically, are intimidated by and hesitant to explore aggressive methods of communication.

Over the years two characteristics have stuck with Canacintra's image: its strong antiforeign, especially anti-American position, and its very close relationship with the Mexican state. Its nationalism has been such that the small subsidiaries of American companies, included in its membership, found their participation embarrassing in the 1960s.[41] Canacintra's protectionist philosophy, extending back to its original formation, influenced it to oppose the government's decision to join the General Agreement on Trade and Tariffs, and succeeded in preventing Mexico from joining it in 1980.[42]

The close relationship of Canacintra to the government, at least in comparison with other organizations, has taken on somewhat mythic qualities. Dale Story noted that "Canacintra is still reported to have suspiciously close relations with the state and with the dominant political party, the PRI. For example, it is often rumored that presidents of Canacintra are assured important government posts after their terms expire."[43] As Story himself suggests, these assertions are rumors, nothing more. Because publicly owned firms are strongly represented in its membership, they influence Canacintra's position, and this makes other groups suspicious.

The ideological posture of Canacintra vis-à-vis the other two major industrial organizations is sometimes exaggerated. Its position is neither consistently opposed to, nor in alliance with, other interest groups. Its posture toward the state has fluctuated from supportive to opposing, depending on the leadership and the general conditions of the private-public relationship. For example, at the beginning of the

Echeverría admininstration, under the presidency of José Terrones Langone, a leader with family political connections, Canacintra praised state enterprises and the government itself. By the end of his administration, Canacintra was no exception to the private sector's antagonistic posture toward Echeverría, and its president in 1976, Joaquín Pría Olavarrieta, became a leading critic of Echeverría's administration.[44] A comparative survey of attitudes among Canacintra and Concamin leaders toward López Portillo found Canacintra's was much less favorable than Concamin's attitude.[45]

It is difficult to conclude whether or not Canacintra's ideological predilections significantly separate it from other semiofficial groups. Scholars of a Marxist persuasion tend to believe its behavior is exceptional and aberrant, that normally the private sector acts as a powerful united front.[46] This view ignores subtleties leading to important weaknesses within the private sector with consequences for private-public relations. For example, it is quite likely that Canacintra's traditionally antagonistic relationship with the banking community made its members more favorably inclined toward bank nationalization. The nationalization decision itself confounds traditional Marxist analysis. Even Canacintra, made up primarily of smaller organizations, is internally divided, despite the denials of its leadership. Carlos Mireles, president in 1984, strongly disagreed with the suggestion that Canacintra was not representing the membership, and that large companies controlled his organization.[47] His assertion may well have been true at that moment, but only a decade ago, when the president of Canacintra objected to joining the CCE, numerous regional leaders publicly opposed him.[48] Whatever ideological differences exist among the three organizations, the state in the 1980s does not appear to be overtly manipulating these differences.[49]

The independent private-sector interest groups are led by three top organizations: the ABM, the Mexican Insurance Association (AMIS) and Coparmex. ABM and AMIS have much in common, while the deviant sister in this group is Coparmex. Because of their relatively small national membership, AMIS and ABM function like private clubs.[50] AMIS, founded in 1946 and one of the peak organizations by the 1960s, fits this label more accurately and consequently is almost unknown to the public. ABM, on the other hand, though small in numbers, has always been very visible, so much so that Robert Shafer could claim that it was possibly the most prestigious of all private-sector organizations in the 1960s.[51]

ABM's most significant claim to distinction is the role it has played vis-à-vis the state. Exaggerating somewhat, one might say that among voluntary organizations ABM and the banking community are to the state what Canacintra is to the state among semiofficial federations. Like Canacintra, ABM has a special relationship to the state, to the extent that ABM has better representation among political entrepreneurs than any other national chamber. Formally, these ties are expressed through ABM's direct representation on the National Banking Commission, the National Securities Commission and the Mexican Stock Exchange.[52]

ABM has played a special mediating role between the state and the rest of the private sector. In an opposing way, however, Coparmex also has played a distinctive role, serving as a model for organizations antagonistic to, and highly critical of, the state. It has taken the lead in politicizing elements in the private sector.

Coparmex was founded in 1929 in reaction to a government policy decision which leaders of the Monterrey Group opposed. Besides their distaste for the 1928 labor law, businessmen founded Coparmex because they considered present interest-group organizations weak and timid; they believed government intervention in the economy excessive; they hoped to incorporate all types of businessmen regardless of economic sector; they wanted an organization independent of public power; and they were affiliated philosophically with the aggressive attitude of Monterrey entrepreneurs.[53] Members of the original organizing committee included Eugenio Garza Sada, Virgilio Garza, Antonio L. Rodríguez, and Joel Rocha.[54] Over the years, Coparmex became identified with the interests of the Garza and Sada families and with Monterrey. Consequently, groups in the state of México and the Federal District have been antagonistic to the organization.[55] Again, geography becomes an obstacle to unity in the private sector—in this case, within formal interest institutions.

During its early years Coparmex faced many difficulties recruiting members, for several reasons. First, most businessmen already were required to belong to a semiofficial organization, so membership in Coparmex appeared redundant. Second, Coparmex did not ask favors of the government in the same way as Concamin or even ABM did.[56] Third, its antagonistic position scared off many entrepreneurs. Last, its identification with the Monterrey Group proved an obstacle for some. From the 1920s until the 1950s Coparmex was very weak, suggesting that its negative qualities far outweighed its attractions. By the 1960s, however, once the semiofficial organizations became stronger and the private sector itself began to flex it muscles, the idea of an organization committed to greater independence from the government, and to a strong visible posture of defending the private sector ideologically, was more appealing. In the 1970s Coparmex's membership increased from 13,000 to 18,000.[57]

The ideological and political qualities of Coparmex are illuminated by José María Basagoiti, former president of the organization:

> The organization that I lead, Coparmex, is the only private sector organization in Mexico that has social and political interests. Our role is to educate our members to be aware of the social and political realities and to read broadly in these areas. When anyone is interested in this aspect of the private sector's relationship with the government they join our organization. They don't go elsewhere.
>
> Other organizations are not thinking about the political scene, but only about economic conditions. This is due in part to the difference between the two types of organizations. Unlike the other industrial organizations, we are really an entrepreneurs' union. The other organizations are obliged by law to be members. Anyone who joins this organization does so freely out of his personal choice and not because of any government regulations. As a consequence, I believe that these other entrepreneurial organizations are in a sense appendages of the state. We are much more independent.[58]

Public officials are in agreement with Basagoiti's description. They suggest that Coparmex's goals have produced a tense relationship with the state. In fact, the frankest politicians readily admit that the reason the government puts pressure on Coparmex is that it promotes a sense of activism the state finds threatening.

Coparmex's sense of activism is incorporated in its original concern with social responsibility. For Coparmex leaders, social responsibility goes beyond helping the community and includes an obligation to understand and participate in the resolution of social and political problems. Coparmex itself claims that one of the three essential reasons for its formation was the "lack of specific preparation among entrepreneurs in Mexico in facing the necessities" confronting businesspeople.[59] This view of its purpose is part of the changing definition of an entrepreneur discussed in the initial chapters. Coparmex began to put this innovative philosophy visibly into effect in the 1970s, although certain less-known positions marked it early in its history as a committed "political" interest group in the North American mode. For example, the organization actually sent funds to support the rebellion of General Saturnino Cedillo in 1939, the last significant violent uprising against the government.[60]

As an important organizational actor in the political arena, Coparmex came into its own during the administration of Luis Echeverría. Analyses of Echeverría have begun and will continue to attribute many significant changes in the political system to his administration's style, content, and direction—among them, his contributions to private sector-state relations. Coparmex took the lead in the initial months of his administration in complaining to the state about its lack of consultation with the private sector.[61] The leader of Coparmex during that period, Roberto Guajardo Suárez, used a language totally different from his predecessors.[62] Coparmex introduced a tone for private interest-group criticism that has since been emulated by other federations, including semiofficial organizations. Coparmex's contribution to a changing private-sector behavior cannot be underscored enough.

It is ironic, therefore, that during the period of political flux in the 1970s and 1980s, Coparmex itself became a subject of internal dissension, revealing weaknesses apparent in the larger private sector. Roberto Guajardo Suárez became the focal point of two opposing views within the organization. A leader of this organization from 1960 to 1973 (the longest continual leadership of any major interest group), he was forced to resign by its conservative elements because of a conflict with President Echeverría, who tried to paint him as unpatriotic—a technique repeated in different circumstances by José López Portillo and Miguel de la Madrid.[63] The culmination of his battles with the president came when Echeverría forced him to read his criticisms at a public meeting, and then used the occasion to criticize the private sector. Yet behind the scenes Echeverría quickly established an open channel with him, lunching with him weekly, all the while that he was receiving unfavorable press coverage for his denunciations.[64] Ironically, Guajardo Suárez was doomed by being insufficiently radical. He resigned because he did not wish to be identified with the hatred and violence promoted by certain entrepreneurial elements in Coparmex.[65]

In 1976, in one of the rare cases of direct capitalist control of an interest organization, the Monterrey Group took over Coparmex by placing one of their own in the presidency, Andrés Marcelo Sada Zambrano, a personable, outspoken advocate of the radical Coparmex line. He called publicly for businessmen to involve themselves in politics and to dispute openly the state's control over societal values.[66] Still, even by the end of López Portillo's administration, Coparmex did not advocate the last logical step of its confrontational political positions toward the state, formation of a political party.[67] Its identification with opposition candidates was sufficiently bothersome that the government attempted in 1984 to bully it into more traditional behavior, blatantly threatening its legal status.[68]

An argument can be made that organizations like Coparmex learn their political behavior by looking at examples north of the border. Without a doubt, many socializing experiences contribute to the propagation of North American attitudes among Mexican businessmen. More concrete, however, is the model offered by the American Chamber of Commerce (CAMCO) in Mexico. Although most observers classify it as an American-run organization, it has participated in several broad policy questions of a political nature. Basáñez believes CAMCO encouraged the division within the Monterrey Group that eventually produced a hard-line faction.[69] More importantly, CAMCO involved itself notably in a boycott of Mexico's major daily, *Excélsior*. This is important not only because of CAMCO's leadership role, but because it provided a politically interventionist model Mexican organizations might copy.[70]

Mexico's private sector, like any large societal group, is bound to have divisions. These divisions weaken its position with the state, just as internal dissensions within the state sap its unity. To tie independent organizations more closely together with semiofficial organizations, seven leading groups—Concanaco, Concamin (including CNIT), Coparmex, ABM, AMIS, CNA (the National Agricultural Producers Council) and the CMHN—formed an umbrella organization known as the Coordinating Council of Businessmen (CCE). It was formed in 1976, after eighteen months of negotiations in the private sector. The key forces behind its birth were the Monterrey Group and the American Chamber of Commerce, another example of North American involvement.[71]

The CCE's purpose is to coordinate activities of the most prominent private-sector organizations. It exists to exchange information and unify criteria and points of view: it is not a substitute for the other organizations.[72]

On paper, the CCE appears to be the apex organization of the Mexican private sector. In reality, however, entrepreneurial power in Mexico lies with the CMHN. As one informant explained, the CCE can be described more accurately as the political arm of the private sector. It tries to do what Coparmex does, only it attempts to obtain a consensus among all private-sector opinion leaders.[73] To carry out its opinion-making activities, the CCE utilizes subsidiary organizations to defend the private sector, to analyze ideological tendencies which influence public opinion, and to pursue legal studies to preserve liberty and guarantee human rights.[74]

The CCE's major weakness, like the organizations themselves, is its unrepresentativeness. The CMHN, which actually dominates the CCE, is controlled directly by major capitalist families. In terms of the formal power structure, the CCE is constituted on an inegalitarian basis. The CMHN has some 30 members, yet it formally receives the same representation on the CCE as Concanaco, which has more than 200,000 members. The CCE has tried to avoid the geographic maldistribution found among other organizations' leadership, requiring that 42 percent of its executive council be from the provinces.[75]

The CCE has had a mixed record of success as a formal channel for private-public sector relations. It tried at the end of the Echeverría administration to call a national strike in support of Sinaloa and Sonora farmers whose lands were to be nationalized. Most observers classified the strike as a failure. As Basáñez suggests, the ability of the private sector to mobilize large-scale support has not been impressive.[76] One explanation for their inconsistent effectiveness has been offered by Jorge Sánchez Mejorada, a former CCE president, who noted that the "purpose of the CCE of course is to lobby, but the style in which they carry out that task needs to be conciliatory."[77]

Throughout the decisionmaking process in Mexico, the most visible actors are often less influential than the hidden ones. Whereas the CCE is supposed to perform the traditional activities of a pressure group for the entire private sector, the power behind the throne is the semisecret CMHN. It was formed in 1962, largely in response to the Mexican support of the Cuban government, the government's tolerance of the National Liberation Movement, the nationalization of electricity, the Mexicanization of the mining industry, and the limitations on foreign capital.[78] Without question it is the most elitist of the major organizations. Thirty individuals make up the council, and their decisions are made collectively. It does not have a president, and it operates behind the scenes.

Originally it was made up of two groups—members of major economic families and some of Mexico's leading professional managers. Among the latter were César Balsa Carralero, real estate developer and president of the María Isabel and El Presidente hotels; Anibal de Iturbide Preciat, long-time manager of the Banco de Comercio chain (Comermex); and Ernesto Robles Levi, president of Bacardi Rum for twenty-five years. Individuals from both categories were prestigious leaders because of their wealth and/or the firms they ran. Foreigners were not permitted, and representatives of small enterprises were excluded.[79]

The CMHN has been thought to have considerable influence, although no concrete evidence exists to support that view. As one observer described it, "The council is not an ordinary business organization—it does not pronounce publicly on major issues; it does not even have an office—yet the consensus that emerges from its secret deliberations determines the private sector's political role."[80] The way it operates, who it represents, and its level of contact with the state undoubtedly have an impact on private-public relations in Mexico. Interviews with present and former members of this select group of Mexican businessmen provide a fascinating picture of its operations and its potential influence on the state.

For all of its purported influence, the impact of the CMHN is limited by many failings, most of which are the fault of entrepreneurs themselves. One prominent businessman who represents an important northern group raises the first of these deficiencies: the "Mexican Council of Businessmen has a very high-level representation with the Mexican government. But really, these are like private clubs in the old days, and they are only made up of people connected to very powerful companies. This is much different in the United States. . . . The members of the council always think they have the last word in representing the private sector, but in my personal opinion they really don't represent us."[81] Leaders of various chambers in the 1980s agreed with this statement.

CMHN's first major weakness is that it is perceived as being, and actually is, dominated by representatives of large industrial groups only. It is obvious from the number of comments offered in my interviews that considerable resentment exists against larger groups. This resentment, and a belief that small firms' interests differ from large firms', suggest that the majority of Mexico's entrepreneurs are not comfortable with being represented by large firms. Like the gap between the leadership of the various organizations and their membership, there is a gap between the CMHN and the other interest groups.

The second weakness confronting the CMHN is the consequence of the revolution in business leadership among large capitalists and professional executives. Although the CMHN membership originally was biased in favor of capitalists, it included highly successful businessmen, primarily self-made, whose reputations rode on their management ability, not their accumulation of capital. One such member, representing a management point of view, explained:

> I resigned from the Mexican Council of Businessmen when they decided that they no longer wanted people with experience to express themselves and vote on the council, but were only interested in members who represented an important economic force in the country. The position of Bernardo Garza Sada was that only those who represent large economic consortiums should be members of the council. . . . I am not resentful in leaving the council, but I think we need people with experience and expertise, not just people with large capital. I think also that a person with my type of experience can deal with the government because I do not have a personal interest in the outcome."[82]

The CMHN is unrepresentative in two ways: it reflects the position of large versus small and medium-sized capital, and it has become increasingly homogeneous and elitist by retaining only those members who are owners rather than managers. Although dominated by Mexico City entrepreneurs, CMHN membership is fairly well distributed geographically. However, the large-capitalist bias has several consequences extending beyond the lack of representation. According to one former member of the council, its members criticize the government, but very timidly. He claims that one reason for this is that they are concerned about personal, vested interests, with which professional managers would not have to be concerned.[83] His argument is that a diversity of council members, divided between large capitalists and professional managers, would change the posture of the organization.

One point CMHN members agree on is the access the organization has to the Mexican state, especially the president. As one member put it, "we have constant contact with the president, and we probably have meetings and meals with the secretary of the budget and programming at least once a week, and just last month with the president. I would say that we meet about twice a month."[84] Access itself is an important commodity in the decisionmaking process, and the CMHN obviously has it. Over the long term, how it uses that access is much more important for private-public relations.

Because of its secretiveness, the dealings of the CMHN with the government have never been revealed. The following comments from a member shed new light on the council and, most importantly, on how Mexican businessmen in a peak association communicate to the president:

When people who are members of the council speak, they *speak as individuals* and not as members of the council as a whole. The private sector did not criticize the last two presidents' bureaucratic growth because of their timidity and fear that there might be reprisals from the government.

Now, when they talk to the government about something, they never talk as a group. To me, this is like committing suicide, because when you are isolated as an individual, you weaken your impact on the government. I resigned eight years ago because when we had meetings to decide certain issues and make studies, any criticism that came out of those decisions was *presented individually.* I think that this kind of behavior represents a very myopic attitude on the part of the private sector. . . .

Look, I will tell you something else about the Council of Businessmen. I have found from luncheons with the president that each member of the council will use that as an opportunity to ask the president for an *individual meeting.* In other words, what the council has beocme is a channel for individuals to make contact with the president rather than to represent the interests of the private sector as a whole. (Italics mine.)[85]

Once again a lack of institutionalization, a devaluation of collective versus individual interests, and the use of personal channels of communication are the foremost characteristics of the CMHN's relationship to the state. These qualities are so typical that the state does need to manipulate private-sector weaknesses to negotiate effectively with the business community. Interest groups have built in sufficient weaknesses of their own which impede their unity when confronting the state.

Conclusions

When any occupational group sets out to represent its interests before political institutions its historical and cultural baggage accompanies it. Mexican entrepreneurs have been plagued by various weaknesses, including unequal geographic representation, overemphasis on large industrial groups, domination of inherited large capital, ideological divisions over the method of participation, and a hesitancy to give full authority to professional management. Each of these deficiencies has produced a series of conflicts within the private sector with consequences reverberating through its relationship with the state.

Interest groups provide the formal, institutional structure through which businessmen can present their demands as a collective body. These same groups, like individual businesspeople, behave according to a mentality entrepreneurs share about themselves, their role in society, and their relationship to the state. Mexico's historical pattern bespeaks a large role of the state in developing the private sector, especially its formal interest groups. Even in the early years, however, nonconformist entrepreneurs, especially from the North, saw the need to establish an independent organization where membership was voluntary. This organization, Coparmex, became the prototype of an activist, antagonistic pressure group.

In assisting the private sector to strengthen its representation before the government, the state perpetrated a divided condition on the private sector. Its organizations have been divided beween voluntary and required (semiofficial), a basis for some tension. The typical pattern of Mexico's business interest groups has been to emulate the semiofficial relationship originally set forth by political architects. Coparmex is an exception; other leading voluntary organizations, including AMIS and ABM, have followed their semiofficial brethren along the path of amicable relations.

Coparmex, in advocating a more ideologically opposed and outspoken style of interest-group activity, forces rejection by the state and contradicts most businessmen's image of their own role. Business leaders advocating an activist stance are revolutionaries within their own ranks. To change institutional behavior, businesspeople have had to alter five decades (or more) of patterns the state itself helped to introduce.

As the private sector's economic power has grown, the influence of the semi-official organizations has correspondingly increased. These groups may accurately be called semiofficial because of how they were constituted by the state and the style in which they continue to relate to the state, but they have reached an autonomous stage in their growth. They no longer need the state's explicit help. By the mid-1980s, these organizations had taken on more features typical of Coparmex. In a sense the original design of the state has turned into a Frankenstein monster, since the private-sector interest groups no longer require the assistance of their creator and have turned on it.[86]

A score card of interest-group influence (admittedly poorly researched) fails to illustrate an obvious victory for Coparmex's radical approach to private-public relations. Coparmex has been successful in threatening the political monopoly of the state at various levels and locales in Mexico in the 1980s, highlighting a long-term strategy of support for political opposition sympathetic to its vested interests. In the policy arena, semiofficial federations, or the realistic voluntary associations like ABM, have been more successful. Whether one speaks about semiofficial or independent interest groups, Dale Story's conclusion "that the state does not control the private sector but also private capital does not dominate the state" remains true.[87] Both, however, are likely to increase their interference with one another.

The activity of the CMHN provides one final revelation about private interest groups. Mexican politicians and entrepreneurs are still in the business of negotiating with each other as though nineteenth-century practices had never disappeared. High levels of institutionalization have taken place, and these provide the framework through which the private sector negotiates with the state. These institutional forces, however, are shot through with personal practices characteristic of Mexican political life for more than a century.

Group behavior in Mexico has not reached its maximum fruition, not only because the state does not permit it to do so, but because businesspeople themselves do not utilize the primary strength of any organization—its collective power. Instead, at the very top, entrepreneurs use CMHN's frequent access to the cabinet and the president to communicate their *individual* concerns and requests, rather than speaking forcefully for the entire business community. Many businesspeople recognize these foibles, but change will not come easily; old habits die hard. The state, not the private sector, benefits from the perpetuation of these habits.

8

Families and Firms

Two themes have reappeared throughout this book. One is that divisiveness in the business world stems in part from the differing interests of firms based on their economic size. The second theme is that social origins contribute to the success of Mexican entrepreneurs, especially those with entrepreneurial fathers. A firm's size and ownership contributes to its importance in Mexico.

Two peculiarities Mexico's private sector today share with those of Latin America and other developing societies are the importance of family-owned corporations and the influence of large industrial holding companies, commonly called groups in Mexico.[1] These two characteristics are inextricably intertwined, as if the old and the new are melded into contemporary institutions of Mexican entrepreneurship. These characteristics are crucial because they affect the entrepreneurial culture, the relationships within the business community, the pattern of business-government relations, and the reproduction of private-sector leadership.

Industrial Groups

The most comprehensive definition of the industrial group, as found in Mexico, has been offered by Nathaniel Leff.

> The group is a multicompany firm which transacts in different markets but which does so under common entrepreneurial and financial control. More generally, this pattern of industrial organization has two essential

features. First, the group draws its capital and its high-level managers from sources which transcend a single family. The capital managers may come from a number of wealthy families, but they remain within the group as a single economic unit. The group's owner-managers typically include some (but by no means all) members of the family within which the group's activity originated.[2]

Leff goes on to say that these groups invest and produce in several product areas rather than in a single product line. One reason each production phase is organized separately within the holding company is for tax purposes.[3]

Industrial groups have a long history in Mexico, the most notable example being the Monterrey Group. The alliance of various firms began to accelerate, as a nationwide trend, in the mid-1960s. Originally, most groups were organized along a single product line, but that pattern gradually altered, and by the 1980s, of the 121 major groups, all were substantially diversified, even though they usually remain identified with a core product.

The economic influences of industrial groups are many, but in the relationship between the public and private sectors, access to decision-makers, influence on policy, and availability of credit stand out. In the first place, major industrial groups receive preferred treatment from politicians. As Vernon notes, "of considerably more importance in the day-to-day contacts between business and government are the dozen or so major groups." What Vernon found to be true in the 1960s is doubly so today as the number of firms and interests seeking government assistance expands. Firm size influences channels of communication.

> I have considerable contact with high government officials, but remember I represent very important interests. This is almost always a difficulty for people with small and medium-sized companies. For example, I have a friend who is in a small business and needs certain papers from the trade ministry to change his import requirements. Instead of having an interview the next day as I would be able to obtain, it took him a whole week to arrange this. If you are big, the government is willing to see you immediately. If you are small, they treat you otherwise.[5]

Size also creates natural resentment between small and medium-sized companies versus large firms. As indicated in the previous chapter, members of the leading industrial and commercial chambers believe their concerns often go unrepresented because larger firms control interest-group leadership.

Accessibility can also be translated more readily into influence. It is not the openness of communication channels per se which gives large firms their influence, but the economic power they exert over the private sector. In 1981, the largest 100 firms accounted for 59 percent of the sales and 73 percent of the capital.[6] Their level of control over capital was nearly twice as great as the 100 top firms' in the United States. Because their economic power has been so dominant, the Mexican bureaucracy must pay particular attention to their demands. Yet, given the present conditions of Mexico's economy, the attention paid to these industrial groups may be misplaced. As a local business leader from the state of México explains, smaller and medium-sized firms, and those in the commercial rather than industrial sectors, may be more critical to the capitalist model's viability.

> The industrial sector is most significant because of the number of people they employ and the tax revenues they provide to the government. But the commercial sector is more important today than in the past because now we can create jobs for much less capital investment, even though our tax base is still smaller. . . . Because there are many more of us in terms of numbers, the potential for our influence has increased.[7]

Economic size rather than numeric strength continues to determine both political access and influence. Many businessmen I interviewed recognized the significant contributions of small and medium-sized businesses to Mexico's economic recovery. Little evidence exists that these firms are exerting more influence than their large industrial-group counterparts. The patterns of behavior which form the culture of private-public relations will alter slowly, even though the influence of smaller firms has undergone some transformation. If business's political participation increases through the rest of the 1980s, then smaller firms may translate their numeric strength into an increasingly powerful political tool and economic policy leverage.

Large holding groups had an impact on the availability of credit before the 1982 bank nationalization. Throughout this book I have stressed the significant role bankers have played in the private sector-government relationship. Even industrialists themselves believe bankers have exerted an unusually significant influence over Mexican government policy. Bankers, therefore, took on a role separate from their typical function as dispensers of scarce capital. They operated in Mexico as sophisticated influence peddlers, brokers between politicians and the private sector.

Major banks share the characteristics of large industrial holding companies, dominating their respective economic sector. In the twentieth century, financial resources have been concentrated in a few institutions. For example, in 1910, the National Bank of Mexico (Banamex), the Bank of London and Mexico (Banca Serfin), and the central Mexican banks controlled 47 percent of the capital. In 1955, Banamex, the Bank of Commerce (Bancomer), and Banca Serfin controlled 43 percent of all capital. By 1980, Banamex and Bancomer alone had 49 percent of the capital, and if Banca Serfin, Comermex, and Fomento Industrial Somex were added to these two leading banks, five companies could claim 73 percent of the capital. Again, the level of concentration in Mexico was much greater than that found among United States banks.[8]

It can be assumed that Mexican government officials treated large banks, like major industrialists, preferentially. The influence of holding companies could be enhanced if they formed an alliance with a leading banking chain. As early as the late 1950s this pattern had already emerged. According to Mosk, older firms were associated with banks though interlocking directorates, and the banks treated well-established industrialists and large commercial firms as favored clients.[9] The purpose of the tie between banks and holding groups is to obtain guaranteed access to capital, traditionally a scarce commodity in Mexico's economy. Industrial groups control banks through direct ownership or through individual board membership.[10]

These multiple, interlocking relationships between leading industrial groups and banks is well illustrated in the following tables. Table 8-1 briefly describes the fifty leading Mexican firms and banks, ranked (somewhat subjectively) on the basis of their economic influence from 1920 to 1980.

The rankings themselves are not so important; rather, we can conclude with considerable assurance that any of the companies listed in Table 8-1 have been in the top fifty for some or most of the years they have operated since 1920. A clear illustration of bank and holding company ties can be seen with the Banca Serfin chain, Mexico's fourth largest prior to 1982. It has representation from the Garza Sada family, who in turn control two major industrial groups, Grupo Industrial Alfa and Grupo Visa. In the case of Bancomer, controlled by the Espinosa Iglesias family before nationalization, various groups were represented on its board, including the Desc Group, the Cremi Group, and the Aurrera retail chain. The Legorreta family, which controlled Mexico's second largest chain, Banamex, has sat on the boards of numerous leading firms, including Cervecería Modelo, whose founder, Pablo Díez

Table 8-1. Ownership and Control of Mexico's Top Fifty Firms and Banks

Name of Firm	Ownership	Field	Rank
Aeronaves de México, S.A.*Data*: Founded 1934. Of the 128,000 shares in 1958, the government owned all but 4.	Government	Transportation	28
Aeropuertos y Servicios *Auxiliares* *Data*: Founded by the federal government in 1965. No private-sector representation.	Government	Transportation	47
Anderson Clayton *Data*: Founded 1934; went public 1966; important board members have included Alberto González Uriarte, Miguel M. Blásquez.	Anderson/C.	Manufacturing	25
Aseguradora Mexicana, S.A. *Data*: Founded 1937; government control 1942; original founders included individual investors and the Mexican Mortgage Association.	Goverment	Insurance	39
Aurrera, S. A. *Data*: Founded 1965; Jewel Co. (USA) owned 36%, Bancomer 34%, and Banamex 7% of stock in 1982; important board members have included Plácido Arango Arias and Jerónimo Arango Arias, who served as president.	Private	Retail	15
Banca Serfin, S.A. *Data*: Founded 1977 with a fusion of the Serfin chain, the Banco de Londrés y Mexico, and Financiera Aceptaciones, S.A. Banco de Londrés founded in 1863. Some of its board members have included León Signoret, Alfonso Michel, Manuel Gómez Morín, Antonio L. Rodríguez, Juan Cortina, Pablo Díez Fernández, Adolfo I. Riveroll, Enrique Sada Muguerza. Since fusion, board has included Eugenio Garza Laguera, Jorge Larrea Ortega, Max Michel Suberville, Carlos Pérez Maldonado, Manuel L. Barragán, Ignacio	Private	Banking	—

Table 8-1. (*continued*)

Name of Firm	Ownership	Field	Rank
Araguren Castiello, and José Calderón Ayala. Francisco F. Maldonado served as president. Before nationalization it ranked fourth in banking. No single family dominated this chain, but the Garza Sada family came to control 30% of the stock.	Private	Banking	—
Banco de Comercio, S.A. (Bancomer) *Data*: Founded 1932 by Salvador Ugarte. Controls many other insurance companies and financial institutions. Original investors were the Espinosa Iglesias and Jenkins families. Top officers have included Salvador Ugarte, Manuel Espinosa Iglesias, and Ignacio Castillo. Board members have included Raúl Bailleres, Ernesto J. Amescua, Mario Domínguez, Julio Lacaud, Manuel Senderos, Maximino Michel, Octaviano Longoría, Luis G. Aguilar, Jerónimo Arango, and Eduardo Bustamante. The largest banking chain. Controlled by the Espinosa Iglesias family prior to nationalization.	Private	Banking	—
Banco Nacional de México, S.A. (Banamex) *Data*: Founded 1854. In 1911, eighth most important firm in Mexico. Dominated by the Legorreta family. Top officers have included Graciano Guichard, Agustín F. Legorreta, and Luis G. Legorreta. Board members have included Pablo Díez Fernández, Atanasio G. Saravia, Carlos Prieto, Antonio Ruiz Galindo, Jr., Gastón Azcárraga, Ernesto Spitalier, and Pablo Jean. Second most important bank before nationalization.	Private	Banking	—

Table 8-1. (*continued*)

Name of Firm	Ownership	Field	Rank
Celanese Mexicana, S.A. *Data*: Founded 1944; went public in 1947; Celanese had 43% of shares; other major stockholder is Banamex. Original founders included Gastón Azcárraga, Alfredo Aboumrad, Pablo Díez Fernández, Pablo Jean, Ernesto Spitalier, Carlos Prieto, and Julián Bayon; important board members include Federico Ortiz Alvarez, Luis G. Legorreta, Eduardo Suárez, Prudencio López, and Carlos Prieto Fernández.	Private	Manufacturing	14
Cementos Mexicanos, S.A. (Grupo) *Data*: Founded 1920; went public in 1976; controlled by Grupo Cementos Mexicanos; important officers have included Rodolfo J. García and Pablo Salas y López; board members include Juan R. Brittingham, Marcelo Zambrano, and Salvador Sada Gómez.	Private	Manufacturing	50
Cervecería Moctezuma, S.A. *Data*: Founded in 1894 in Orizaba; for many years operated by the Suberbie brothers; later owned by Raúl Bailleres and a group of French investors, then by son Alberto Bailleres; important officers since 1959 have been Raúl and Alberto Bailleres; board members have included Anibal Iturbide, Justo F. Fernández, Manuel Senderos, Carlos Trouyet, Plácido Arango Arias, Juan B. Riverol, Augusto Domínguez, Estaquio Escandón, and Luis G. Aguilar; major stockholder is Bancomer; went public 1946; presently part of Grupo Cremi (Bailleres).	Private	Manufacturing	21

Table 8-1. *(continued)*

Name of Firm	Ownership	Field	Rank
Cervecería Modelo, S.A. *Data*: Founded 1922; part of Grupo Cervecería Modelo; founder and president, Pablo Díez Fernández; major stockholder is Banamex; important board members have included Luis Legorreta and Juan Sánchez Navarro. Díez Fernández cofounded Celanese.	Private	Manufacturing	9
Chrysler de México, S.A. (Fábricas Automex) *Data*: Founded 1938; founder Gastón Azcárraga Vidaurreta; Vicente Aríztegui Perochena company officer; Chrysler owns 99% of stock; went public 1963.	Chrysler	Manufacturing	10
Comercial Mexicana, S.A. *Data*: Founded 1946; went public 1972; officers include Martín García Urtiaga; board members have included Javier Ruiz Galindo.	Private	Manufacturing	21
Comisión Federal de Electricidad *Data*: Founded in 1933; no private-sector representation.	Government	Utilities	4
Companía de las Fábricas de Papel San Rafael y Anexas, S.A. *Data*: Founded 1894; in 1911 one of the top fifty companies; controlled by Grupo San Rafael and Banamex; officers have included Emilio Spitalier and Fernando de la Macorra (father José founded firm with Tomás Braniff O'Gorman). Luis Legorreta García has been a board member.	Private	Manufacturing	49
Companía Fundidora de Fierro y Acero de Monterrey, S.A. *Data*: Founded 1900 by a group of Mexicans and one North American, including Antonio Basagoiti, León Signoret, and Vicente Ferrara; top officials have included Carlos Prieto, Adolfo Prieto, Evaristo Araiza; important board	Private/Gov't	Manufacturing	12

Table 8-1. (*continued*)

Name of Firm	Ownership	Field	Rank
members have included Luis G. Legorreta, Miguel S. Macedo, Evaristo Ariza, Maximino Michel, Manuel L. Barragán, Mariano Hernández, Issac Garza, and Adolfo Zambrano. Ranked thirtieth in 1911, third in 1968, and third in 1981. Flagship of the Alfa Group. Government bought 25% of shares in 1972 and intervened again in 1974 to prevent bankruptcy, at which time it gained majority control, becoming part of Sidermex. Declared bankruptcy in 1986.	Private/Gov't	Manufacturing	12
Compañía Hulera Goodyear Oxo *Data*: Founded 1927; founding president was Angel Urraza; stock controlled by Goodyear and Cydsa Group.	Private	Manufacturing	40
Compañía Mexicana de Aviación, S.A. *Data*: Founded 1924; went public 1949; only Mexican founder was Gustavo Espinosa Mireles; subsidiary of Pan American, 1930; Pan Am sold its shares to Mexican investors, including Abelardo Rodríguez and Aaron Sáenz, in 1944; in 1968, Pan Am sold remainder of shares to Cresencio Ballesteros and Manuel Sosa de la Vega. Government took over in 1980s.	Private/Gov't	Transportation	23
Compañía Nestlé *Data*: Founded 1934; José Represas and José Represas, Jr., company officers.	Nestlé	Manufacturing	30
Compañía Nacional de Subsidios Populares (Conasupo) *Data*: Founded in 1949; no private-sector representation.	Government	Retail	4

Table 8-1. *(continued)*

Name of Firm	Ownership	Field	Rank
Condumex (Grupo) *Data*: Founded 1952; went public in 1957; became Grupo Condumex in 1977; originally Nacional de Conductores Electricos; founders include Eduardo Prieto López; investors included Anaconda-Ericsson Inc., whose 20% stock share was bought out by Atlantic Richfield in 1977; Banamex controlled the largest amount of shares in 1982, and Nafinsa had 16%. Board members have included Gastón Azcárraga, Rafael Mancera, Prudencio López M., and Alejandro Alvarez Guerrero.	Private	Manufacturing	35
(Descuento Sociedad Fomento Industrial, S.A.C.V.) (Desc) (Grupo) *Data*: Founded 1973; went public in 1975; RCA owned large share of stock; in 1982, the largest shareholder was Fomento de Valores, S.A.C.V. with 48%, followed by Banamex with 11%. Largest individual shareholders were Armando Ruiz Galindo and Manuel Senderos Irigoyen, two of the original founders. Seven members of its board were on the CMHN; three members of its board were on the Banamex board. Other important board members have included Agustín F. Legorreta Chauvet, Alberto Bailleres González, Gastón Azcárraga Tamayo, and Rómulo O'Farrill, Jr.	Private	Manufacturing	11
Diesel Nacional *Data*: Founded 1951 by the federal government, Fiat, and a group of individual investors.	Government	Manufacturing	18
El Puerto de Liverpool, S.A. *Data*: Founded 1944; went public in 1965; stockholders included foreign and domestic owners; board	Private	Retail	34

Table 8-1. *(continued)*

Name of Firm	Ownership	Field	Rank
members have included Armando Garza Sada, Graciano Güichard, and Max Michel, son of founder, and several members of Suberville family.	Private	Retail	34
Empresas ICA, S.A. *Data:* Founded 1947 by Bernardo Quintana Arrioja with a group of graduates from UNAM. Family-owned firm; leadership passed to Bernardo Quintana Issac with death of father. Largest construction firm in Latin America.	Private	Construction	8
Empresas La Moderna, S.A.C.V. *Data:* Founded 1936; went public in 1964; presently part of the Grupo El Aguila y La Moderna; Important board members have included Eduardo Bustamante, Eugenio Erana García, and Carlos Maldonado Elizondo.	Foreign	Manufacturing	19
Empresas Tolteca de México, S.A.C.V. *Data:* Stockholders foreign and domestic. Former officers included Bernardo Quintana Arrioja. Board members have included Alfredo del Mazo Quintana.	Private	Manufacturing	43
Ferrocarriles Naciones de México *Data:* Founded 1908. The federal government took control in 1937. No private-sector representation since 1940.	Government	Transportation	13
Fomento Industrial Somex, S.A.C.V. (Somex) *Data:* Includes Sosa Texcoco, founded 1943, with government and private ownership. Founding president was Atanasio G. Saravia. Board members have included Luis G. Legorreta, Pablo Macedo, Eduardo Brittingham, Jerónimo Arango, and Pablo Díez Fernández. Government control by 1978.	Government	—	29

Table 8-1. *(continued)*

Name of Firm	Ownership	Field	Rank
Ford Motor Company, S.A. *Data*: Founded 1925; 100% owner- ship by Ford Motor Co.	Ford	Manufacturing	9
General Electric de México *Data*: Founded 1924; went public in 1968; Mexican board members have included Carlos Sánchez Me- jorada; GE owned 90% of the stock in 1982.	GE	Manufacturing	43
General Foods de México *Data*: General Foods held 80% of the stock.	General Foods	Manufacturing	30
General Motors de México *Data*: Founded 1935; General Mo- tors held 100% of stock.	GM	Manufacturing	26
Grupo Chihuahua *Data*: Flagship firm, Celulosa de Chihuahua, founded 1952; went public in 1956; stock controlled by Vallina family, also tied to Banco- mer. Board has included José An- tonio Vallina, Rafael Vallina Fernández. Eloy S. Vallina Lagu- era officer of firm.	Private	Manufacturing	22
Grupo Cydsa, S.A. *Data*: Founded in 1965; one of four holding companies of the Monter- rey Group. Went public 1974. Flag- ship firm is Celulosa y Derivados, with Goodrich and Rohn Poulenc as investors. Goodrich had 40% of stock in 1982, followed by Serfin and Banco del País (Banpaís) bank- ing chains with 20% and 14%. The largest individual investors are Andrés Garza Sada (4%), Beatriz Zambrano de Sada (4%), and Adrián Sada Treviño (3%). Com- pany president was Andrés Marcelo Sada Zambrano. Board members have included Bernardo Garza Sada, Antonio Madero Bracho, Agustín Garza Laguera, and Fer- nando Sada Malacara.	Private	Manufacturing	28

Table 8-1. (*continued*)

Name of Firm	Ownership	Field	Rank
Grupo IMSA, S.A. (Industrias Monterrey, S.A.) *Data*: Founded 1936. Board members have included Fernando Canales Salinas, uncle of Ernesto Canales Santos, major Alfa stockholder.	Private	Manufacturing	45
Grupo Industrial Alfa, S.A. *Data*: Founded 1974; most important holding company of the Monterrey Group. Largest stockholder is Ernesto Canales Santos with 47%. Other important shareholders are Jesús Delgado Garza, Armando Garza Sada, Lorenzo Garza Sepúlveda, and Rafael R. Páez Garza. Chief officer has been Bernardo Garza Sada. Board members have included Adrián Sada Treviño, Eugenio Garza Laguera, José Calderón Ayala, Andrés Marcelo Sada Zambrano, and Dionisio Garza Sada. Largest privately owned firm in Mexico. Flagship firm was Hojalata y Lamina (Hylsa), founded in 1942.	Private	Manufacturing	3
Grupo Industrial Bimbo, S.A. *Data*: Founded 1966; went public 1980. Major stockholders are Banamex and the following three families: Servitje (41%), Mata (25%), and Sendra (13%). Important officers have included Roberto and Lorenzo Servitje. Board members have included Jorge Orvanaños Zúniga and Claudio Terreín de Coorignies.	Private	Manufacturing	25
Grupo Industrial Saltillo *Data*: Founded 1966. Went public 1976. Holding company includes Companía Industrial del Norte. Board members have included Bernardo Garza Sada and Claudio X. González Laporte.	Private	Manufacturing	31

Table 8-1.   *(continued)*

Name of Firm	Ownership	Field	Rank
Grupo Industrias Unidas *Data*: Major stockholder and officer is Alejo Peralta.	Private	Manufacturing	29
Grupo Sidermex (Altos Hornos) *Data*: Founded 1942; important board members include Jorge B. Marcos Giacoman, Antonio Ruiz Galindo, Jr., Agustín Legorreta, and Juan Sánchez Navarro.	Government	Manufacturing	2
Guanos y Fertilizantes de México, S.A. (Fertilizantes Mexicanos) *Data*: Founded 1943 by the federal government.	Government	Manufacturing	13
Industrias Nacobre, S.A.C.V. *Data*: Founded 1950. Stock held in 1983 by Atlantic Richfield (40%), Deutz, S.A.C.V. (Pablo Deutz holding company 13%), and Ba- namex (10%). Important officers have been Eduardo Prieto López and Pablo Deutz, Jr. Board members have included Eustaquio Cortina Portilla and Claudio X. González Laporte.	Private	Manufacturing	50
Industrias Purina, S.A.C.V. *Data*: Founded 1978. Went public 1978. In 1982, Ralston Purina owned 49% of the stock, followed by Sociedad Industrial Hermes with 39% (a firm tied to Carlos Hank González's interests). Com- pany officials have included Carlos Hank Rhon, son of Carlos Hank González.	Private	Manufacturing	50
Kimberly Clark de México, S.A.C.V. *Data*: Founded 1925. Went public 1961. Major stockholder is Kim- berly Clark. Board members have included Cresencio Ballesteros Ibarra, Pablo L. Deutz, Jr., Antonio Ruiz Galindo, and Javier Pérez Rocha. Top company officers have included Claudio X. González Laporte.	Private	Manufacturing	41

Table 8-1. *(continued)*

Name of Firm	Ownership	Field	Rank
La Provincial, Companía General de Seguros *Data*: Founded 1936. Board members have included Manuel Gómez Morín, Miguel R. Cárdenas, Roberto Casas Alatriste, Franz Mayer, and Adolfo I. Riveroll. Presidents of the company have included Maximino Michel (El Palacio de Liverpool) and Alberto Bailleres (Cervecería Moctezuma).	Private	Insurance	38
Multibanco Comermex *Data*: Founded 1934 as the Banco Comercial Mexicano; reformed 1977 with the fusion of several financial groups. Belongs to the Grupo Chihuahua, headed by Eloy S. Vallina, president until the nationalization. Board members have included Eduardo Suárez, Carlos Trouyet, Alberto Bailleres Chávez, Anibal de Iturbide, Augusto Domínguez Amescua, Eugenio Garza Laguera, and Isaac Riveroll Beasley. Was the fourth largest banking chain before nationalization.	Private	Banking	—
Petroleos Mexicanos *Data*: Founded as a consequence of the nationalization of 17 foreign firms in 1938, 93% of all production.	Government	Petroleum	1
Productos Pesqueros Mexicanos, S.A.C.V. *Data*: No information.	Government	Fishing	41
Salinas y Rocha, S.A. *Data*: Founded 1933; went public 1981. Board members have included Octavio Rocha, Luis Latapi Toussaint, and Roberto Zambrano Lozano. Top officials include Blanco Vigil.	Private	—	37

Table 8-1. (*continued*)

Name of Firm	Ownership	Field	Rank
Sociedad Industrial Hermes, S.A.C.V.	Private	Manufacturing	44
Data: A holding company controlled by the Hank González family. Most important firm is Campos Hermanos, S.A., founded in 1938 by the Campos Domínguez brothers with 100,000 pesos capital. Purchased by Carlos Hank Rhon in 1976. Carlos Hank Rhon is president of Hermes.			
Sosa Texcoco (*see Fomento Industrial Somex*)			
Teléfonos de México, S.A.	Private	Communications	12
Data: Founded 1909. Went public in 1951. Originally Empresas de Teléfonos Ericson. Government and private ownership. Board members have included Antonio Ruiz Galindo, Agustín F. Legorreta, Eloy S. Vallina, Carlos González Nova, Francisco Trouyet, and Justo F. Fernández.			
Tubos de Acero de México, S.A.C.V.	Private	Manufacturing	29
Data: Founded 1952; public in 1953. Stockholders include Grupo Pagliai, the government, and foreign investors. Top officials have included Bruno Pagliai, Ernesto Fernández Hurtado, and Carlos J. Díaz. Board members have included Anibal de Iturbide, Carlos Abedrop, Eduardo Bustamante, Antonio Ruiz Galindo, Eloy S. Vallina and Carlos Trouyet.			
Valores Industriales, S.A. (Grupo Visa)	Private	Manufacturing	8
Data: One of the four major holding companies of the Monterrey Group. Founded 1936. Went public 1978. Major company in group includes Cervecería Cuauhtémoc, S.A., founded 1890 by Issac Garza, José A. Muguerza, and Francisco			

Table 8-1. (*continued*)

Name of Firm	Ownership	Field	Rank
Sada. Stock of the brewery controlled by Garza-Laguera families. Top officials have been Eugenio Garza Laguera and Eugenio Garza Sada, who has also headed Visa. Board members of Visa included Jose F. Muguerza, José Calderón Ayala, Alejandro Garza Laguera, Bernardo Garza Sada, and Francisco Maldonado. In 1982, important individual stockholders included Lorenzo Garza Speúlveda, Adrián Páez Garza, and Olton Páez Garza. Guillermo Ballesteros Ibarra served as president.			
Vitro, S.A. *Data*: Founded 1936. Went public 1976. Major stockholders in 1982 were Banpaís (17%), Serfin (13%), Adrián Sada Treviño (5%), Nelly González de Sada (5%), and Adrián Páez Garza (2%). Board members have included Alejandro Garza Laguera, Dionisio Garza Sada, Rogelio Sada Zambrano, and Eduardo G. Brittingham. One of the Monterrey Group holding companies.	Private	Manufacturing	16
Volkswagen de México, S.A.C.V. *Data*: Founded in 1964; 100% owned by Volkswagen.	Volkswagen	Manufacturing	33

Fernández, in turn sits on Banamex's board; Companía de las Fábricas de Papel San Rafael y Anexas, which Banamex has a large interest in, and whose chief officer, Emilio Spitalier, has sat on Banamex's board, while Luis Legorreta García served on the firm's board; and Companía Fundidora de Fierro y Acero de Monterrey, whose chief executive officer, Carlos Prieto, traded board membership with the Legorretas. In fact, the Legorretas are known to sit on at least eight of Mexico's top company boards. The connections in board membership between these three banking chains are found among other leading firms and banks.

Family-controlled companies originally became tied into banking firms to obtain capital unavailable within the family. These banking and firm relationships are basically symbiotic, since each benefits from the relationship—the firm because of their preferred credit position, the bank because it has an established clientele of blue-ribbon firms. In addition to regular commercial banks, each major group is also tied to a *financiera*, an investment bank. Each banking chain incorporates an investment bank within its own conglomerate, and often securities and insurance firms—as in the case of Banamex—are included. Because they lack connections, new firms "typically will find it difficult to obtain adequate funds from commercial banks. It is only logical, under these conditions, that businessmen should develop a means for providing themselves with what are in effect captive sources of capital."[11]

The interrelationship between bank and firm ownership further demonstrates why many independent firms might take a differing attitude from their large entrepreneurial peers toward bank nationalization. Medium-sized and small firms do not necessarily believe their interests are compatible with larger firms', especially when it comes to obtaining credit. The structural feature of large Mexican firms' establishing special alliances with major banks must be considered in an analysis of the private sector and its relationship to the state. These alliances produce divisiveness and jealousies among groups within the private sector. From this point of view, the nationalization might be looked upon as a decision that strengthened rather than weakened the Mexican business community, removing a point of contention from within the private sector.

The private sector shares an interesting characteristic with the public sector and other groups in Mexican society, a scarcity of information. In developing societies, control over information is a powerful political weapon. Industrial groups maintain ties with financial groups because each has its own outside connections through which information can be gathered. These multiple sources of information are invaluable to both groups.[12]

Bankers not only have served as conduits of information for Mexican firms but until 1982 were a key channel between the private sector and the state. I argued previously that one important consequence of the bank nationalization for the private-public relationship was the removal of this important channel. The elimination of bankers as a broker between the private sector and the state only further complicates their relationship. Antonio Ortiz Mena provides an excellent example of bankers' influence on their relationship:

The state and the banking system are interrelated in two ways. First, bankers have always given their point of view to the state, and in turn, the government takes their views into account. Secondly, they are an excellent conductor or conduit of views from the private sector as a whole. In many cases, bankers served as mediators to persuade the private sector of the advisability of certain government policies. For example, in 1975, the social security law was changed in such a way that the private sector would become responsible for paying half of the amount put away for each employee, which previously had been paid by the state. In my opinion, the bankers were the ones who convinced the entrepreneurs that it was a good policy for the employer to do this. As a result, there were no major political consequences from this significant policy change.[13]

The tie between banks and industrial groups is only one characteristic of leading firms revealed in Table 8-1. Another feature of Mexican firms, unaffected by nationalization, is the makeup of the boards. Three important questions can be raised about board membership. First, to what extent do families continue to dominate boards? Board membership is revealing because stock ownership information was unavailable until 1982, and mostly unavailable after 1982, unless the firm is publicly traded. Second, to what extent have large firms developed alliances with other companies similar to their relations with banks, as part of their desire to maintain preferred forward and backward economic linkages? Third, to what extent are politicians represented on company boards, so as to provide a more direct tie to the state?

When Derossi completed her study in the early 1970s, she asked her sample of industrialists about the makeup of their boards. Her data showed that 25 percent of all board members were either relatives or shareholders; 31 percent were nonrelative experts or professional managers; 21 percent came from other companies; and bankers accounted for the remaining 23 percent.[14] She found that nearly two-thirds of the industrialists in her sample sat on the boards of other companies, but unfortunately she did not identify politicians. She also discovered that the majority of firms were still family owned.[15]

If we examine the data in Table 8-1 we find that Derossi's earlier assertions for industrial firms applies to every economic sector and type of firm, whether manufacturing, retail, banking, transportation, or insurance. Again, parallels among the political, intellectual, and business worlds readily come to mind. Politicians use personal and family alliances to build up their cliques and establish their political influence. The boards of intellectual magazines similarly reveal individuals who have personal, social, and even kinship ties, sometimes extending back more than one generation. The most exaggerated form of family influence can be found on important company boards. "Dynasties of entrepreneurs sit on each other's boards of directors, combine their resources through reciprocal deals and matrimonial alliances, and consciously support the family tradition."[16]

An examination of the leading firms listed in Table 8-1, excluding government-owned and operated companies, shows a definite pattern of alliance between major groups, and therefore major families. If boards are any indication of control, Mexico's business management at the very top is confined to a rather small group of individuals. Stock information available suggests that is typically the case. For example, what does the board membership of Mexico's largest bank, Bancomer (Table 8-2), reveal during the forty-year period from 1940 to nationalization?

Data from Table 8-2 support many of the suppositions concerning interlocking directorates between banks and major holding firms. Bancomer is no exception to representation found on the boards of directors of the other leading banking chains. In the first place, a single bank has ties to more than one major industrial group. In fact, the data in this figure and from other firms and banks unquestionably demonstrate that most major groups, instead of seeing themselves as directly competitive, share multiple ties with one another. Over and over again the leading firms, the largest groups, and the most powerful families appear on the board of Bancomer. Of the twenty-one most influential families listed in Table 8-4, five, or nearly a fourth—Aguilar, Aranda, Bailleres, Espinosa Iglesias, and Senderos—are represented. Of the most important groups, nearly all—including Bailleres, Diéz Fernández, Michel, Pagliali, Ruiz Galindo, Trouyet, and Sáenz—are repeatedly represented. Many of the individuals on the Bancomer board are in turn related to other board members by marriage, so that long-lived companies seem to have incestuous leadership from one generation to the next. Equally interesting is the fact that Bancomer is well represented on other bank and insurance company boards, particularly banks allied with the Cremi Group (Banca Cremi) and the Sáenz Group (Banco Industrial y Comercio). On the other hand, it is easier to determine its competitors by who is excluded, namely the Banamex chain.

The other question raised at the beginning of this section is the extent of politicians' representation on the boards of private-sector

Table 8-2. Board Members of Bancomer, 1940–80

Names	Companies (*families and/or groups*)
Luis G. Aguilar	Cementos Atoyac (Lacaud), Banco Industrial (Bailleres), Cervecería Moctezuma (Bailleres), Banco de Industria y Comercio (Sáenz Group), Cía Mexicana de Refractorios Greene (Trouyet Group), Luis G. Aguilar, S.A. (Aguilar).
Ernesto J. Amezcua	La Provincial Insurance (Michel), La Nacional Insurance, Cía Mexicana de Refractorios Greene (Trouyet Group), Cervecería Moctezuma, twice president of Concanaco.
Jerónimo Arango	Cía Industria Orizaba (Grupo Cidosa), Sosa Texcoco (Somex).
Raúl Bailleres	Cremi Group (banking, insurance, beer), Buda Group.
Eduardo Bustamante	Banco de Industria y Comercio (Sáenz Group), La Moderna, Tubos de Acero (Grupo Pagliali).
Miguel R. Cárdenas	La Provincial Insurance (original shareholder), Cía Hulera Euzkadi (Urraza), Banco de Industria y Comercio (Sáenz Group); Banco de Industria (Bailleres).
José F. Castello	Crédito Mexicano (Bancomer); possibly related to Aaron Sáenz through marriage.
Mario Domínguez	Buda Group (Bailleres), related to Amezcua family through marriage, Cía Mexicana de Refractorios Greene (Trouyet Group), Cremi Group (Bailleres), twice president of Mexican Bankers Association; original shareholder of La Provincial Insurance (Michel).
Manuel Espinosa	Frisco, Productos Químicos (Grupo Vallina).
Julio Lacaud	Banco Industrial (Sáenz Group), Cementos Atoyac (Trouyet Group), Cía Mexican de Refractorios Greene (Trouyet Group), and Pan American de México (insurance).

corporations. Banks, as I have asserted earlier, are better in this regard than firms in general. Bancomer, over several decades, has maintained ties with two politician-entrepreneurs: Aaron Sáenz and Eduardo Bustamante. Bustamante himself is a protégé of Manuel Goméz Morín, who obtained Bustamante's first job as a college graduate in the treasury department. Gómez Morín is the archetypal politician-turned-successful investor in the 1920s and 1930s. Bustamante also came under the influence of Aaron Sáenz, first as his financial adviser when Sáenz served as governor of Nuevo León, then as his personal

Table 8–2. (continued)

Names	Companies (families and/or groups)
Octaviano Longoría	Empresas Longoría (Longoría), Banco Continental, Nacional de Drogas, related by marriage to Antonio L. Rodríguez.
Maximino Michel	Companía Fundidora de Fierro y Acero de Monterrey (Prieto), El Puerto de Liverpool, Banco de Londrés y México (owned 22% of shares at one time, Garza Sada and Garza Laguera), Aceros Esmaltados (Grupo Somex), Cía de las Fábricas de Papel San Rafael (de la Macorra), La Provincial Insurance, Sofimex (Gómez Morín, Sada Muguerza, Urraza).
Manuel Muñóz Castillo	Banco Industrial (Sáenz Group), president of Concanaco.
Elías Pando	Industrias Pando, S.A.C.V. (Pando).
Juan Sánchez Navarro	Altos Hornos (government), Cervecería Modelo (Díez Fernández), Química Hooker, Tubos de Acero (Grupo Pagliali), president of CCE and Concanaco.
Manuel Senderos	Desc Group (Ruiz Galindo), Spicer (Trouyet Group), Seguros La Comercial (insurance), Cervecería Moctezuma (Bailleres), Industrias Peñoles (Bailleres).
Antonio Signoret	Brother on board of Banco Mineral y Mercantil of Monterrey (Cremi Group).

Note: This is only a partial list of board members for these years. Many of the individuals listed have been board members for periods exceeding twenty years.

Source: Data are taken from biographical information and financial reports too numerous to mention.

secretary in the cabinet in the early 1930s, and finally as director general of Sáenz's bank from 1942 to 1945, before Bustamante became subsecretary of the treasury.[17]

Bustamante represents an important type of Mexican politician-entrepreneur. As the evidence in Chapter 7 illustrates, his pattern is neither typical nor on the increase. On the other hand, the entrepreneur-turned-politician, or the reverse, like Bustamante, is often the protégé of a mentor who has followed a similar route. This may be why the interchange remains stable. Before an exchange pattern becomes commonplace, it will take an innovative generation of politicians and entrepreneurs to cross openly the artificial boundaries between Mexico's political and economic worlds, just as a younger generation of intellectuals have begun to turn away from the typical intellectual-state model of government service.[18] Until large numbers from one sector or the other take this step, their disciples will follow the traditional pattern of separate careers.

It is equally valuable to examine an important Mexican firm to test these assumptions. One of the Mexico's oldest firms, Cervecería Moctezuma, S.A., provides a typical example. A partial listing of its board members (Table 8-3) illustrates the same patterns that can be found with Bancomer. The firm is controlled by the Bailleres family, so their group's holdings will be overly represented on the board. This is obviously the case, as about half the board members hold positions in other Bailleres family-controlled firms. Also interesting is the fact that its primary financial ties have been through Monterrey banks eventually incorporated into the Banca Cremi chain, part of the Cremi Group, which itself controls the Cervecería Moctezuma. However, the company maintains strong financial representation on its board from two other major chains, Multibanco Comermex, the northern chain run by the Vallina family, and Bancomer, controlled by the Espinosa Iglesias family. The brewery, therefore, has banking ties with multiple banks. Again, as in the case of Bancomer, the Bailleres family includes strong representation from a half-dozen or more major entrepreneurial families, including Michel, Ruiz Galindo, Sáenz, Suberbie, Trouyet, and Vallina, who represent every economic sector, including retail, banking, insurance, and manufacturing.

Family Influence

The information in Tables 8-1, 8-2, and 8-3 illustrates the linkages among banks, major firms, holding companies, and entrepreneurial families. Most important, these tables illustrate the continuation and extent of family control in Mexico's major enterprises. For this reason, it is essential to understand the nature of family ownership, how it has evolved in recent years, and the extent of its influence at other levels of the economy.

With the exception of the Monterrey Group, very little literature, biographical or otherwise, exists about entrepreneurial families and their ties.[19] Mexican capitalism cannot be fully understood without studying in detail the families that have developed its industry and commerce. It is especially interesting to contrast the Anglo-Saxon individualism which has been identified commonly with North Ameri-

Table 8-3.   Board Members of Cervecería Moctezuma, S.A., 1952–82

Name	Company (group and/or family)
Luis G. Aguilar	Cementos Atoyac (Lacaud), Banco Industrial (Bailleres), Luis G. Aguilar, S.A. (Aguilar), Banco de Industria y Comercio (Sáenz), Cía Mexicana de Refractorios Greene (Trouyet Group).
Ernesto J. Amezcua	La Provincial Insurance (Michel), La Nacional Insurance, Cía Mexicana de Refractorios Greene (Trouyet Group), twice president of Concanaco.
Jerónimo Arango	Cía Industria Orizaba (Grupo Cidosa), Sosa Texcoco (Somex).
Alberto Bailleres	Cremi Group (banking, insurance, beer), president of Cervecería Moctezuma, board of Cía Mexicana de Refractorios Greene (Trouyet Group), Desc Group (Ruiz Galindo), La Provincial Insurance (Michel), Multibanco Comermex (Vallina), El Palacio de Hierro, CMHN.
Raúl Bailleres	Cremi Group (banking, insurance, beer), Buda Group.
Ernesto Couttolenc	Banco Minero y Mercantile (Cremi Group).
Augusto Domínguez	La Provincial Insurance (Michel), Multibanco Comermex (Vallina), president of the Mexican Bankers Association.
Norberto A. Domínguez	El Palacio de Hierro (Cremi Group).
Eustaquio Escandón	Multibanco Comermex (Vallina), Banco Mineral y Mercantil (Cremi Group), original member of the CMHN, president of Concanaco.
Justo F. Fernández	General Foods, Teléfonos de México, original member of the CMHN.

can capitalism to the attitude of family solidarity that flavors the culture of Mexican capitalism.[20]

In the nineteenth century an economic oligarchy controlled Mexico's political and economic resources at the state level. These families were intertwined through marriage and sanguinal ties with many other kinship groups. No better example existed at the turn of the century than the Olegario Molina family, which dominated political and economic resources on the Yucatán peninsula.[21] As I demonstrated earlier, Mexico's economic and political leaders separated further after 1920. As entrepreneurs pursued economic interests, important local businesspeople continued to produce successful descendants, although their impact was diluted by Spanish immigration and by small

Table 8-3. *(continued)*

Name	Company *(group and/or family)*
Joaquín Gallo Sarlat	Banca Cremi, El Palacio de Hierro, Industrias Peñoles (Bailleres).
Anibal de Iturbide	Multibanco Comermex (Vallina), Aceros Escatepec, Cía Industria de Orizaba (Grupo Cidosa), Ponderosa Industrial (Vallina).
Gabriel Mancera Aguayo	Cía Hulera Euzkadi, Cía Mexicana de Refractorios Greene (Trouyet Group), Salinas y Rocha, S.A., brother of Miguel, director general of the Bank of Mexico, 1982–1988.
Juan B. Riveroll	Sanborn Hermanos, S.A. (Trouyet Group), Grupo Nacional Provincial Seguros, La Nacional Insurance, Industrias Peñoles, three times president of the Mexican Insurance Association.
Manuel Senderos	Desc Group (Ruiz Galindo), Spicer (Trouyet Group), Seguros La Comercial (insurance), original member of CMHN, Industrias Peñoles (Bailleres), Bancomer (Espinosa Iglesias), Financiera Comermex (Vallina), Cía Industrial de Orizaba (Cidosa Group), E. R. Squibb.
Hipólito Signoret	Banco Minero y Mercantil de Monterrey (Cremi Group).
Emilio Suberbie	Grupo Suberbie, stockholder in Extractos y Maltas (Grupo Suberbie).
Salvador Ugarte	Bancomer (Espinosa Iglesias).

numbers of revolutionary politicians who turned to the world of business in the 1920s and 1930s.

If postrevolutionary Mexico witnessed a gradual separation between the political and economic worlds, the years after 1940 claimed the beginnings of a full-scale industrialization of the Mexican economy. In the United States, during a comparable period of growth, major companies rapidly went public, selling their stock to numerous outside investors. In Mexico, very few corporations went public, and when they did, the extent of public ownership appeared limited. Some analysts suggest that family ownership in the United States may not be as uncommon as typically is believed. For example, in the 1930s, Joslyn's study indicated that nearly half of leading United States businessmen were owners or executives in the same business as their fathers.[22] More recent power elite theorists argue that studies of United States kinship networks and holding companies of important families would show they have much greater involvement in many companies than a superficial glance would indicate.[23] Unfortunately, analysts' arguments pro and con provide very little concrete evidence to support their assertions.

Observers of the Mexican scene suggest that family ownership and control is still substantial, and that generalizations about the extent of familial influence on the private sector are unwise. Derossi concluded from her sample in the early 1970s that the overwhelming majority of industries appeared to be family owned, even though most had changed to corporations. When asked how many had relatives on their boards or in executive positions, only 46 percent responded negatively. Moreover, the number of actual shareholders was limited. Derossi found that two-thirds of Mexico's industrial firms (in her sample) were owned by twelve or fewer shareholders, hardly authentic public ownership.[24] Nationally, Derossi found that approximately 60 percent of the firms were family owned, and her figures attributed very few differences among Mexico City, Nuevo León, and other regions.[25] In a 1984 study of Guadalajara, Mexico's third largest industrial concentration, 41 percent of the firms were family operated, 19 percent had mixed family and institutional control, and only 39 percent were operated as genuine corporations.[26]

Knowledgeable Mexican entrepreneurs all agree that family ownership and control are stronger in the provinces than Mexico City. Even the state of México, with its huge concentration of manufacturing firms, is not immune to continued familial influence. According to a private-sector leader, the "majority of the businesses in the state of México are still family owned, although they tend to be the smaller firms. Also, some of these family businesses have begun associations with individuals outside of [the state of] México who have similar product interests."[27]

Explanations vary for why family control remains dominant in spite of a rapidly expanding economy. Most explanations, however, come back to cultural variables. For example, in her examination of a single powerful Mexican entrepreneur, Lomnitz found that the traditional businessman did not place much confidence in "modern technology, favored centralized authority and was disposed to involve relatives in business."[28] She discovered fifty-nine relatives working for or economically dependent on her one successful entrepreneur.

A second reason for continued family influence relates to the question of trust, a variable influential in politics and all aspects of society in Mexico. Several variations on trust as the primary cause of extended family control have been offered. One version is that the family unit itself is stronger in Mexico than in the United States. Kinship reinforces the individual's devotion to the success of the firm and, according to owners, increases loyalty.[29] Another view is that the organization and behavior of the family itself is transferred to the firm. As one Mexican businessman explained, entrepreneurs still "continue this sort of oligarchic control, which is patterned very much along the lines of how the Mexican family operates, with the father making the decisions in a very authoritarian manner. I think one of the reasons for this pattern remaining unchanged is cultural."[30]

Larissa Lomnitz has taken this argument furthest, suggesting that the private and public sectors are similar in their internal organization. In her view,

> dominant groups are organized in two competing sectors vying for control of the system, namely the public sector and the private sector; both are organized into hierarchies. Above their rivalry, both sectors (plus the hierarchy of the labor sector) are interested in the maintenance of the system as such: this is expressed in the proliferation of an intricate mesh of social networks based on kinship and friendship, where information, goods, and services are traded along horizontal channels of reciprocity within and between sectors.[31]

I have provided much evidence to support Lomnitz's statement for the public sector. Some of the information in Tables 8-1, 8-2, and 8-3 lend support to her assertions concerning the private sector. To test the presence of these characteristics in the business world, it is worth examining the holdings and kinship ties of some of Mexico's leading entrepreneurial families (Table 8-4).

The data in Table 8-4, from some twenty of Mexico's leading families since 1920, illustrate (in an incomplete fashion) the extent of family control over the leading firms listed in Table 8-1. The data in Table 8-4 also demonstrate the extent to which certain families, even without kinship ties, share economic control with one another. For example, from the brief data included, it is obvious that some type of connection exists between the following families: Aguilar and Bailleres; Alemán and Azcárraga, Azcárraga and O'Farrill; Bailleres and Ruiz Galindo; Bailleres and Vallina; Ballesteros and Ruiz Galindo; Ballesteros and Garza Laguera; Díez Fernández and Garza Laguera;

Table 8-4. Mexico's Leading Entrepreneurial Families

Family Name	Family History
Aguilar	Family head was Luis G. Aguilar, founder of a firm Luis G. Aguilar, S.A., a pharmaceutical company. Served on many major boards at least since mid-1940s, including Cementos Atoyac (Lacaud family), Banco Industrial (Bailleres family), and Cervecería Moctezuma (Bailleres family). Son, Luis Aguilar Bell, was on the board of Sanborn Hermanos, a major retail chain.
Alemán	Family head was Miguel Alemán Valdés, son of a revolutionary general, who served as president of Mexico, 1946–1952, and was an investor, never a company officer or board member. After his death in 1983, son Miguel Alemán Velasco began operating the family fortune. His major holdings have been in Televisa with the Azcárraga and O'Farrill families; he also has large holdings in real estate, including the Continental Hilton, and is alleged to be the primary investor in Tubos de Acero.
Arango	Family head was Jerónimo Arango Díaz, an industrialist who served on the boards of Bancomer and Cía Industrial Orizaba. Son, Jerónimo Arango Arias, Jr., original member of the CMHN, served on the board of Bancomer (Espinosa Iglesias family), and has been an officer of Aurrera, in which family has an interest. Brother Plácido Arango Arias is vice-president of Aurrera, and on the board of Central de Malta, S.A. (Bailleres family).
Azcárraga	Family head was Emilio Azcárraga Vidaurreta, married to Laura Milmo, from a family tied to the original Fundidora of the Monterrey Group. President of Telesistema Mexicana, jointly controlled by O'Farrill and Alemán families. After death in 1972, nephew Gastón Azcárraga Tamayo has taken leadership, serving as president of Fábricas Automex, S.A., and member of CMHN. Major investor in Celanese Mexicana with Pablo Díez Fernández. Gastón is on board of Desc Group (Ruiz Galindo).
Bailleres	Family head was Raúl Bailleres, who founded the first mining financial institution, Crédito Minero y Mercantil, S.A. Led a group of investors which acquired majority control of El Palacio de Hierro and Cervecería Moctezuma. Formed Buda investment group with the Ugarte, Domínguez, and Amezcua families. Nephew Alberto Bailleres González served on the CMHN and as president of La Provincial Insurance. His uncle's bank is now part of the Banca Cremi chain. Alberto is a board member of Multibanco Comermex (Vallina family), Cervecería Moctezuma, and Desc Group (Ruiz Galindo family). Has stock in Desc Group, Industrias Peñoles, and Cía Mexicana de Retractorios Greene.

Table 8-4.   (*continued*)

Family Name	Family History
Ballesteros	Founder of family interests is Cresencio Ballesteros Ibarra, original member of the CMHN and president of various companies, including Companía Mexicana de Aviación, S.A., Mexico's largest airline. Founded own construction firms, member of the board of Desc Group (Ruiz Galindo family). Brother Guillermo founded Constructora Ballesteros, has served on the board of Seguros América Banamex (Legorreta family) and has been president of the Visa Group (Garza Laguera). Has stock in Desc and Kimberly Clark.
Braniff	Family fortunes begun by Tomás Braniff O'Gorman, immigrant from United States who built important railroads in Mexico. President of major firms at turn of century, including Cía Industrial de Orizaba (Cidosa Group), Fábrica de Papel de San Rafael, and Banco de Londrés y México. Grandson in finance and real estate. Not on the boards of any major corporations in the 1980s.
Cortina	Juan Cortina Portilla, head of the family, is a descendant of a long line of distinguished Mexicans. Tied by marriage to the Legorreta, Suberbie, and Pastor families, all important investors in Mexican firms and banks. An original member of the CMHN and president of the Mexican Bankers Association, Cortina was president of the Banco de Londrés y México (Serfin chain). His brothers Manuel and Eustaquio are important too, and Eustaquio is on the board of Industrias Nacobre (Pablo Deutz family).
de la Macorra	The family made its fortune in the paper business when José de la Macorra, a Spanish immigrant, founded its flagship firm, Companía de las Fábricas de Papel San Rafael, in 1894. Sons Fernando and José de la Macorra y García Barzanallana have presided over the original firm and many other paper companies.
Díez	Spanish immigrant Pablo Díez Fernández founded Cervecería Modelo in 1922, now one of Mexico's largest privately owned companies. Cofounder of Celanese Mexicana in 1944, and major stockholder. Served on the boards of top companies, including Banamex (Espinosa Iglesias), Banco de Londrés y México (Garza Laguera and Garza Sada families), and Sosa Texcoco (Somex).
Espinosa	Manuel Espinosa Iglesias began career as a messenger boy for William Jenkins. President of the Mexican Bankers Association, he served for many years as director general and president of Bancomer, the largest banking chain. Children Manuel, Angel, and Guadalupe serve on the board of Frisco. In 1982, was on the board of Pigmentos y Productos Químicos (Vallina family).

Table 8-4. (*continued*)

Family Name	Family History
Garza	Easily the most prolific entrepreneurial family. The original head of the family was Isaac Garza Garza, who married Consuelo Sada Muguerza, sister of Francisco Sada Muguerza. Founded Cervecería Cuauhtémoc in 1890, Fábrica de Vidrios y Cristales, and the Cía Fundidora de Fierro y Acero, all major firms of the Monterrey Group. Among his more prominent children are Issac Garza Sada; Eugenio Garza Sada, president of the board of Cervecería Cuauhtémoc, Hojalata y Lámina, and Empaques de Cartón Titán; and Roberto Garza Sada, president of General Aceptaciones (Banca Serfin). Grandchildren include Dionisio Garza Sada Sada; Bernardo Garza Sada Sada, founding president of Grupo Industrial Alfa and CMHN member; Eugenio Garza Laguera, son of Eugenio Garza Sada, member of the CMHN, president of the Grupo Visa, and member of board of Multibanco Comermex (Vallina family) and Union Carbide (Ballesteros family); Alejandro Garza Laguera, director general of Cervecería Cuauhtémoc. Family includes many other children and grandchildren through marriage.
Hank González	A self-made man, Carlos Hank González combined a career in politics as governor of the state of México and head of the Federal District. Began business career with candy factory, moved into trucking with White Truck factory. Controls Sociedad Industrial Hermes, a holding company for other firms. Son, Carlos Hank Rhon, is president of this firm and has served on the boards of Industrias Purina, and Seguros América Banamex (Legorreta family). Like the late Miguel Alemán, Hank González does not personally sit on company boards.
Larrea	Family head is Jorge Larrea Ortega, original member of the CMHN. Interests in mining, steel, and construction. On the board of Cementos Anahuac (Trouyet group) and Banca Serfin (Garza Laguera family). President of Industria Minería México, S.A. Carmen Larrea López owns 6% of Compania Hulera Euzkadi.
Legorreta	Family head was Agustín Legorreta Ramírez, president of Banamex until his death in 1937. Family interests in the bank were taken over by his nephew Luis G. Legorreta García, president for many years until 1970. Luis served on the boards of Sosa Texcoco (Somex), Celanese Mexicana (Díez Fernández and Azcárraga), Cervecería Modelo (Díez Fernández), Compañía de la Fábricas de Papel San Rafael (de la Macorra family), and was vice-president of the Compañía Fundidora de Fierro y Acero de Monterrey (Garza). Agustín Legorreta's son, Agustín Legorreta López Guerrero, took control as president when his cousin Luis retired. Served as an original member of

Table 8-4. (*continued*)

Family Name	Family History
	the CMHN. Son Agustín F. Legorreta Chauvet employed as director general of Banamex until nationalization, and as a board member of Teléfonos de México and Companía Mexicana de Aviación (Ballesteros). Married to Mónica Cortina, daughter of Juan, past president of the Banco de Londrés y México (Banca Serfin) and original member of the CMHN.
Pagliai	An Italian immigrant to Mexico in 1941, Bruno Pagliai built up one of the most powerful groups in Mexico before his death in 1983. President of Asarco (American Smelting and Refining Co.), one of the top companies from 1911 (ranked second) to the 1970s. Original member of the CMHN, Pagliai ran many steel-related firms, including Tubos de Acero de México (Alemán) and Grupo Pliana.
Prieto	Family founder was Adolfo Prieto y Alvarez de las Vallinas, a Spanish immigrant who worked with Antonio Basagoiti (José María's grandfather) in the 1890s. When Basagoiti cofounded Companía Fundidora de Fierro y Acero de Monterrey (Garza), Prieto ran the firm, serving as president from 1936 to 1945. Since he had no heirs, his nephew, Carlos Prieto Fernández de la Llama, took over leadership of the family fortunes, as well as the presidency of the Fundidora. Carlos has served on the boards of Banamex (Legorreta), and Celanese (Azcárraga and Díez Fernández). Son Carlos Prieto Jacque was president of the Banco General de Monterrey, and is on the board of Central de Malta (Bailleres family).
Quintana	Original family head was José Miguel Quintana Ávalos, businessman, banker, industrialist, and intellectual. The economic fortunes of the family did not blossom until Bernardo Quintana Arrioja, great-nephew of José Miguel, formed an engineering and construction firm with his classmates from UNAM, which eventually evolved into the Grupo ICA, a holding firm of eighty companies and 88,000 employees. Bernardo headed his firm from 1946 until his death in 1984, was an original member of CMHN, and presided over Empresas Tolteca and Industrial del Hierro. Related by marriage to Carlos Sanchez Navarro. Son Bernardo Quintana Issac has taken over management of family firm and has sat on the board of Grupo Financiero Atlántico.
Ruiz Galindo	Antonio Ruiz Galindo, formerly minister of industries in the Alemán administration, founded a furniture company, DM Nacional, in 1929. Among the boards he served on were Altos Hornos de México and Tubos de Acero (Pagliai). In the 1960s he was president of Concanaco. His sons are very much involved in the family businesses, and Antonio Ruiz Galindo Gómez, Jr. presides over Desc, a holding corporation of nine companies,

Table 8-4. (*continued*)

Family Name	Family History
	eight of which are joint ventures with North American firms, including Monsanto. An original member of the CMHN, Antonio Jr. has served on many boards, including Banamex (Legorreta), Teléfonos de México, Union Carbide (Ballesteros), Kimberly Clark, Asarco (Pagliai), and Spicer (Trouyet and Manuel Senderos).
Sada	Original family head was Francisco G. Sada Muguerza, first president of Concanaco and cofounder of the Companía Fundidora de Fierro y Acero and the Mercentile Bank of Monterrey. Children include Andrés G. Sada García, board member of Vidrio Plano and Desc (Ruiz Galindo); Camilo G. Sada García, president of Hojalata y Lámina, S.A.; Diego G. Sada García, director general of Troqueles y Esmaltes, S.A. and on board of Grupo Industrial Alfa; Luis G. Sada García, first president of Coparmex and board member of Cervecería Cuauhtémoc and Roberto G. Sada García, president of Vidriera Monterrey. Grandchildren include Fernando Sada Malacara, vice-president of Grupo Cydsa, Adrián G. Sada Treviño, president of Grupo Vitro, and Andrés Marcelo Sada Zambrano, president of Grupo Cydsa and member of the CMHN.
Sáenz	Aaron Sáenz Garza, the founder of the family's fortunes, epitomizes the postrevolutionary politician who makes good in business. The most-successful politician (four times cabinet secretary) from the 1920s and 1930s to reach the top of the business world, Sáenz went into the construction and sugar business, later founding the Banco de Industria y Comercio. Known to have had business interests with former President Calles, his sister is married to Calles' son. His daughter is married to Julio Hirschfield Almada, an industrialist, whose son married into a third-generation Calles family. Son Aaron Sáenz Couret is also on the board of Companía Mexicana de Aviación (Ballesteros).
Senderos	Manuel Senderos Irigoyen joined at the ground floor of many powerful firms. An original founder of Desc with Antonio Ruiz Galindo, he owns 4% of the stock. He was an original member of the CMHN and has been president of Seguros La Comercial, Spicer (Trouyet), and Financiera Comermex (Espinosa Iglesias). Among the boards he has served on are Bancomer (Espinosa Iglesias), Cervecería Moctezuma (Bailleres), Banca Cremi (Bailleres), Industrias Peñoles, and E. R. Squibb. Son Fernando was on Desc board.
Trouyet	Founder Carlos Trouyet began his career at a French bank in Mexico in 1917, then worked under prominent investor J. Lacaud. Founded the Banco Comercial Mexicano, later Multi-Banco Comermex, Mexico's fourth-largest before

Table 8-4.   (*continued*)

Family Name	Family History
	nationalization. Member of the board of Cervecería Moctezuma (Bailleres), Tubos de Acero (Pagliai and Alemán), and Aceros Escatepec before death in 1970. Son Francisco Trouyet Hauss has served on the boards of Desc (Ruiz Galindo), Spicer (Manuel Senderos and Trouyet), and Teléfonos de México.
Vallina	Family head was Eloy S. Vallina García, a Spanish immigrant from Oviedo, who managed Trouyet's Banco Comercial Mexicano after founding it with Trouyet and a group of friends in 1933. He and Trouyet started the Chihuahua group in the 1950s, but Vallina founded Celulosa de Chihuahua, the flagship firm. Married daughter of Pío Laguera, sales manager of Cervecería Cuauhtémoc. Helped purchase Teléfonos de México and was on the board of Banco Minero y Mercantil (Bailleres). Murdered in 1960; his son Eloy S. Vallina Laguera took over the presidency of Multibanco Comermex and became an original member of the CMHN. Has served on the boards of Industrias Peñoles (Bailleres) and Banca Serfin. Children are now on group's boards.

Díez Fernández and Espinosa Iglesias; Legorreta and Ruiz Galindo; Sáenz and Calles; Senderos and Trouyet; Trouyet and Vallina; Trouyet and Bailleres; and many more.

Another way of examining the continued influence of entrepreneurial families is to analyze the backgrounds of the board members of the leading fifty firms in Mexico. Data from the MEBP demonstrate that the board members of these top firms are more strongly related to leading entrepreneurial families than are board members generally of important firms. Of the leading entrepreneurs holding board positions in the most powerful fifty firms and banks, 74 percent were the children of entrepreneurs, and 26 percent were the grandchildren of successful businessmen. Only one-fifth were not direct descendants of entrepreneurs, compared to two-fifths of board members of less influential firms. Expressed in slightly different terms, of the leading entrepreneurs serving on top company boards, only 10 percent were not from second, third, or fourth generation enterpreneurial families.

Mexican entrepreneurial families have had to go beyond their extended family boundaries for capital. Instead of relying on a North American method, the stock market, they have chosen a transitional pattern somewhere in between the traditional entrepreneur's self-contained posture and the modern public corporation. Cresencio Ballesteros, a leading family head, explains how the search for capital has altered single-family ownership of major firms:

> It really is impossible to develop a company today without going public. The emphasis on family control still exists, especially in Monterrey and in Guadalajara, where the people who have inherited these firms from their fathers and grandfathers can continue to control the major shares of stock. But all of them, including those in [the state of] México and the Federal District, really need investment from outside in order to grow. We should be aware of the fact that even if they are not on the stock exchange, these companies make use of outside investors. I personally do not know any large industry in which all of the shares are now in the hands of a single family.[32]

What Ballesteros has to say is very important for understanding the nature of firm ownership and the role of entrepreneurial families in Mexico. In the first place, the more visible features of the Mexican firm are not necessarily the most notable. The informal means by which leading firms obtain capital is crucial to understanding the interlocking nature of these firms. Whereas most firms have had to seek outside capital, instead of doing it on the stock exchange they have gone to a selected number of investors, thus limiting investment to a small, select group of individuals. Although many investors (especially women who have inherited this wealth) do not sit on the boards, individuals who have pursued business careers hold multiple board directorships, and very often direct the fortunes of companies which they or one of their select investors control. Intermarriage is the most common form of maintaining economic control over large companies, clearly exemplified by the Garza and Sada families. As one analyst described the Monterrey industrial groups, only rarely is the stock of any of the larger groups traded on the stock exchange; transfers are effected through sales within the family or by inheritance.[33] The pattern of the Monterrey groups is no longer typical; trust had to be expanded to investors and managers outside the family.

Many leading Mexican entrepreneurs have given up operating their own companies or, as in the case of Miguel Alemán, never actually directed firms they controlled. In order to sit on the board of a major corporation, one has to pass informal muster as deserving of another's trust. It is almost as if, in terms of leadership, major Mexican firms operate as cartels, doling out their trust to select individuals.

Mexico's family-controlled firms have been an obstacle to public ownership and professional management. The so-called management revolution in business initially proceeded in Mexico at a very slow pace. This modernizing tendency has become increasingly necessary as firms expand. A multifirm owner explains why:

> I believe the tendency of families to run their own enterprises is very definitely changing in Mexico, and this has come about as these firms need more competent people than the families can provide. I have people working for me at the management level in all of my firms who are not family members. As a family, we do still retain close relationships. For example, since August, my family enterprises have purchased a bank, the Latino Bank, where my uncle is president. This institution serves to finance our collective industries.[34]

A consequence of the continued importance of family ownership is the unwillingness of many capitalists to switch their philosophy completely in favor of professional management. Self-made managers still have not found a completely accepted niche in the Mexican business world. One Mexican entrepreneur likens the resistance of owners to professional management to the landlords who resisted modernization at the turn of the century. He claims, "objectively I think they realized that this trend was coming, but in their minds they just could not bring themselves to let go."[35]

The other significant consequence of continued family control over major corporations is its impact on capital formation, specifically the stock exchange. The head of the Mexican stock exchange explains the detrimental influence of family ownership on Mexico's brokerage business:

> I think the control of family businesses has been changing, but very, very slowly. We have about 150 companies listed on the Mexican Stock Exchange, but there are more than 20,000 middle-sized and large companies who potentially could benefit from public stock ownership. Of these 20,000, I think at least 5,000 of them should actually be on the stock exchange at present. These are companies which need resources to expand their operations. In general terms, the middle-sized companies continue to be completely dominated by individual families.[36]

However, a number of major companies also are family controlled and could use the stock market to expand their capital. Examples include Pedro Domecq wines and liquor and Comercial Mexicana, one of the largest retail chains in Mexico. The most important company in Table 8–1 that is still totally family-owned is Empresas ICA. Bernardo

Quintana Arrioja, founder of the company, acknowledged that the process of transferring from family to public ownership in the stock market has been quite slow. He has pursued a limited expansion on a closed ownership model, allowing employees to participate in a stock plan, but this approach is atypical in Mexico.[37]

The stock market has not expanded in Mexico for other reasons. According to several entrepreneurs a mentality exists in Mexico, inherited from Spain, that undervalues investment in stock and overvalues investment in real estate.[38] Another reason is that Mexican capitalists share the misconception that they must own at least 51 percent of the stock in order to influence company policy. Until large investors' desire to control a high percentage of the stock changes, it will be difficult to open up the stock market fully. Finally, it is apparent from interviews with several traditional entrepreneurs who favor family control, that certain prominent businessmen psychologically resist giving up absolute control. Rómulo O'Farrill, scion of Televisa and numerous publishing ventures, explained that he had "never been that enthusiastic about the stock exchange and having stock in my company bought and sold."[39] He appeared to find the whole idea distasteful, as if his conceptualization of a Mexican entrepreneur excluded outside investors.

Two additional economic consequences are nurtured by family-owned and -operated enterprises. There is a suspicion that family control breeds nepotism and inefficiency. Some of the more successful firms, notably the Alfa Group before its economic difficulties, demonstrate that family management is not detrimental. A more significant consideration is the homogeneity of management. One can argue that heirs do not necessarily exhibit the level of risk-taking found among self-made entrepreneurs. One wonders if family managers are as willing to explore new ideas as successful outsiders would be. Finally, one analyst notes that family-owned groups rarely disperse their profits, rather than recycling them in the same corporate holdings. Therefore, their distribution of income is internal, having less influence on the rest of the economy.

The Monterrey Group

To illustrate the impact of family control, and its actual operations, a brief history of the Monterrey Group is instructive. In the nineteenth century, eleven landholding families financed most of Monterrey's incipient manufacturing firms. Those families were Armendáriz, Belden, Calderón, Muguerza, Ferrara, Hernández, Madero, Milmo, Rivero, Sada Muguerza Garza, and Zambrano.[41] The descendants of all these original families are present in the extended family ownership and management of the dozens of firms in the Monterrey Group in the 1980s.

The Sada Muguerza, Garza, and Muguerza families started out with beer and steel through the Cervecería Cuauhtémoc and the Cía Fundidora de Acero y Fierro de Monterrey. They began to branch out into product areas that had forward and backward economic linkages to their original product line, for example, glass. Some of the families consolidated their control over the original joint ventures, while others branched out into additional manufacturing fields. By the 1920s the original founders or their descendants were well established in banking and insurance in the northern region. Their network of companies expanded rapidly in the 1960s as the third generation came of age. The general outlines of family holdings remained basically consistent until 1974. In September 1973, the most important descendant of the original families, Eugenio Garza Sada, was assassinated. The motive for his murder has never been clear, although many observers, including some outspoken members of the clan, believe members of his own extended family were responsible.[42]

Garza Sada's death served as a wedge for breaking up the Monterrey Group into four separate but complementary conglomerations. By April 1974 the divisions were final.[43] Despite the partition, these four components still rank individually among the top fifty Mexican firms or groups (see Table 8-1). The first of these, and most notorious, is the Alfa Group whose main firms are Hojalata y Lamina, S.A. (Hylsa), founded in 1942, and Empaques de Cartón Titán, formed in 1926. This group does not directly control any major banking chain, but it maintains ties with Serfin. The group's interests are primarily controlled by the Garza Sada family, whose founding chief executive was Bernardo Garza Sada, nephew of the assassinated family head.[44] A secondary component of Alfa is the Fomento de Industria y Comercio (Ficsa), primarily a producer of plastics and glass. Its president, Rogelio Sada Zambrano, represents the Sada Zambrano side of the family, and they have affiliated with the Banpaís banking chain, whose president in the 1970s was Adrián Sada.

The second component of the original group, known as Vitro, is focused on glass, originally to supply the brewery with bottles. It maintains ties with the Alfa Group through representation of the

Garza Sada and Sada Zambrano families on its board. The Garza Laguera family, which controls the third group, Visa, also sits on its board. Moreover, before 1982, Serfin and Banpaís were the largest company stockholders. The third subdivision took the name Valores Industriales, S.A. (Visa), keeping the original brewery. In 1974, when the split occurred, the brewery's stock was still controlled by descendants of the five original founders, but the largest blocks of stock belonged to the Garza Lagueras and the Garza Sadas.[45] The Visa Group is also known as the financial heart of all the Monterrey groups, since the Garza Lagueras, the children of Eugenio Garza Sada, controlled Banca Serfin. The fourth and final conglomerate, the Cydsa Group, is primarily concentrated in chemicals. It has been presided over by Andrés Marcelo Sada Zambrano, brother of Rogelio, who sits on the board of Vitro. The major firm in this holding company is Celulosa y Derivados, and its investors have again included the Serfin and Banpaís banks, as well as members of the Garza Sada family.

The outstanding operational feature of the Monterrey Group before and after its subdivision is its desire to maintain its independence from the federal government, and even from other groups. A strong aura of individuality has surrounded the Monterrey Group because of its geographical concentration and isolation. In the average Mexican's eyes, Monterrey personifies the private sector. Despite the multiplicity of kinship and economic ties, Monterrey offers an image of independence and isolation. Enersto Canales, who feels its culture as part of his own personal makeup, describes this special identity: "Monterrey is a region isolated from the center, in comparison, for example, with other parts of Mexico such as Guadalajara, which is very integrated with the center. On the other hand, it is more comparable with Yucatán. It is characterized by a strong sense of capitalism and an emphasis on the private sector."[46] Monterrey capitalists are unusual not only for their self-sustaining qualities, but for the fact that unlike other prominent business groups, such as those found in Guadalajara, they are not deeply involved socially or through marriage with Mexican politicians. According to one source from Monterrey, to live in Mexico City is to live in exile, for they have little desire to be part of the capital's social and economic life.[47]

Isolation and independence has heightened special characteristics associated with the Monterrey Group. One of the most detrimental has been the arrogance of some individual families. This attitude has been perceived at certain historical points by not only leaders of the public sector, but also ordinary citizens and businesspeople, and limits the group's political potential to obtain support from possible private-sector allies in opposing government policies. Gabriel Zaid repeats a revealing anecdote about one of the leading family groups, the Garza Sadas.

> Some time ago this family bought a sizable share of stock in the leading newspaper in Monterrey. The editor of that newspaper, who became tired of the editorial control exerted by the family, decided to try and wrest control from them. At the next stock meeting, he applied a formal rule requiring each individual to have their stock on their person in order to be allowed in, to prevent the entrance of the family. Since the family had no proof of ownership on their person, they couldn't get into the meeting. For revenge, the family decided to break the newspaper and sent out word to all of the companies in Monterrey to withdraw their advertising from the newspaper. Everyone thought the editor was crazy and that the newspaper would be out of business within a month. Instead, so many businesses in Monterrey wanted to show their independence from the Garza Sada family that instead of withdrawing their advertising, they purposely maintained it in order to demonstrate their independence from this arrogant family.[48]

The cohesiveness of the leading Monterrey families gives them a certain strength, yet as Zaid's story makes clear, even their local peers resent the very closeness and arrogance that has made them so visible economically and, more recently, politically. Their relations with the state itself are worthy of a separate study, but a brief descriptive narrative gives interesting glimpses of how an industrial holding company, versus an individual entrepreneur, relates to the government. The general assumption about their relationship to the government is that the Monterrey group want to negotiate with the state as their equal, believing that they have more to offer the government than the government can give them in return.[49] The near-bankruptcy of the Alfa Group, however, probably has tempered their view since the 1980s.

The independent attitude of the Monterrey group, which characterizes many entrepreneurial families, was not common in the nineteenth century. The political and economic fortunes of Mexico's oligarchy at the turn of the century were deeply intertwined; those in Monterrey were no exception. Their first great ally was Bernardo Reyes, governor of Nuevo León and a regional kingmaker during that era.[50] Unfortunately, like so many other economic leaders in 1910, the Garza Sada family misjudged the Revolution's outcome, and sided with the reactionary interests under Victoriano Huerta. They were related to General Enrique Gorostieta, Huerta's treasury secretary. General Pablo González, a Constitutionalist, seized their brewery in retaliation, and they fled to the United States for two years.[51] Eventually, in 1916, the brewery was returned to the family. They were able to accommodate themselves to successive postrevolutionary governments, but since the 1920s they never succeeded entirely in overcoming their sense of alientation from the new class of politicians.[52]

The Monterrey families also had ties with the Madero extended family, whose branches can be found in Durango, Coahuila, and Chihuahua. Of course the Madero family itself had very little use for Francisco, Mexico's first revolutionary president (with the exception of several brothers). Once the Revolution succeeded, they and related Monterrey families claimed ties to him.[53] Economic ties with several generations of the Madero family have continued through the 1980s, but superficial ties with the Madero factions were not helpful politically after 1920 because most Maderistas did not retain political influence. The interdependence of economic and political power between Monterrey and the Mexican state has never been closer than prior to 1900.[54]

During the 1920s the Monterrey group maintained a low political profile, concentrating on expanding their product lines. They were so politically uninfluential during this period that they exerted no control even over state offices in Nuevo León. In the 1930s they came in conflict with President Lázaro Cárdenas but not in any overt political manner. In the following decade the Cuauhtémoc Brewery group began applying their economic power in exchange for political favors. According to one historian, they made a pact in 1940 with the government to support the official party candidacy of Manuel Ávila Camacho for president in return for regional political favors.[55] This view further suggests that the brewery group went beyond their regional interests to persuade other leading entrepreneurs to reach an informal understanding with the government, an agreement that became the basis of their political pact with the state for the next forty years. In a secret agreement with Miguel Alemán, Ávila Camacho's campaign manager, they promised to withdraw their support for a strong opposition candidate, General Almazán, in return for control over the gubernatorial and mayoralty nominations for Nuevo León and Monterrey.[56] Once Ávila Camacho was elected, Alemán reneged on his side of the bargain, demonstrating once again the state's strength in operating independently—at least in the electoral arena—of major private-sector interests.

Tension had governed the relationship between the government and the Monterrey group, but they did not become active politically until the 1950s. During this decade, members of the Garza Sada family and other Monterrey groups openly supported the National Action Party founded by Manuel Gómez Morín, a disgruntled former government official with major private-sector investments. After López Mateos became president (1958–1964), the Monterrey clan joined the Cruzada Regional Anticomunista, a political action group strongly opposed to the government's free textbook program. Their confrontation with the state on this major social issue stirred considerable public interest, especially from the growing middle class, foreshadowing the Monterrey group's confrontational style of the 1970s and 1980s.

By the late 1960s the Monterrey group had acquired sufficient economic strength to exert political influence over state offices for the first time. In 1967, Eduardo A. Elizondo Lozano, considered by many to be the Monterrey group's "man," took office as governor of Nuevo León. Elizondo definitely was not a typical PRI candidate, having come from a business-oriented family and, most importantly, having married the daughter of Manuel L. Barragán, the grey eminence of local politics, a self-made banker and investor who sat on many of the group's boards. Elizondo started out in the law firm of Santos de la Garza, whose owner was an active Panista. He later served as president of the Regional Bank of the North, a Garza Sada company. Even if they were responsible for his gubernatorial designation, the Monterrey group could not keep him in office when Echeverría ousted him in 1971. Some observers suggest that Echeverría removed Elizondo to discredit Monterrey's entrepreneurs.[57] The governor selected for the 1973–79 term, Pedro Zorilla Martínez, was barely on speaking terms with the group during his last three years in office.[58]

At the national level the relationship equally was strained between President Echeverría and the Monterrey group families. Before 1973, however, the Monterrey clan had good relations with the federal government, attributable to the personal relationship between Eugenio Garza Sada and the president. They came to know each other through Víctor Bravo Ahuja, rector of the Technological Institute of Monterrey, when Echeverría went to Bravo Ahuja's university to solve some student problems in 1968.[59] Because of its increasing estrangement from the federal government, the Monterrey group strengthened its ties with PAN by pushing a more conservative faction as presidential candidates within the party. In 1972, according to some analysts, their man, José Angel Conchello, became president of the party.[60]

Conchello, a native of Monterrey, at one time worked in public relations for the Moctezuma brewery (Bailleres Group), but has no known personal or professional ties with the Monterrey group. The group allegedly tried to disrupt the legitimacy of the government, and of Echeverría personally, by starting a successful rumor campaign that the president was plotting a coup to stay in power.[61]

The group's relations with the federal government took a turn for the better in 1977, when the recently inaugurated José López Portillo formed an alliance with them to increase employment and expand manufacturing.[62] As part of this economic and political pact, the Monterrey group built many new manufacturing plants in less-crowded locations.[63] On the other hand, the government encroached on the private sector's monopoly in Monterrey, building a Pemex plant, the first major publicly owned industry in the city.[64]

In 1981, the group saw another candidate they favored, Pablo Emilio Madero Belden, win PAN's presidential nomination and in 1984 take the party's mantle as president. In the following year, members of the Monterrey group decided to abandon efforts to rely solely on traditional channels to influence government policy, allying themselves in the electoral arena with the political opposition. They chose to do this in the 1985 off-year congressional elections in the North and in the gubernatorial campaign in Nuevo León. In a bitterly fought contest producing numerous charges of fraud, PRI's candidate defeated that of PAN. What is most important about this campaign as a reflection of the business community's relationship to the government is that the PRI was forced to choose a candidate similar to PAN's. It could be argued that their electoral strategy, on a local level, achieved more favorable results than informal pacts established with individual presidents.

In the past, some elements of the Monterrey Group have followed a different strategy in their relationship with the government. Most commonly used are informal channels between business leadership and top government officials, especially between the president and a leading entrepreneur. The most recent application of this strategy took place between the Alfa Group and Bernardo Garza Sada in their relationship with José López Portillo and the Mexican state. But four years into López Portillo's administration, Alfa was on the verge of bankruptcy. The causes of its near-bankruptcy, and the impact of its failure, reveal important characteristics about the Monterrey group and about the larger relationship between the public and private sectors.

The Decline of Alfa

The near-failure of Alfa takes on special importance for the business community for three reasons. First, José López Portillo had used the Alfa Group and his personal friendship with Bernardo Garza Sada to restore the confidence in the business community that his predecessor had destroyed, and to reestablish the traditional cooperative arrangement between the state and the private sector formalized in the Alliance for Production. The near-bankruptcy of Alfa cast doubt on the success of a government-business alliance to expand the economy and increase employment. Second, the Alfa Group is the flagship group of the larger Monterrey industrial holdings. Because of its visibility, any actions it took reverberated psychologically throughout the business sector. Finally, its psychological impact only complemented its economic position as the leading firm in Mexico and in Latin America. From 1974 to 1980 its growth was impressive. During those years the company grew more than 1,000 percent, increased its sales by 950 percent, and expanded its subsidiaries to over 150 and eighteen states. Its employees increased from 33,000 to 50,000 during the same period.[65]

The reasons for Alfa's fall are many, but a widespread consensus among businesspeople and government leaders exists as to the leading causes. The first revolves around the personnel Alfa hired during its rapid expansion stage. Similar to the argument that Mexican political technocrats lack broad hands-on political experience is the assertion that Alfa was obsessed with the formal credentials of young executives, especially if they were foreign-trained, rather than their actual experience. As Lawrence Rout suggests, they would "always pick the kid with the Harvard MBA over the guy who really knew the business. The Alfa man had to look good on paper."[66] Alfa's recruitment policies became intertwined with its expansionist goals. They abandoned their traditional prudent policy of integrating firms with similar or complementary products.[67] Thus, Alfa executives faced two problems. First, many of the lower-management people had no practical experience. Second, upper management, while experienced, took charge of firms about which they knew very little. Enrique Krauze, a leading intellectual who runs his own business, explains that Alfa

> bought businesses like someone would buy candies for their children.
> For example, they bought this huge meat-packing firm that had been
> run by a single person for more than forty years. They brought in a

bunch of young experts, with all sorts of technical training and MBAs from Harvard and Columbia, but they didn't know anything about the realities of the meat-packing industry. The shift from a family-controlled operation to an administrative bureaucracy drove this business into bankruptcy. I think that Alfa placed far too much confidence in credentials and not enough in practical experience. In my own business, I have the tendency to hire experienced people who do not have technical qualifications in the belief that they probably can do a better job.[68]

In making these recruitment and management choices, Alfa alienated the other three subdivisions of the Monterrey Group by violating an informal rule established in 1974—each subdivision would not pirate away the other's executives.[69]

Alfa not only immersed itself in management problems but also overextended itself economically. As late as 1981 Alfa still was offering salaries far above the norm for Mexico's top firms. It added premiums of a million to one-and-a-half million pesos for educating these pirated employees' children, plus expensive paid vacations and other executive perquisites. Their policy created a grave distortion in executive salaries for the business community in general. According to one investigator, many small companies were ruined trying to keep their executive salaries on par with Alfa.[70]

In all its economic activities Alfa, as a representative of the Monterrey Group in general, was perceived as arrogant.[71] While this perception moderated the impact of Alfa's near-bankruptcy (many businessmen were not upset to see Alfa in difficulties), it exacerbated the larger business community's negative attitude toward the privileged position of holding companies in general. Holding companies, at the insistence of the Alfa Group, received huge tax breaks from López Portillo's administration.[72]

At the time the Alfa Group ran into serious financial difficulties in 1982, the psychological and economic consequences for Mexico's private sector seemed devastating. The extent of these consequences, especially on a psychological plane, depended very much on the age and experience of the business leader. My interviews among businessmen suggest that when we assess the impact of individual events—both political and economic—on their views of the private sector and their relationship to the Mexican state, generational divisions are significant. Individuals well-versed in Mexico's economic history saw Alfa as an aberration rather than a decisive indicator of Mexico's entrepreneurial potential. They also saw the government's rescue of Alfa (from its international creditors) as having historical continuity, it had been repeated many times previously. Emilio Alanís Patiño, a distinguished economist, drew this analysis immediately after the news of Alfa's condition:

> The impact of Alfa on Mexico is critical and has become a subject of public discussion. Now the public realizes that Alfa is much bigger than they thought. The Left likes to use Alfa's failure as an opportunity to attack the capitalist system as a whole. For people of my generation, however, Alfa's failure is not new. About forty years ago there was a Mexican group led by a Dr. Antonio Sacristán, an immigrant who arrived from Spain with business experience. He founded an organization called Financiera Sociedad Mexicano y Crédito Industrial, and persuaded many businessmen to join his group. This was a very diverse group, which during World War II had the support of the government and Nacional Financiera. They had control of about seventy small and middle-sized industries—just as Alfa did in recent years. The government ultimately had to intervene when this group ran into serious economic troubles. This is an important precedent for what happened to Alfa, and the only difference is that proportionately Alfa was much larger than this group.
>
> My point is that this type of failure has always been a problem as well as a consequence of rapid economic growth. That failing group later became the government financial group now called Somex. The government had to intervene to prevent unemployment and they actively took over some of the small firms in order to save them.[73]

The government stepped in for several reasons, the most important being to save employment. Repeatedly, the Mexican government has embarked on Chrysler-like programs to rescue various private enterprises. Unlike the United States government with Chrysler, Mexico's government has often ended up the proprietor of these same firms, some of which, despite extensive government investment, fail. When government intervention occurs at frequent intervals, and the rescued firms are notable, the relationship between the private and public sectors is fundamentally altered. In the short run the government is placed in a stronger position vis-à-vis the private sector, since it assumes the role of a last-ditch benefactor to troubled companies.

Major private-sector failures place into question the entire economic strategy both the state and the private sector have generally pursued since 1940. Despite the support they received from the public sector, leading industrialists lost their chance to use capital-intensive manufacturing firms as a leading edge for the capitalist development model. That may be the deeper lesson of Alfa's failure.[74] If it is logical to expect political leadership to pursue economic interests favorable to the private sector because they deem such policies essential to their own political survival, then allowing the private sector to falter temporarily to weaken it politically is counterproductive of the state's long-term health.

For the average Mexican, Alfa's failure affected confidence in the private sector. It would be comparable to General Motors or Exxon going under in the United States. A country's largest company has visibility and influence extending beyond any economic and political power it wields. It is a weather vane for the private sector as a whole. Mexicans, rightly or wrongly, perceived Alfa's health as mirroring that of the general business community. Again, perception is much more important than reality. According to one astute public official with extensive experience in the financial field, "all of this demonstrates very clearly to the educated Mexican that they must not be as well organized, or intelligent, or powerful a group as was suspected, otherwise why would they be in this situation. The result, therefore, is that their failure has a tremendous impact on public confidence, in the same way that the devaluation had an important impact on the lack of confidence in the government."[75]

Finally, Alfa had an economic influence on the private sector, both financially and in terms of management style. Before its difficulties, other holding companies had begun buying up firms, imitating it. Initially held up as an organization worthy of emulation, after its failure it served as an example of what not to do. Furthermore, one international consequence of Alfa's bankruptcy was to make credit much more difficult to obtain abroad. If foreign banks could not make successful loans to Mexico's leading firm, then, as one of Mexico's leading entrepreneurs suggested, that put credit to all Mexican firms in doubt.[76]

As the distance in time from Alfa's problems in 1982 grows, their impact decreases. By 1983 Mexican entrepreneurs discussed Alfa's failure as though it were a legend, something that took place far in the past.[77] Business leaders' reactions to Alfa obviously are tempered by time, as well as age and experience. Care must be taken to avoid overemphasizing the significance of any event when examining it at close range. A crisis image melts away rather rapidly, and although each event surely finds a place in the minds of all business leaders, any single event—unless its impact is economically catastrophic like the Great Depression's—does not seem to have a long-term impact on Mexican entrepreneurs' perceptions.

The perception of Alfa itself has a long-term impact, positive and negative, on Mexico's economy and on private-public sector relations. Mexicans saw Alfa's predicament in two ways. The least generous view is expressed by Carlos Tello, who believes that the private sector as a whole was not grateful for the government bailout.[78] If Tello's interpretation is correct—and politicians' memories are long—Alfa's impact on the private sector-state relationship will extend well into the future. Politicians may become resistant to helping out companies in difficulty—unless, of course, they continue to weigh the political consequences of unemployment highly. The dislike of Alfa as arrogant is the public's second view, not confined to politicians. Gabriel Zaid believes that many people in northern Mexico were ecstatic at Alfa's failure because of the way it had treated other firms, including other Monterrey holding companies.[79] From this point of view, the impact of Alfa's failure may not be as damaging to the private sector as might appear.

Conclusions

Holding companies play a role in every industrialized capitalist nation. In the United States they seem to have emerged at an advanced stage in our economic evolution, after the decline of entrepreneurial families and the rise of technocratic management and public, corporate ownership. In Mexico, holding companies were initiated by dominant economic families and have developed simultaneously with the rise of corporate ownership and the increase of professional management.

Mexico's private sector bears some resemblance to its political system. Structurally, both have absorbed many features of modern Western culture, but like the Japanese, Mexicans have held strongly to traditions extending back to the nineteenth century and earlier. One of those traditions, unfettered by the artificial boundaries between public life and private interests, is the role of the family and the value of kinship as a determinant of trust. North Americans like to think that in their culture choices are detached, based on merit and impersonal criteria. Our reality is not nearly as close to that as we like to pretend, but personal criteria do play a lesser role than in Mexico, and in the United States when personal ties do influence choices, friendship is a more common influence than kinship.

The commonalities between the political and economic models in Mexico are instructive. Political families in Mexico are common—

nearly one out of every three politicians at the national level is a close relative through marriage or blood of another national public figure (MPBP) However, the pool of political families is relatively large compared to the extended entrepreneurial kinship groups, and a small elite does not continuously dominate Mexican political life over multiple generations. Political families appear on the scene, and disappear from prominence, circulating within the larger pool—although "juniors" (the children of politicians) are becoming increasingly frequent at cabinet levels. To reach the top in Mexico, politicians must go well beyond the extended family to develop alliances with other potential political leaders, some from notable families but the majority without such origins. Businesspeople use a different approach. To acquire additional resources, human and capital, to keep their lead and expand ahead of the competition, they have sought out allies. However, the majority of those are from elite extended families controlling other economic resources.

Public leadership, because of its very functions and its necessity to appeal to the widest of audiences, is more fluid than private-sector leadership. However, contrary to the expectations and predictions of economists in the 1960s, Mexico's private sector shares an important characteristic with the public sector. One expects that as a political system modernizes, social mobility increases and the presence of limited families, generation after generation, should decline, as was true in the United States. As my work on Mexico's political leadership makes clear, no such trends have taken place since the 1930s, and if anything, family generational ties may be on the increase. Furthermore, Mexicans predicted the decline and demise of the family firm. Without a doubt, family control has become diluted as the need for resources has increased, but the data suggest that families' *actual* control has diminished only very slightly, and an examination of the most influential firms reveals the interlocking nature of leading entrepreneurial families in Mexico.

Interviews with prominent businessmen, and the case study of the Monterrey group, bring out the importance of the individual businessman or family in Mexico. Their significance as individual actors reverberates in the relationship between the public and private sectors. As the preceding chapter made evident, Mexico, like most capitalist countries, has institutionalized its channels of communication through formal interest chambers. Often, when the Mexican private sector makes significant negotiations or compacts with the government, it does so on a personal, individual basis.

Carried to an extreme, the reliance on personal friendship in the private sector, and between the private and public sectors, alters the formal, often more visible relationships between the various groups. Personal and family ties are firmly built into the fabric of business and political life in Mexico. Their long-term consequences are many, but one important implication is that impersonal relationships and organizations are slow to become institutionalized formally. The fact that the government negotiates with a Eugenio Garza Sada or Bernardo Garza Sada instead of a collectivity of firms, or even a firm, encourages a tenuous quality in the agreements between the two parties.

The cohesive quality which the retention of family ownership and control gives the private sector is both a strength and a weakness. The private sector can maintain a greater sense of unity when negotiating with its opponents. On the other hand, its very impermeability makes it an obvious target for criticism from the public in general. Smaller and medium-sized entrepreneurs are disgusted by the arrogance of large firms and disgruntled with their excessive control over private-sector interests. As Mexicans familiar with the stock market made clear, public capital will never be forthcoming until families sell off a greater proportion of their investments, and investors learn to appreciate the value of impersonal ownership of a respectable company, rather than of knowing its individual leaders and owners.

The state, I believe, will continue to be in the driver's seat in its relationship with the private sector, at least in the immediate future. At this point, the private sector does not control sufficient political and economic resources to act independently. The private sector, as illustrated by the Monterrey group, one of the most cohesive protagonists of the hard-line position against the state, is exploring many other options for negotiating with the state. But the private sector must capture a larger audience of Mexicans as sympathizers and allies before it can bargain more effectively. The persistence of family control and influence stands in the way of the private sector taking that fresh and significant step.

9

Private-Public Relations

The entrepreneur's self-image, self-definition, origins, education, historical setting, and attitude toward political participation and the role of the state offer many insights into the relationship between the private and public sectors in Mexico. Other variables also explain the peculiar nature of this relationship in Mexico and elsewhere. Theories or hypotheses offered to explain the importance of any one variable over another do not provide a satisfactory portrait of entrepreneurs' relations to the state. Taken together, a more complete picture begins to emerge.

Domestic Influences on Private-Public Relations

Analysts of the Mexican scene, and entrepreneurs and politicians themselves, suggest six central explanations for the patterns which exist between the two. These explanations include (1) the role of an autonomous Mexican state, (2) the control of a power elite, (3) the intervention of interest groups, (4) structural conditions, (5) cultural values, and (6) the influence of constitutionalism. Each of these explanations, some better-grounded in general theory than others, is difficult to explain fully in the Mexican case because, as a long-time pioneer in the field has concluded, "much of the relationship between government and business is not visible except to participants."[1]

Autonomous State Theory

The most helpful theoretical interpretation of the relationship between the Mexican state and private sector can be found in the literature on state theory, especially among those authors who see the state as an autonomous actor. In her excellent survey of state-theory literature, Theda Skocpol argued that recent theorists have generally conceptualized the state as either a collectivity of officials who formulate and implement distinct strategies or policies, or as an independent actor whose independence needs to be given more serious attention.[2] She goes on to point out that "government itself was not taken very seriously as an independent actor," especially in comparative research. States can be defined in a variety of fashions. They do indeed correspond in actual functions to a diversity of activities ascribed to them, but in the Mexican case, my concern is with the interpretation that the Mexican state is an autonomous actor.

States can be considered autonomous if they formulate and pursue goals that are not simply reflective of the demands or interests of social groups, classes, or society, but are attributable to the collective or individual goals of government officials themselves.[3] If the existence of an autonomous Mexican state is accepted, certain consequences in its relationship to the private sector can be identified. Many recent analysts admit to the existence of Mexican state autonomy, but considerable disagreement exists as to its extent and limits. Some believe that the state has relative autonomy from short-term business interests but acts in the long-term interests of Mexico's private sector.[4] This interpretation implies that any long-term policy commitment by government has been determined by some actor other than the state itself. The weakness of this argument, however logical it may seem, is the assumption a priori that the state has not made these choices of its own volition. One prominent international business-group leader points out that "the government may think more like the private sector, rather than the private sector actually having an impact on the policy orientation of the government."[5]

Miguel Basáñez has presented a more radical interpretation of state autonomy, the thesis that the Mexican state is not the instrument of the private sector even though the state has favored the latter's interests.[6] His view seems much closer to the truth, although it remains largely unexplored. An important exception to this statement, including the work of Basáñez himself, is a revealing historical analysis by

Douglas Bennett and Kenneth Sharpe. They argue very convincingly, with evidence from case studies, that the state is characterized by its own interests. They do not believe that specific interests can be automatically attributed to the state; rather their argument is that conditions peculiar to Mexico encouraged the state to behave in certain ways.

They suggest that three principal explanations apply to Mexico. First, the weak condition of the private sector itself explains state intervention, an interpretation I emphasized in the preceding chapters. This view corresponds closely to other analyses which I will discuss under *Structural Interpretations*. Second, state intervention institutionalized a larger, visible role for the state in the economy. Whereas Bennett and Sharpe stress the institutionalization of pragmatic state involvement, I would carry that one step further, as I will in the constitutionalism argument, noting the socializing impact of past decisions on the formation of politicians', entrepreneurs', and the general public's values. Finally, they believe that each presidential administration alters state orientations, an interpretation with which few Mexicanists would disagree.[7]

In their overall approach, Bennett and Sharpe tend to explain the choices of the Mexican state in relation to the private sector by using the United States as a model. They have identified several important variables for the Mexican state, but their analysis tends to downplay significant traditional, cultural-political roles which allow government officials to move the state into the economic sphere more easily than in the United States. As I suggested previously, Mexican values—especially those of entrepreneurs and politicians—establish boundaries for state autonomy, both restrictive and expansionist. Carried to an extreme, one can argue that state autonomy might be extremely weak if not for the fact that Mexicans expect an activist state, thus giving political actors more room to make policy choices.

According to some scholars, the key to understanding the relationship between the state and the private sector is government initiative.[8] This view implies that the state is in control of the relationship, and that the pattern between the two groups is determined not so much by government reactions to private-sector demands as by policies the government itself initiates. This is not to suggest that the state is a completely independent actor. The independence of the state is limited by its goals and its survival needs as a political institution. The primary goals of the Mexican state since 1920 have been political stability and economic growth. These two goals are intimately intertwined and are essential in explaining its relationship with the private sector. As the Purcell's noted, the "government sees its role as that of encouraging private investment and business activity *as long as it leads to economic growth.*"[9]

This caveat is the key variable, because not only do politicians believe that economic growth is inherently important, they realize that the key to political stability, and to their own leadership, is a growing economy. The neo-Marxist view, and that of other scholars, is that the state functions as a mediator, maintaining a balance between those actors or classes which are essential to the capitalist system, primarily labor and entrepreneurs.[10] This mediating role is compatible with the state as an autonomous actor; what is unproven is the assumption that the capitalist class determines the state's goals.

The Power Elite

One of the explanations used to support the view that the state is not an autonomous actor, and that private-sector interests are synonymous with the state's, is that a ruling class or power elite, dominated by the wealthy, controls government. Other more sophisticated interpreters of power elite theory argued early on that members of the power elite may not act in the interests of the ruling classes when holding government offices, but might formulate their own interests and act to support them.[11] Regardless of whether power elite theory supports or contradicts the concept of an autonomous state, the concept of a power elite is tied to, and more fully explains the validity of, state autonomy—especially as it relates to the private sector.

Unfortunately, most of the literature supporting the existence of a power elite is based on studies of the United States, where information that might prove this assertion is more readily available. The most balanced utilization of this theory is that of G. William Domhoff, who does for the power-elite literature what Skocpol does for state theory. In the first place, Domhoff avoids some of the criticisms made of earlier works, including the works of C. Wright Mills, by redefining the concept of a power elite. In his words, it is the "leadership group or operating arm of the ruling class" and "is made up of active, working members of the ruling class and high-level employees in institutions controlled by members of the ruling class."[12]

In his survey of the North American literature, Domhoff concluded that considerable evidence exists to demonstrate that members of this power elite hold a great many positions in government, especially in the executive branch of the federal government.[13] When we examine the existence of a power elite in other societies, whether or not we accept its presence in the United States, the general assumption is that such groups are more likely to exist in Third World countries where pluralism is weak and social inequalities are strong. However, Mexico is an exception, and wealthy entrepreneurs there control or occupy very few government positions. These findings support Peter Smith's assertion that Mexico "appears to have a fragmented power structure that is dominated, at the upper levels, by two distinct and competitive elites."[14] The reasons for this separation are not stronger pluralism or less-prevalent inequality, but cultural and historical factors not found in the United States.

Power elite theorists all attempt to identify the backgrounds of those individuals who occupy important political offices. For example, Kay Trimberger believes that state autonomy is possible only if political elites are not recruited from the dominant entrepreneurial classes and do not form close pesonal and economic ties with this group after reaching office.[15] Mexico basically meets this criterion. The relationship between the private and public sectors is affected not only by the flow of leadership from the private to the public sector but also by the reverse pattern. One can argue that certain reforms in the private sector have been impeded because too many political elites "have clients in the private sector, too many *camarillas* include members of the private sector, and too many ex-politicians have economic interests."[16]

Some Mexicanists believe that an important characteristic of Mexico's power structure is the high level of cohesion among dominant groups. They claim that the cohesion itself is a product of "an agreement reached between the governing group and the economically dominant groups concerning the role of the state and the entrepreneurial sectors in the process of development."[17] As I have documented in previous chapters, the private sector and the state are not in agreement about their roles, and these disagreements exacerbate tensions in their relationship. Furthermore, the fluidity of their values introduces other fissures weakening a cohesive image. Power-elite analysts stress that the alliance between the dominant classes and Mexico's political leadership has prevented progressive leaders within the state who are allied with other political actors from accomplishing their goals. Progressive private-sector leaders face the same problems as their political counterparts. They are stymied in the same way the state is. They are opposed not only by dominant elements within the public sector but by equally strong elements in the private sector.

Possibly, as one public official suggested, the tensions between the public and private sectors are the most visible aspect of their relations. Public criticisms of each other by both the private and public sectors receive widespread press coverage. This being the case, the argument goes, Mexicans overlook less visible, but potentially more significant ties between the two groups.

> There is an enormous and continuing contact between both sectors, and in many circumstances it is because of personal friendships and family ties. In Mexico, one impression is that the close relationship between the private sector and public sector is not known because it is overshadowed by the posture taken by the leadership of the private-sector organizations. Their positions are not necessarily a true reflection of the individual attitudes of important businessmen.[18]

The Interest-Group Approach

A third interpretation of the private sector-state relationship relies on several versions of interest-group theory. One view is that the private sector is one interest group among many that attempt to influence state decisionmaking.[19] The ways Mexico's private sector pursues those interests, compared with similar groups in the United States, are altered significantly by the fact that most of the decisionmaking authority rests with the executive branch, especially in the hands of the president himself. Traditional interest-group theories must be reinterpreted for the Mexican case. The greater centralization of authority in the Mexican system means that theories of interlocking business and political leadership carry more weight.

The general belief expressed in Third World literature and in studies focusing on the United States is that individual businesspeople and business interest groups exert considerable power over government policy decisions, despite mounting evidence to the contrary.[20] It is clear, however, that attempts by the Mexican private sector to emulate their North American counterparts in interest-group roles are making it more difficult to balance political power.[21] Mexico's political leadership is partially responsible for the private sector's changing vision of its relationship to the state, having introduced electoral reforms in the political arena, thereby conveying a changing image of executive political authority and the role of the legislative branch.

Some Mexican entrepreneurs have been so caught up on these changes that they are behaving as if the United States model had already arrived, without considering the realities of Mexico's political environment.

To make interest-group analysis fit the Latin American and Mexican cases, social scientists have popularized a corporatist model in which the state coopts important interest groups, establishing their organizations and controlling their leadership. Much more evidence for the value of this approach exists for organized labor and peasants in Mexico than for the business community. Van R. Whiting, Jr. states unequivocally that corporatism is inappropriate to the analysis of Mexican private sector-state relations. As evidence for his assertion, he claims the state does not exercise control over the leadership of the major business confederations or over their internal affairs.[22] Dale Story's study of Canacintra is less unequivocal but essentially supports the same view.[23] All the evidence in this book demonstrates that the state does not control leadership or organizations.

Whatever the disagreements about the condition of private-sector interest groups and their relationship to the state in the 1980s, little controversy exists as to the strength of the private sector in the decades following the Revolution. As William Glade writes,

"the other new actor in the political drama first appeared in a modest role during the national economic recovery of the 1930's, although as an interest group it was barely visible in policy circles prior to the 1940s. By Alemán's time, . . . the business-industrial interests had plainly joined the chorus of voices to which the state paid heed, though by no means can it be assumed that this new group, either then or later, overpowered the other contending interests."[24]

In the context of interest-group theory, Nora Hamilton raises a very useful historical point, suggesting that during the 1930s the government tried to control an interest group by incorporating it into the private sector: "one means utilized by the government to control the military was to provide high level officers with the incentive and material means to go into business, with the hope that their political ambitions might be diverted to entrepreneurial channels."[25] She also believes that government officials took advantage of the same opportunities, suggesting that recruitment from the public to the private sector became an accepted means of replenishing entrepreneurial ranks. Hamilton provides some prominent examples but does not give sufficient evidence to support this generalization. Her assertion, however true, has several important consequences for private-public sector relations.

In the first place, the most potent interest group historically, one properly incorporated in many respects in the 1920s and 1930s under corporatist theory, is the military. If many career officers opted for the private sector in those years, it weakened them vis-à-vis the state, and strengthened what was at best a marginal interest group, the business community. However, if such an exchange between the two groups did take place, it did not continue to the present. No evidence exists whatsoever of strong ties between career officers and the private sector for many decades.[26]

Hamilton's thesis may also shed more light on the stability of the state, from two points of view. First, as intimated in the discussion of power elite theory, an exchange of leaders between the public and private sectors potentially strengthens ties between them—since ex-politicians share some interests with entrepreneurs—and provides channels for contact between entrepreneurs and their ex-colleagues in the political arena. Second, but less obvious, the public sector itself would be internally weakened if middle-aged politicians at the end of each administration had no place to go. Their ability to ease successfully into the private sector has a positive impact on public-sector stability.

Interest-group theory is also valuable in suggesting the importance of other actors who complicate the relationship between the two sectors. Potentially some of the most important, and as yet unmentioned, are multinational corporations. Their impact on this relationship has been examined separately, as was organized labor's, in a decisionmaking context. Basáñez believes that since 1968, the three actors who have dominated the political arena and are in conflict with one another are: the public sector, the private sector, and what he calls the dissident sector, which includes intellectuals.[26] As the media expands their political influence, the potential impact of intellectuals increases.[27]

Structural Interpretations

A fourth explanation for the outstanding features of the relationship between the two sectors can be lumped together in a sort of structural-conditions interpretation. No overall theory has focused on these characteristics to explain the peculiarities of the private-public sector relationship. An argument receiving some sophisticated discussion in economic literature posits that the structural weaknesses present in the Mexican economy immediately following the Revolution determined the role of the state vis-à-vis the private sector. As William Glade suggests, the chief constraints on the state's role "were those set by resource availabilities," permitting, in his view, the evolution of a relatively autonomous state.[28]

Economic conditions in Mexico in the 1920s were largely the result of the Revolution. There is little disagreement among scholars that it brought about adverse economic conditions, creating an environment in which the remnants of the business community, in terms of both economic power and leadership, remained weak and in disarray. Scholars do not agree, however, on whether the ties between political and economic elites were broken. The most widely accepted view is that "protracted economic devastation, then, severed the links between economic power and political influence, helping to pave the way for a regime in which control of the political machinery itself was paramount in the country's economic and social order. The political process per se became preponderant and laid the basis for the directive economic role of the state."[29]

Mexico found itself in the 1920s in a political and economic vacuum; the traditional rules of the game had been broken, and the new rules of the game, including the relationship between the public and private sectors, were yet to be determined. Within the vacuum, a new generation of military-political leaders redefined the state's role, in the context of their belief that the objective of Mexican public policy was the evolution of a modern capitalist economic structure.[30] Bennett and Sharpe describe how this pattern evolved.

> "Following on the Revolution, the Mexican state came to take on the role of making capitalism work for Mexico, and, in the context of Mexico's being a dependent, late-starting industrializer, this task required, for any degree of success, both major restrictions on the demands of the lower classes and the forceful entry of the state into areas of the economy where the private sector was unwilling or unable to enter, or had entered and failed."[31]

The historical weakness of the private sector is only one structural explanation for this pattern, perhaps the most important of the so-called structural variables. Another explanation is Mexico's inequality. Social and economic inequalities have made it necessary, according to this view, for the state to play a role different from what it might play in a society where these conditions were less exaggerated. The state must, therefore, balance different and competing groups and interests, and to achieve success, must itself become an actor.[32]

The view that the state operates to moderate potential inequalities in a capitalist development strategy, and does so in a traditional environment in which the Mexican private sector shows little concern for its social responsibilities, complements the view that the state performs necessary functions the private sector is incapable of accomplishing. In other words, the state attempts to alter social as well as economic characteristics. As a consequence the state has built up its own set of values, a public culture if you will, over three generations of political leaders. On the issue of state economic intervention, this public culture reflects "expectations of a role for private investment that was not fulfilled."[33]

Over the last five decades Mexican government policymakers have been socialized to accept a large state role. Indeed, a case can be made that the state often responds to political or economic crises with more intervention, as in the 1982 bank nationalization.[34] Each time the state encroaches on the private sector, whether symbolically or pragmatically, it alters structural patterns between the two, setting in motion significant reverberations in their relationship.

Cultural Interpretations

Public officials, in part influenced by the ambience of a pro-statist culture, have guided the state along its historic path. In addition to structural weaknesses in the private sector, and a cultural ambience among politicians supportive of state intervention which explains the evolution of the public-private relationship, a general cultural variable may contribute to how they view each other.

The most important cultural explanation for the dominant role the state has played in Latin American societies is offered by Glen Dealy. He suggests that public power, that is, the control over public resources both human and financial, has always had more prestige in Latin cultures than control over private resources.[35] Thus, the state holds distorted attraction for potential leaders and opinion-makers, and its prestige creates an expectation that the state will play a visible and active role in society. This is a widespread value, according to Dealy, and therefore, leaders in both the private and public sectors share some similar expectations about the state's role.

A complementary attitude, which accentuates how the state might deal with the private sector in Mexico, is the presence of authoritarianism in all Mexicans' value systems. Studies of Mexican values have a long way to go, but general agreement exists among Mexicans and North Americans that authoritarian beliefs are still deeply embedded in most Mexicans' minds, including childrens'.[36] One recent study of a selected occupational group suggests democratic values may be in the ascendancy, but the authors' conclusions are contradictory.[37] The point is that generally, a more authoritarian culture accepts a stronger, more authoritarian state. Therefore, a political leadership that decides a priori to function as an independent political actor encounters a more receptive audience than in a culture in which those values are weaker.

Constitutionalism

Early in the twentieth century, Mexico, unlike most other Latin American cultures, insured a special relationship between the state and the private sector through a unique variable that can logically be labeled constitutionalism. In previous chapters I made reference to the contradictory qualities of the private-public sector relationship. No single factor is more important in explaining these contradictions than the Constitution of 1917, which suggests how the political leadership could evolve a philosophy advocating both economic liberalism and capitalism on the one hand, and state dominated social justice and economic growth on the other. The essence of these contradictions has been well summed up:

> In the end, the constitution embodied contradictory views and conceptions vis-à-vis the roles of the individual and the state and the relationship between the two. On one hand, it reiterated all the essential concepts of a federal democratic government that had been present in the 1857 Constitution. . . . On the other, the constitution integrated two new concepts: primacy of the executive over the legislative and the judicial powers; second, it placed social interest above individual freedom. The latter point was expressed repeatedly.[38]

In the 1920s and 1930s the concepts of a mixed economy and the public good became intertwined. As one prominent Mexican economist suggests, state intervention generally was looked upon favorably, and it was based on the principle of collective well-being, a concept found in the 1917 Constitution.[39] Moreover, the Constitution made clear the quasi-governmental role of organized labor and peasants, but it left open the pattern between the state and the private sector.[40] Not surprisingly, the state, interpreting constitutional provisions for labor and peasants, attempted to establish its relationship with entrepreneurial groups following the model used with these other two actors.

The Constitution wields an influence beyond the codification of some patterns in state-group relationships. It is well known that the political leadership uses the rhetoric of the Constitution to support its own interpretations of desirable goals for all Mexicans and, moreover, often considers itself the guardian of constitutional values. Several generations of politicians, including those most influential in establishing the capitalist development strategy and the basis for the private-public relationship, were "true believers" in a large state role in the economy.

These generations learned their views about the state in the tumultuous period following the Revolution. Values were changing. The learning environment was exciting and dynamic. Most of the future leaders were young lawyers socialized in an ambience in which Mexican jurists accepted public utility, that is, the importance of communal interests, as a basic legal principle.[41] An exceptional representative of these generations, Antonio Carrillo Flores, who helped to formulate economic policies of adminstrations in the 1960s—the high point for the success of Mexico's mixed-economy philosophy—unequivocally emphasizes that state omnipotence was a very important idea conveyed through the educational system to his generation. They learned this value from notable intellectual-politicians like Narciso Bassols, who drew on the 1917 Constitution for this view.[42] In his own writings Carrillo Flores would say, "The economic participation of the state, far from being the major problem, is one of the best pillars to save and strengthen democratic institutions, such as we conceive them, and the social system of private property established in the Constitution."[43]

It has been established that the overriding value of Mexico's postrevolutionary political generations, in power from 1940 through 1970, was political peace.[44] In a practical sense the political leadership thought peace could be achieved in several ways. First, they hoped to follow a conciliatory policy—that is, to use the state to balance the power of competing interests. Stability was their leitmotif. One member of this generation described this philosophy as "never taking an extreme position either to the Left or to the Right, but developing a sense of balance or equilibrium."[45] This philosophy was put into effect and is precisely the reason why the 1982 nationalization of the banks had such an impact on the historic equilibrium. Second, the generation which took power after 1940 clearly understood the need to mold a homogeneous political elite to insure its own stability, a concept shared by other postrevolutionary leaders.[46] Mexico's leaders used a public educational system and their own skills as teachers to instill this conformity within broad ideological boundaries among three successive generations.[47]

Foreign Influences on the Private-Public Relationship

All these causes of the characteristics of the relationship between the state and the private sector share one similarity: they are domestic in origin. Many scholars, however, argue that an important variable in Mexico's economy is foreign investment and foreign-managed firms. Because the impact of foreign capital is substantial, it is likely to affect the very nature of the relationship between the domestic private sector and the state.

An examination of the influence of foreign capital, or the relationship between multinational corporations and the state, is not within the purview of this study. It is essential, however, to identify certain characteristics, both behavioral and institutional, of foreign capital in Mexico, and how those qualities modify the domestic private sector's relationship to the state. Raymond Vernon saw North American economic control as never "far from center stage in the interplay between the public and the private sectors."[48] This statement was far more true historically than at present, since at the turn of the century the domestic private sector was quite weak, and foreign investment, compared to its present scope, was quite broad. For example, in 1914, of the largest twenty-seven manufacturing industries, eighteen were completely foreign and twenty-five had some measure of foreign ownership.[49]

Today the distribution of ownership is substantially different. In the first place, of the fifty largest manufacturing firms between 1968 and 1981, only seven were foreign-controlled or dominated.[50] If a larger sample of firms is examined, foreign control over investment appears larger. The extent of foreign control depends on the figures cited. Basically, however, four important facts emerge. First, between 1970 and 1980, foreign control over Mexico's productive industrial capacity was as low as 32 percent or as high as 52 percent, although most authors put it at approximately one-third.[51] Second is the importance of state ownership (a variable not present at the turn of the century), accounting for 12 to 15 percent of Mexico's total industrial capacity, a figure that increased dramatically after the 1982 bank nationalization. Third, among the largest firms, foreign control comes largely from the Untied States.[52] Finally, it is important to note that students of external investment believe it is growing substantially in Mexico and that the increase of foreign investment in the 1960s and 1970s was at the expense of Mexican companies.[53]

How and to what degree multinationals influence public policy has been analyzed by others. The presence of a sizable foreign private sector in Mexico is important not only because of its potential or actual influence over decisionmaking, but because it can either bring the domestic private and public sectors closer together or cause them to move further apart. For example, Mexican receptivity to multinational corporations, within a nationalistic context, has interesting consequences. Nationalism is very appealing to most Mexicans, regardless of income or occupation. As Glade and Anderson suggest,

> policies designed to reduce the scope of foreign economic activity have had great popular appeal in Mexico, an appeal which serves to unify the always divisive components of the Revolutionary coalition. Thus, while Mexico's stress on capitalistic industrialization, with its attendant effect of creating a new class of wealth, may seem a betrayal of the radical aspirations of the Revolution, it is also consistent with one of the primary consensus values of the Revolutionary elites. Public policies which promote economic self-sufficiency in Mexico, then, may be supported both by the radical intellectual and by the conservative entrepreneur, though each for his own reasons.[54]

Given these feelings among Mexicans in general, it is possible for the state to alter its relation to the domestic private sector using foreign investors as a foil.

On the other hand, some Mexican businessmen believe their nationalism creates a significant distinction when working with the Mexican state. Their view is that nationalism not only works against foreign companies' influencing government but also allows Mexicans a level of intimacy with the state unobtainable by foreign entrepreneurs. Cresencio Ballesteros, a powerful leader of the construction industry and member of the elite Mexican Council of Businessmen (CMHN), believes that if foreign entrepreneurs tried to influence government policy directly, the consequences would be disastrous and produce the opposite of the result they desired. Furthermore, he argues that "if we can talk privately with the government as Mexican entrepreneurs, we can examine our mistakes and our achievements, and we can do this because whether we are from the public sector or the private sector, we are all Mexicans. This is something not true of the foreign investor."[55]

Other ideological influences also abound. I suggested earlier that the work of Dilmus James illustrates that Mexican firms are competitive with foreign firms in obtaining technology, yet they believe themselves inferior.[56] A sense of inferiority is not only part of their overall self-image but can play a role in their relationship to the state. If Mexican entrepreneurs observe that multinationals can obtain concessions from the state, they might expect the state to treat them similarly. Still another view sees foreign private-sector influence aiding the consolidation of capitalist ideology among all members of the domestic entrepreneurial class.[57] In other words, multinational corporations are socializers of domestic entrepreneurs.

Whereas multinational corporations sometimes strengthen the position of the domestic entrepreneur in his relationship to the state, multinationals have been known to exploit divisions within the domestic private sector for their own interests. Miguel Basáñez asserts that in the 1970s the American Chamber of Commerce, the most important representative of North American firms in Mexico, promoted and organized opposition to the state among Mexican multinational corporations. They were trying to wrest control of the private sector away from the CMHN, using internal divisions within the Monterrey industrial group to accomplish their goal.[58] One of the important consequences of their effort was to encourage a faction in the Monterrey Group, led by the Alfa holding company, to pursue a more activist policy through Coparmex. As demonstrated previously, Coparmex's posture toward the state has been a primary cause of tension between the state and the private sector since the late 1970s.

Ironically, most Mexican entrepreneurs interviewed were adamant in their belief that multinational corporations have little if any effect on their relationship to the state. Mexican public figures were more sanguine about possible effects, but generally agreed with businessmen. The importance of multinational corporations' presence may lie less in their short-term structural influence on private-public relations than in their long-term consequences for the ideology of the Mexican entrepreneur. A former official articulates this impact rather astutely:

If you believe that the foreign investment in Mexico has a cultural impact as you mentioned, it is one of the positive influences, to the degree that it creates a broader sense of loyalty to human beings everywhere, rather than to a chauvinistic concept of nationalism. One could expand on this idea and say that this attitude affects the view of the domestic private sector toward the Mexican government. It must be true that something happens from the influence of the foreign private sector. It is impossible to be otherwise. In my opinion, foreign investors must have an impact on the attitudes of individuals toward their own governments, if you are aware of the attitude which your colleagues from other countries have toward their government. Once you exchange views in terms of the attitude which one businessman has toward his government, then those views are going to have an impact on your own. Obviously, as an entrepreneur I would learn the rules of your political game in the relationship between the two sectors in your country, and I would be interested in why those rules exist. In effect, when we both exchange this type of knowledge, it is bound to have an influence on the manner in which businesses conduct their relationships with the government, especially if you are a close collaborator with businessmen from another culture. The values which affect the manner or behavior of the businessman are learned in part by how an economy behaves in its respective culture.[59]

The proximity of the United States to Mexico, the success of its economic model, and the penetration of North American media and culture into Mexico indirectly convey aspects of North American business-government relations to Mexicans. For example, Newell and Rubio believe that in the late 1970s, Mexican businessmen were becoming very concerned about the extent of government influence in their economy, even though by comparison to Italy or France Mexico's public sector was still relatively small.[60] Mexicans, however, were comparing theirs to the degree of state influence in the United States.

The Mexican businessperson's image of the United States, whether obtained indirectly through conversation and the media, or through direct experience there, cannot be easily ascertained, nor is that image's impact assured. As one prominent Mexican businessman, who worked for Sherman Williams in the United States and then became president of a Mexican firm affiliated with Phelps-Dodge, recounted, "Even though I had a personal experience in the United States, and I was affected by things that I saw in the United States, such as the Truman-Dewey election, they have not really had any influence on my attitude toward my own government and its relationship with the private sector."[61]

Each of the aforementioned foreign business influences on the private-public relationship are, with one exception, indirect. This may explain why Mexican businessmen and public figures see foreign businesses, especially dominant North American groups, as having little if any impact on their relationship to the state. Another reason why important North American businessmen are perceived to have a negligible impact on this relationship is that cultural influences work in both directions. As one Mexican explained, there are two types of North Americans in Mexico. The first type, and most important, are those who have lived in Mexico for many years. They speak Spanish, acquire Mexican customs, and even think like Mexicans, making it difficult for them to identify with the United States and its private-sector policies regarding Mexico. The second group, in Mexico only temporarily, could potentially have a certain cultural influence, but because their presence is short-term, they exert far less influence over their Mexican peers than the previous group.[62]

The other reasons why Mexican businessmen believe North American firms have little impact in Mexico is that these firms' interests are different, they are sensitive to their position in Mexico, and one organization, the American Chamber of Commerce, expresses their views. A former Mexican chamber leader, experienced in the actual process of private sector-government relations, summed up the general attitude of Mexican businessmen: "Because foreign companies' communication with the Mexican government is essentially unified and channeled through the American Chamber of Commerce, I do not think that they have much influence on the relationship between the domestic entrepreneur and the government. Furthermore, they are very careful in their attitude and in their relationship to the government."[63]

Foreign businesses exert additional influences on the private sector's relationship to the state. Generally, they are likely to have a long-term effect through the American Chamber of Commerce's programs promoting private-sector values among Mexican youth. Such programs strengthen an environment favorable to entrepreneurs in Mexico and increase self-confidence among businessmen. Any change in entrepreneurs' self-image, as documented earlier, is likely to affect how they behave toward the state.

A second type of impact is organizational. Mexican businessmen admit that the structure of North American businesses has been admired by many Mexican managers, and they have restructured their internal organizations in imitation of the United States model. Internally, United States management models have little effect on the private sector's relationship to the state. An exception to this could be the impact Mexico's leading industrial group Alfa had on the psychology of the entrepreneur and his self-image vis-à-vis the state. As I indicated earlier, most Mexicans believe Alfa's near-bankruptcy in 1982 could be explained in part by an inappropriate replication of United States organizational trends. A clearer example, with direct consequences for private-public sector relations, was the participation of United States corporations and the American Chamber of Commerce in a 1972 boycott of *Excélsior*, Mexico's leading daily newspaper. Essentially, multinational corporations initiated an advertising boycott among many Mexican firms, responding to what they perceived as the paper's unfavorable attitude toward private enterprise. Their actions forced the government to step in and make up the difference in *Excélsior's* revenues.[64] In effect, not only did multinationals initiate a policy that created tensions between the Mexican government and the private sector, but also, equally important, foreign businesspeople schooled Mexicans in a North American technique.

At this point it is important to reemphasize, as in the discussion on entrepreneurs' self-image, that often what is more important to the relationship between the private sector and the state is the perception, rather than the reality, of what influences are important. Mexican businessmen do not believe multinationals have much impact on their relationship to the state. Whether foreigners exercise as little influence as claimed is debatable, but the Mexican business community firmly believes its assertion. Therefore, the homogeneity and intensity of that belief itself is weighed as an important variable in my analysis.

The Influence of the State

These many characteristics that affect the behavior of the private and public sectors toward each other provide a more accurate picture of the larger context in which the two parties must operate. As each develops its posture toward the other, it has a variety of weapons it can use to strengthen its bargaining position. Although I believe the relationship is symbiotic, the state appears to have had the upper hand.

The Mexican state has some advantages in the relationship not found in the United States—political, ideological, and economic. Politically, the Mexican state's most important weapon is the existence of a well-defined state ideology, incorporating such values as economic growth, submission to the state, industrialization, national unity, and a mixed economic model. Its ideological preferences are supported by a growing sense of nationalism that makes "it more and more difficult to pass judgment on political centralism, paternalism and economic policy; in effect, the public sector is immune from independent criticism."[65]

Nationalism made it possible for the government to pursue a policy that favored infrastructure expenditures in support of their goal of industrialization, while simultaneously legitimizing the maldistribution of wealth and the lack of social services.[66] In other words, the intertwining of nationalism with a state ideology has allowed the state to favor or curb private-sector interests. The important point to remember is that the state has the ability to define the national interest and to make it acceptable to the Mexican people.

Given the condition of its ideology, although by no means homogeneous, the state is at an advantage vis-à-vis the private sector. Entrepreneurs, or any other group, find it difficult to criticize the state, especially on the issue dearest to their interests, government economic intervention. Susan Purcell explains why: "Since state ownership and control is sanctioned and encouraged by nationalist sentiments of both the regime and the population in general, the private sector can do little to challenge effectively the continuous expansion of such ownership and control without appearing to be 'unpatriotic' and 'unrevolutionary.'"[67]

Although the stress here is on public-sector advantages in controlling the business community, it is worth noting that the government limits its options in its relations to the private sector. If the state needs to strengthen its ties with the private sector, its own ideological rhetoric restricts its ability to do so. As a representative of the Monterrey group suggests, prominent industrialists have to be discrete in seeking out help because the government does not want to be seen as an obvious ally of the private sector.[68]

Another political strength of the public sector is the authoritarian quality of the leadership—notably, their political discipline. Many students of the Mexican political system have commented on the ability of government officials to maintain a united front, allowing much in-house dissension but frowning strongly on public displays of disagreement. Several important ideological currents exist within the political leadership, differences with significant effects on the private-public relationship. These differences are more apparent in the 1980s than at any other time in recent decades, but the government generally confronts the private sector unified. The private sector, which by definition is independent, cannot exert similar discipline over its members, a fact the government can and has exploited to its advantage.

The government's structural advantage is represented in another way. Because it has historically initiated various business organizations, it has a greater potential for manipulating and mobilizing private-sector opinions than if they had been autonomous. Independent entrepreneurial organizations do exist, and are increasing in strength, but the majority of the private sector's views are channeled through institutional structures established by and for the benefit of the state.

The state also has another advantage, stemming from its actual power and the Mexican view that power over public resources is prestigious. Because educated Mexicans believe the state's power is far superior to that of any other group in their society, government exercises a magnetic quality in attracting capable adults. The state obviously is not the sole recruiter of ambitious Mexicans, but in recent decades, at least among potential entrepreneurs, its position sways many future leaders to join its ranks. Mexican intellectuals, in their relationship to the state, offer interesting parallels. They too complain that it is very difficult for individual intellectuals to resist the appeal of the state's power.[69] Even for young people in Monterrey, where the private sector has been most successful in creating an environment favorable to its interests, the state retains a strong attraction. Ernesto Canales, who was educated there, describes the impact on his peers:

"Many people of my generation who were serious intelligent students became involved with the government. The government has grown so much in its power that it is obvious that if you want to have power in Mexico, you need to go into the public rather than the private sector. So the attitude has changed from the 1950s to the present. I am talking about a social group of course, with whom I had contact, especially from Monterrey, but also my friends from Mexico City went through this same evolution in attitude."[70]

Power in Mexico is intimately tied to the complexities of the private-public sector relationship, especially communication. According to some entrepreneurs, the government does a good job of listening to private-sector demands but is not really hearing its complaints. These entrepreneurs argue that the government's ability to listen lulls people into believing that they are affecting government policy. Listening skills are a positive feature of the government's relation to the private sector, but few businessmen believe entrepreneurs have much impact. They suggest that "the only thing the government respects is power."[71]

The government's strongest weapons in its battles with the private sector are economic. Essentially, the government confronts the private sector on its own ground. One of the Mexican economy's structural characteristics, whose political impact has for the most part been ignored, is the role of government-owned enterprises. The expansion of parastate enterprises has been phenomenal since 1970. Mexico's public sector contains three separate but complementary institutions: traditional government agencies (comparable to their counterparts in the United States), parastate firms under congressional budgetary supervision, and another group of publicly owned firms not under congressional control.[72] Since 1970, two important developments have exaggerated the importance of the public sector. First is the discovery and exploitation of vast oil resources. Because oil is under a parastate agency, and because its impact on the export economy is overwhelming, it is difficult to subordinate the public sector to private enterprise.[73] Second, the nationalization of the banks in 1982 pushed public-sector economic control to an all-time high, assuring it of economic preponderance.

The state is able to use its economic resources as a weapon because its involvement is so great and it uses private management criteria, so that it directly competes economically with the private sector. This orientation in the public sector came about when "technically trained managers expanded the original industries which the government acquired into chains. They opened up opportunities for other technicians. . . . However, with this change, they lost the objective of what public administration is really all about. So what happened in the publicly controlled economic sector is that it grew faster than did the private sector itself."[74]

This philosophy pervades the public management of the banking system since the government takeover in 1982. As the government-appointed head of the third-largest banking chain in Mexico explained, "things today are managed with some social criteria, and we are competing with each other, not cutthroat competition, but the same techniques that were being used by the private banking system are still in use today. We want to show profits as an example of our efficiency."[75]

The Mexican state has long used its control of credit as a carrot and a stick with the private sector. In the early 1960s, the government's control over long- and short-term credit was pervasive and selective.[76]

Until 1982 the National Finance Bank, established in 1934, played the most important role among public financial institutions in advancing industrialization. With the nationalization of the banks, the government acquired nearly exclusive control over all domestic sources, of credit. Its ability to allocate resources to one entrepreneur and deny them to another is a significant economic weapon. Even before the nationalization, economists could correctly claim that the state's use of development banking as a political weapon altered the relationship of the government to the rest of the society.[77]

The government's ability to employ political criteria to distribute a scarce resource like credit also enters into its allocation of subsidies. One can argue that the government does not misuse its power to withhold subsidies, but instead creates a dependent relationship between the private sector and the state by making these resources available to privileged entrepreneurs. Much of the private sector's success rests on subsidized utilities and raw materials from government-run companies.[78] United States companies like to form partnerships with the Mexican government because that makes it much easier to obtain the permits so necessary to do business.[79] The same rationale obtains for domestic firms, which might find the advantages of partnership outweighing the disadvantages. The Mexican entrepreneur is caught in a dilemma. If one does not cooperate with the government one may place oneself at a disadvantage vis-à-vis one's competitors. Yet by cooperating with the state, "entrepreneurs are traitors to their own condition since they are helping the government accomplish its goal in relation to the private sector."[80]

Again, some very important parallels exist between the private sector's and intellectuals' relationships to the state. The state controls, even more heavily, resources supporting intellectual activities. For example, they subsidize newsprint, a key resource for publishing, which is a source of employment for numerous intellectuals. Moreover, political managers have been known to allow the National Finance Bank to overlook a borrower's mortgage payments for many years, and then suddenly, in response to a change in editorial policy, threaten to call in a publisher's loan.[81] Very few cases exist of these sanctions being applied. It is the threat of withholding a resource that characterizes the state's treatment of intellectuals. Purcell alludes to several companies who may have fallen afoul of the state because of politics, although no empirical examples of this are in evidence.[82] The Mexican state uses the same techniques and establishes the same tone in its relations with entrepreneurs as it does with intellectuals.

A dependent relationship between the private sector and the state produces advantages and disadvantages for both. The advantage to the state is the enhancement of the divisions that already exist within the private sector. As one entrepreneur argues, the secret of the government's relationship to the business community is to divide it, a policy they have been very successful in implementing.[83] Entrepreneurs may find themselves moving in a direction similar to intellectuals' in their relationship to the state. In the future, businesspeople may find themselves split over the extent to which they should collaborate with the state, although they have traditionally favored cooperation rather than disagreement on historically important issues. Many businesspeople, however, will not express their actual views publicly, because they are already too dependent on the public sector and fear reprisals from politicians.[84] This fear, rather than the state's concrete actions against them, affects—and flavors the environment of—the interactions between the public and private sectors.

The Influence of the Private Sector

Obviously, the Mexican state has many weapons it can draw on to maintain its control over the private sector. Yet the private sector is not without its own means of forcing concessions from and limiting the alternatives of the state. The most powerful pressures the private sector can bring to bear are economic in nature. Without question, the private sector's control over capital is its most viable threat against the state.[85] It is important to remember that the state is committed to economic growth and industrialization, goals requiring considerable capital formation. In spite of the dependency between the state and the private sector in achieving these two goals, the private sector, not the government, has provided the most domestic investment. According to Roger Hansen, 70 percent of Mexican domestic investment since 1940 has been generated by the private sector.[86] Unlike the state, which has rarely applied some of its potential threats, the private sector has not hesitated to use this weapon. In the 1970s businessmen tried to legally transfer assets to the United States, an important step in forcing the government to devalue the peso in 1976.[87] In the 1980s, when the business community began to lose confidence in the government's ability to control inflation, more than twenty-three billion dollars in savings and investment capital left the country.[88]

Other economic weapons available to the private sector include short-term suspension of productive activities through strikes, a technique it used during the Echeverría regime.[89] Owners' strikes do not have a long history of success in Mexico. Generally, they have been tried only regionally. Other sectors of the economy have not supported them, nor have they received unified, national backing. Thus, it is fair to say this is a potential weapon and not a threat with proven consequences.

The love-hate relationship between the public and private sectors is further complicated by the fact that many individuals who are representatives of the state, or who previously held high-level state offices, have personal investments in the private sector. The private sector can generally limit the extent of any alteration in its relationship to the state by counting on politicians' interest in protecting their own capital. Many years ago Raymond Vernon identified this "conflict of interest," suggesting that it affected the behavior of the public sector and was a limiting variable in changing the two sectors' orientations toward each other.[90] The trouble with businesspeople relying on conflict of interest as a limiting factor is that no one really knows the extent of politicians' involvement in the economy, although it is not nearly as extensive among prominent firms as rumored. While the private sector can rely on politicians' selfishness to protect their interests when policies are being slowly and carefully formulated, an overreliance on politicians' vested interests provides a false sense of security. When a president decides to take matters into his own hands, as José López Portillo did when he announced the 1982 nationalization of the banks, this weapon loses its effect.

Politically, the private sector can confront the state on its own territory. Although Mexico's political system is semiauthoritarian, it does respond to certain powerful interests. One analyst believes that the business community has some effect on the designation of certain cabinet-level officials, or at least can press for their removal.[91] Scattered evidence exists of business leaders expressing opinions about individual political appointments, but very little data support their actual control over such designations, except at the regional level.

Perhaps the most important political tools the private sector can use to its advantage are its organizational skills and its independent financial resources. These strengths give it the most autonomy of all the important potential political actors in Mexico, including organized labor.[92] Not only have they used these resources to support interest-group activities, they have made clear their willingness, especially in recent elections, to support vociferous, antagonistic opposition parties, especially the National Action party, as a means of delegitimizing the official party and the ideology of the state. As a threat this has not been very useful, until the 1980s. With the expansion of opposition and the political difficulties faced by the regime, such threats take on greater importance.[93] This explains why in November 1985, for the first time in Mexican history, businessmen claimed publicly that high government officials were pressuring them to abstain from politics.[94]

A small number of knowledgeable Mexican business leaders who have a clear understanding of their relationship to the state, and the political consequences stemming from it, admit that the only group with any real influence over the state is the private sector. They attribute their power to the human and financial resources the private sector controls. One human resource from which the private sector benefits is hidden: the business community potentially has large numbers of allies among small entrepreneurs. A Mexican public official explains how the state promotes the usefulness of this resource for the private sector:

> The public believes that the government attacks on the private sector are also attacks on little, local businessmen, which involve millions of Mexicans. What is interesting is that I believe the government doesn't know how to distinguish between the big entrepreneur and the little entrepreneur, and the irony is that the small businessman speculates much more and sells goods at a higher price than the large chains criticized by the government.
>
> What really needs to happen in this country is for the government to apply the laws just to corrupt businesses and to stop attacking all businessmen. Because they don't distinguish between various types of businessmen, it is really hurting what the government says and their position in society among all people who are involved in private initiative.[95]

Whereas political activism may be the most dangerous potential weapon in the private sector's arsenal, its use of publicity (defined in its broadest sense) is most influential at the present moment. Certain groups in the private sector, as part of a more activist posture, have decided to make themselves and their views more visible. On a leadership level, not only are chamber leaders more outspoken, but major entrepreneurial capitalists, such as Bernardo Garza Sada, became more visible in the late 1970s. Such a posture is significant because Mexican entrepreneurs have been notable for avoiding public exposure.[96]

Another reflection of this changing attitude is the use of public protests, a technique the private sector began using on a national level in 1976.[97] Its most important manifestation is in the media, rather than through physical demonstrations or economic pressures. According to Dale Story, the entrepreneurs who favored joining GATT could have used publicity to influence the outcome of that decision in the late 1970s but did not do so because they lacked unity.[98]

If the private sector can overcome its internal divisions, it has great potential for using the media to create a favorable image of itself and its values. Representatives of the private sector see the importance of publicity in their battles with the Mexican state. As one leader suggested,

> I think that in the last six years we have become more concerned with the image that the Mexican private sector has in the minds of the typical citizen, especially after the land invasions that took place under President Echeverría. I think there is a sympathy for the private sector in Mexico largely because of the way they have been abused and maltreated by the state. However, we need to use the mass media to help create a much more positive image, which I tried to do as president of the CCE six years ago.[99]

There is no question that the public sector is convinced that ordinary Mexicans are influenced by certain media. Many politicians believe that the Mexican media use yellow journalism to analyze complex political issues, especially tensions between the private sector and the state. Whereas the private sector's poor image historically has put it at a disadvantage in its relations with the government, politicians believe that in the 1980s it has received more favorable treatment, which has been translated into votes for the National Action party. In fact, one of Mexico's most prominent politicians complained vehemently about the Mexican media's irresponsibility toward politicians, suggesting that many government officials are fearful of reprisals from the press if they offend individual reporters.[100]

Government-controlled censorship of the Mexican media is complex. The most viable threats against the media usually are determined by the president himself, and individual politicians rarely control these decisions.[101] The government traditionally conveys its position in the media through advertising and subsidized news coverage. The private sector has, in a more active way, decided to use the same techniques to publicize its relationship with the state. In late 1985 Coparmex paid for an ad claiming that high government officials pressured individual businessmen to abstain from political activities. The government was so sensitive to these charges that the secretary of government felt compelled to respond in Mexico's leading dailies, denying the accusations point by point.[102]

It is important to understand that the private sector dominates media ownership. According to recent analyses, Mexicanists believe that the state has not recognized the long-term ideological impact of the media, leaving it in the hands of some of Mexico's most important capitalists.[103] The state has only rarely sought to restrict this control. The only case in which it directly intervened *financially* in the print media was in 1973 to prevent the sale of the *Sol de México* chain, Mexico's seventh largest, to Cervecería Cuauhtémoc, a flagship company of one of the Monterrey groups. The government itself purchased the company, leaving at the masthead the original owner, who changed his editorial position from open defense of the private sector to a more ambivalent posture.[104]

Most of Mexico's major chains are controlled by leading entrepreneurial families. These newspapers include *El Heraldo de México*, an avowedly conservative publication under the control of the Alarcón family. Gabriel Alarcón also has majority interests in Club 202 (the Diners Club credit card in Mexico), real estate firms, and the Cadena de Oro cinema chain. His newspaper, which has been labeled a mouthpiece of the industrial, commercial, and financial sector in the 1970s, has the second-largest circulation in Mexico City.[105] Another leading Mexican daily, *El Universal*, Mexico's oldest published daily, has been operated since the 1910s by the Lanz Duret family, another of Mexico's leading entrepreneurs. It ranks fifth in circulation among Mexico's daily papers. Finally, *Novedades*, Mexico's third-largest independent daily, has been owned for years by the O'Farrill family, a major stockholder of Mexico's largest television empire.[106]

Another variable influenced by media ownership is stockholders' attitudes toward the state and its relationship to the private sector. Some of the major print media, as illustrated by the O'Farrill and Alarcón holdings, are in the hands of conservative, traditional Mexican entrepreneurs who see their political role as nonactivist.[107] Since students of Mexico's print media believe the press is a primary determinant of the public's image of Mexico's political system, these media's long-term impact ideologically should be quite strong.[108] A concerted but subtle alteration in the tone of press coverage could favor the long-term position of the private sector vis-à-vis the government. On the other hand, if politicians perceive this threat, greater use of censorship is likely to occur.

The private sector also has a dominant position in television. Television is a fundamental medium for attracting support from the Mexican urban middle class to reinforce and propagate the private sector's ideology.[109] Only a few studies examining the relationship between Mexico's media and politics are available, but they indicate that the immediate impact of television on political behavior generally is limited. In Mexico City, however, 30 percent of those who watch television say it influences their voting. Of those who say they are affected by television, 36 percent say they vote for PAN.[110] However, observers believe the long-term impact of television is more substantial. A former Mexican correspondent for *The New York Times* theorizes that television is helping to create and exaggerate cultural differences in Mexico.[111]

The private sector controls most television stations in Mexico. The government only owns one significant national station (although four are under its control). It is allowed by law to use 12 percent of all air time for public programming. The leading firm, Televisa, includes more than forty-five companies in television, radio, press, and publicity. Televisa operates four major television stations. Four entrepreneurial families control it: Miguel Alemán Velasco, Jr., Emilio Azcárraga, Jr., Rómulo O'Farrill, and more recently Bernardo Garza Sada.[112] Each family is among Mexico's top capitalists, and only Alemán has political origins. His father, a classic case of a politician-turned-entrepreneur, however, represents the economically conservative political leadership favoring strong support for a liberal economic model.

The use of media is an important weapon in the hands of the business community and is likely to be used in specific campaigns involving private sector-government conflicts. However, the structural weakness of this weapon—the government's control over censorship and the media's resources—restricts its use. Therefore, its impact on the image of the private sector will be more important over the long term than in short-term conflicts with the state, and campaigns favoring the private sector and its ideology can only strengthen its bargaining position with the state.

Conclusions

The foregoing analysis makes clear that many variables influence the behavior of the private sector in its relationship to the Mexican state. These many influences more fully explain two primary characterizations of the private-public relationship. They further demonstrate that a multitude of variables must be taken into account if one is to draw a clear picture of this relationship. My analysis also indicates that other actors in Mexico's political arena, who might be described as interest groups in North American political literature, share certain qualities in their relationship to the state. Finally, both the private sector and the state have weapons—found universally, or only in Mexico—that they can bring to bear in support of their postures toward each other.

The first of the two common characterizations of the private-public relationship used in Mexican economic literature is that it is symbiotic. Mexican businessmen who are perceptive of their dependence on the state, and believe that their relationship has undergone few changes, use this term. As one businessman explains, "naturally, businessmen constantly complain about the public sector, but in reality we depend heavily on each other. We have had some important exchanges which are really interchanges based on convenience."[113]

Businessmen who see their relationship with the state as symbiotic are not committed to a philosophy of critical activism toward the government. They perceive their survival in Mexico in realistic but traditional terms. They believe that Mexico's economic and political futures are closely intertwined, and without close cooperation between the two sectors Mexico is doomed to return to violence and anarchy—conditions the postrevolutionary system sought, for selfish and selfless reasons, to alleviate.

It is possible that among the various categories of businessmen whose outlines emerge in these pages, one distinct group includes those whose favorable posture toward cooperation with the government outweighs their positions on political activism or social responsibility. These businessmen are socially aware; they understand the importance of politics; but unlike the leader of Coparmex, they see Mexico's salvation as close cooperation between the public and private sectors. The late Bernardo Quintana Arrioja voiced this group's views:

> I think the private sector is trying to go in the same direction as the state in order not to confront it further. We also understand that this is a serious economic crisis, and we expect difficult conditions in the future which we must overcome. We have to join together in order to combat inflation, to become more self-sufficient, to establish an equilibrium in our external monetary policy, and above all to create employment. If we don't do this, it will surely result in instability and it will cause the government serious problems, the private sector problems, as well as

problems for the average Mexican. Much disruption will occur if measures are not taken to improve cooperation between the two sectors.[114]

It is difficult to ascertain the weight of this group in the private sector as a whole. Their position falls between that of the traditional, conservative entrepreneurs, who are unaware of the broader social and political issues, and the activist businessmen, who wish to put much greater pressure on the political leadership to reverse the mixed economic model. Regardless of its strength—and it is substantial—this group acts as a moderating force against radical alterations in the present balance between public and private interests.

The second characterization that most frequently comes to mind when analyzing the relationship between the two sectors is that it is paradoxical. Its irony can best be understood if we think of it as analogous to a mentor-disciple relationship. In all strong mentor-disciple relationships, somewhere along the line the disciple, in this case the private sector, must break away from the confines of its mentor. However much it owes its mentor for creating, molding, and sustaining it through difficult times, it must exert its independence. The state, in turn, is like the proverbial master who cannot understand why his dependent bites the hand that feeds him. Thus, a level of incomprehension emerges on both sides toward each other's behavior.

The irony is that as the private sector became stronger, it came to believe that state economic intervention should be increasingly subordinate to market forces.[115] It began, as a consequence, to question the basic underlying philosophy of Mexico's development—according to some authors, for the first time since the Revolution.[116] The source of this irony, however, raises important broader questions about the structural relationships present in the Mexican political model.

It can be argued that the Mexican private sector-state relationship exposes a significant weakness in a semiauthoritarian, state-led political model. When the state controls a preponderance of resources, and distributes them in such a way as to nurture a set of actors who must perform the functions necessary for the state to grow and survive, it builds into the relationship a self-destructive time bomb that eventually must ignite. My examination of both intellectuals and entrepreneurs reveals a significant pattern, in which state-supported growth leads to vigorous, dynamic cultural and entrepreneurial sectors. Once these subsidized groups reach a certain level of sophistication and power they wish to fulfill goals and dreams that do not necessarily correspond to their mentor's.

Mexico's proximity to the United States influences how the state is viewed, complicating these relationships. In the case of intellectuals, their younger Mexican leaders clearly are deviating from the traditional model of state involvement to one imitative of the intellectual model found in the United States, where intellectuals have remained almost completely independent of the government. Similarly, a group within the Mexican business community—also indirectly influenced by a northern model—wants to alter their relationship with the state, asking it to reduce its traditional role and allow entrepreneurs to grow more powerful and behave independently.

The state has been and continues to be able to restrict the posture of the private sector because, like each political actor the state bargains with, the private sector is heterogeneous.[117] The state realizes the potential political value of these divisions, and when necessary, uses them to its advantage, setting off one entrepreneurial group against the other. Some individual businesses or even sectors have cultivated a close relationship to the state, so much so that they function as channels of communication between the government and the business community.[118]

Finally, underlying the many peculiarities that contribute to the unique evolution of the private sector's relationship to the state in Mexico, none is perhaps more important than an inherent belief in state intervention. The idea that private management must rely on its own ingenuity and initiative as measured by yields, rather than being supported—if not subsidized—from above, is fairly rare.[119] From the point of view of the state, therefore, the private sector has only itself to blame. No better expression of this dilemma can be found than in the words of President de la Madrid himself when he noted, "To be sure, we always encounter very different opinions because a great part of state intervention comes about as a result of requests from private entrepreneurs themselves. In the eyes of some private businessmen, state intervention is beneficial, while for others it is inappropriate."[120]

These changing attitudes in the private sector have altered its traditional relationship with the state. The relationship over the next decade will be tense and dynamic. Tensions between the two are likely to increase. The state is overly sensitive to the private sector: all its disciples—to which opposition parties can be added—simultaneously are demanding concessions. Like organized labor and intellectuals, these parties were nurtured by the state for decades, but now see themselves functioning in a pluralistic, United States model of political participation. The private sector will play a critical role in this participatory culture, influencing Mexico's political future.

Notes*

Preface

1. *Intellectuals and the State in Twentieth Century Mexico* (Austin: University of Texas Press, 1985).

2. For the importance of this rapport, see Richard Sennet and Jonathan Cobb, *The Hidden Injuries of Class* (New York: Knopf, 1972), p. 37.

3. Roderic A. Camp, *Mexico's Leaders: Their Education and Recruitment* (Tucson: University of Arizona Press, 1980) and *Mexican Political Biographies, 1935–1980* (Tucson: University of Arizona Press, 1982).

4. For some preliminary findings, see my "Generals and Politicians in Mexico: A Preliminary Comparison," in David Ronfeldt, ed., *The Modern Mexican Military: A Reassessment* (La Jolla: Center for U.S.-Mexican Studies, University of California at San Diego, 1984), pp. 107–156.

Chapter 1

1. C. Wright Mills, *The Power Elite* (New York: Oxford University Press, 1959).

2. Phillip H. Burch, *Elites in American History*, vol. 1 (New York: Holmes and Meier, 1981), pp. 4–5.

3. W. G. Domhoff, *Who Rules America* (Englewood Cliffs, N.J.: Prentice-Hall, 1967).

4. Robert C. Scott, "Mexico: the Established Revolution," in Lucian Pye and Sidney Verba, eds., *Political Culture and Political Development* (Princeton: Princeton University Press, 1965), p. 380.

5. Wilbur A. Chaffee, Jr., "Entrepreneurship and Economic Behavior:

*Re personal interview. No name indicates the interviewee does not wish to be cited.

A New Approach in the Study of Latin American Politics," *Latin American Research Review*, 11, no. 3 (1976):55–68; the excellent survey of state theory in Peter Evans, Dietrich Rueschemeyer, and Theda Skocpal, eds., *Bringing the State Back In* (Cambridge: Cambridge University Press, 1985), Chapter 1; and Martin Carnoy, *The State and Political Theory* (Princeton: Princeton University Press, 1984).

    6. Burch, *Elites*, p. 19.

    7. Hugh G. J. Aitkens, "The Future of Entrepreneurial Research," *Explorations in Entrepreneurial History*, vol. 1 (1963–1964), p. 5.

    8. Burch, *Elites*, p. 25.

    9. Flavia Derossi, *The Mexican Entrepreneur* (Paris: Development Center of the Organization for Economic Cooperation and Development, 1971), p. 11.

    10. For a good explanation of the controversy, see Van R. Whiting, Jr., "Review of Peter H. Smith, *Labyrinths of Power: Political Recruitment in Twentieth Century Mexico* (Princeton: Princeton University Press, 1979)," *Foro Internacional* 22 (July–September 1981):110–113.

    11. Julio Labastida Martín del Campo, "Grupos dominantes frente a las alternativas de cambio," in *El Pérfil de México en 1980*, vol. 3 (Mexico City: Siglo XXI, 1980), p. 135.

    12. Burch, *Elites*, p. 22; Lewis J. Edinger and Donald D. Searing, "Social Background in Elite Analysis: A Methodological Inquiry," *American Political Science Review* 61 (June 1967):428–445.

    13. Aitkens, "Future of Entrepreneurial Research," p. 5

    14. Plato, *Republic* (New York: Modern Library, 1982).

    15. Friedrich Engels, *The Origin of Family, Private Property and the State* (New York: International Publishers, 1972), p. 229.

    16. Ruth Berins Collier, "Popular Sector Incorporation and Political Supremacy: Regime Evolution in Brazil and Mexico," in Sylvia Ann Hewlett and Richard S. Weinert, eds., *Brazil and Mexico, Patterns in Late Development* (Philadelphia: Institute for the Study of Human Issues, 1982), p. 60.

    17. Georg Wilhelm F. Hegel, *The Philosophy of Right* (London: Encyclopaedia Britannica, 1952), p. 92.

    18. Robert M. MacIver, *Politics and Society*, ed. David Spitz (New York: Atherton Press, 1969), p. 66.

    19. For Mexico, these views are best explained by Miguel Basáñez, *La lucha por la hegemonía en México, 1968–80* (Mexico City: Siglo XXI, 1981); and Van R. Whiting, Jr., "Private Power in Mexico," unpublished manuscript, Brown University, 1983, p. 38.

    20. David Brading, "Government and Elite in Late Colonial Mexico," *Hispanic American Historical Review* 53, no. 3 (August 1973):405–414.

    21. Ruben Vargas Austin, "The Development of Economic Policy in Mexico with Special Reference to Economic Doctrines," Ph.D. dissertation, Iowa State University, 1958, p. 299.

22. Karl Schmitt, "Church and State in Mexico: A Corporatist Relationship," *The Americas* 40, no. 3 (January 1984):353.

23. Leopoldo Solís, "Mexican Economic Policy in the Post-War Period: The Views of Mexican Economists," *The American Economic Review* 61 (June 1971):54; and *La formación del estado mexicano* (Mexico: Porrúa, 1984).

24. Juan Felipe Leal, "The Mexican State: 1915–1973, A Historical Interpretation," *Latin American Perspectives* 2 (Summer 1975):56.

25. Octavio Paz, "Escombros and Semillas," *Vuelta* 9, no. 108 (November 1985):8.

26. Enrique Krauze, "Mexico: el Timón y la Tormenta," *Vuelta* 6, no. 71 (October 1982):21.

27. Daniel C. Levy, *University and Government in Mexico, Autonomy in an Authoritarian System* (New York: Praeger, 1980), pp. 8–11.

28. Daniel C. Levy and Gabriel Szekely, *Mexico, Paradoxes of Stability and Change* (Boulder: Westview Press, 1983), p. 115.

29. Susan K. Purcell, *The Mexican Profit-Sharing Decision, Politics in an Authoritarian Regime* (Berkeley: University of California Press, 1975), p. 5.

30. Ruth Berins Collier and David Collier, "Inducements versus Constraints: Disaggregating Corporatism," *American Political Science Review* 73 (December 1979):968.

31. Dale Story, *Industry, the State and Public Policy in Mexico* (Austin: University of Texas Press, 1986).

32. Nora Hamilton, *The Limits of State Autonomy, Post-Revolutionary Mexico* (Princeton: Princeton University Press, 1982), p. 12.

33. Susan K. and John Purcell, "Mexican Business and Public Policy," in James Malloy, ed., *Authoritarianism and Corporatism in Latin America* (Pittsburgh: Pittsburgh University Press, 1977), p. 194; Austin, "Development of Economic Policy," p. 2.

34. Ibid., p. 243; and Basáñez, *La lucha por la hegemonía en México*.

35. Leal, "Mexican State," p. 60; and Hamilton, *Limits of State Autonomy*, p. 30.

36. Hamilton, *Limits of State Autonomy*, p. 14.

37. Basáñez, *La lucha por la hegemonía en México*, p. 209.

38. Ellen Kay Trimberger, *Revolution from Above: Military Bureaucrats and Development in Japan, Turkey, Egypt and Peru* ((New Brunswick, NJ: Transaction Books, 1978).

39. Smith, *Labyrinths*, p. 215.

40. Personal interview with Pedro Daniel Martínez García, Mexico City, May 16, 1985.

41. John Walton found this to be true in Monterrey, in his *Elites and Economic Development* (Austin: University of Texas Press, 1977), p. 213.

42. Maurice Zeitlin et al., "Class Segments: Agrarian Property and Political Leadership in the Capitalist Class of Chile," *American Sociological Review* 41 (December 1976):1017–1018.

256   NOTES

Chapter 2

1. Friedrich Katz, *The Secret War in Mexico*, (Chicago: University of Chicago Press, 1981), p. 11.

2. Roberto Newell and Luis Rubio, *Mexico's Dilemma, The Political Origins of Economic Crisis* (Boulder: Westview Press, 1984), p. 19.

3. Robert J. Shafer, *Mexican Business Organizations* (Syracuse: Syracuse University Press, 1973), p. 126.

4. Katz, *Secret War*, p. 572.

5. Julio Labastida Martín del Campo, "Los grupos dominates frente a las alternativas de cambio," *El pérfil de México en 1980*, vol. 3 (Mexico: Siglo XXI, 1972), p. 107.

6. Newell and Rubio, *Mexico's Dilemma*, p. 267.

7. William P. Glade and Charles Anderson, *The Political Economy of Mexico*, (Madison: University of Wisconsin, 1963), p. 114.

8. Nora Hamilton, "The State and the National Bourgeoisie in Postrevolutionary Mexico: 1920–1940," *Latin American Perspectives* 9, no. 4 (Fall 1982):40.

9. Ibid., p. 38.

10. Douglas Bennett and Kenneth Sharpe, "The State as Banker and Entrepreneur: The Last Resort Character of the Mexican State's Intervention, 1919–1976," *Comparative Politics* 12 (January 1980):173.

11. Enrique Krauze et al., *Historia de la revolución mexicana, la reconstrución económica* (Mexico: El Colegio de México, 1977), pp. 9–13.

12. Bennett and Sharpe, "State as Banker," p. 172.

13. Jean Meyer et al., *Historia de la revolución mexicana, estado y sociedad con Calles* (Mexico: El Colegio de México, 1977), p. 283.

14. Ibid., p. 297.

15. John M. Hart, *Anarchism and the Mexican Working Class, 1860–1931* (Austin: University of Texas Press, 1987), p. 175.

16. Meyer, *Historia de la revolución mexicana*, p. 326.

17. Vargas Austin, "Development of Economic Policy," p. 234.

18. Lorenzo Meyer, *Historia de la revolución mexicana, el conflicto social y los gobiernos del maximata* (Mexico City: El Colegio de México, 1978), pp. 11–12.

19. James W. Wilkie, *The Mexican Revolution, Federal Expenditure and Social Change Since 1910* (Berkeley: University of California Press, 1967), pp. 71–72.

20. Glade and Anderson, *Political Economy*, p. 121.

21. Shafer, *Mexican Business Organizations*, p. 34.

22. Personal interview with Antonio Martínez Báez, Mexico City, March 6, 1986.

23. James D. Cockcroft, *Mexico, Class Formation, Capital Accumulation, and the State* (New York: Monthly Review Press, 1983), p. 128.

24. Patricia Fagen, *Exiles and Citizens: Spanish Republicans in Mexico* (Austin: University of Texas Press, 1973).

25. Personal interview with Carlos Abedrop, Mexico City, August 29, 1983.

26. Vernon, *Dilemma*, p. 88.

27. Solís, "Mexican Economic Policy," p. 5.

28. Julio Lebastida Martín del Campo, "De la Unidad Nacional al Desarrollo Estabilizador, 1940–1970," in Pablo González Casanova, ed., *América Latina*, vol. 2 (Mexico City: Siglo XXI, 1981), p. 357.

29. Newell and Rubio, *Mexico's Dilemma*, p. 23.

30. Cockcroft, *Mexico*, p. 145.

31. William P. Glade, "Mexico: Party-Led Development," in Robert Wesson, ed., *Politics, Policies, and Economic Development in Latin America* (Stanford: Hoover Institution Press, 1984), p. 98.

32. Menno Vellinga, *Economic Development and the Dynamics of Class, Industrialization, Power and Control in Monterrey, Mexico* (Netherlands: Van Gocum Assen, 1979), p. 33.

33. Vernon, *Dilemma*, p. 100.

34. Wilkie, *Mexican Revolution*, p. 278.

35. Personal interview with Carlos Abedrop.

36. Manuel Camacho, "El poder: estado o 'feudos' políticos," *Foro Internacional* 14 (1974):88.

37. Solís, "Mexican Economic Policy," p. 4.

38. Vernon, *Dilemma*, p. 108.

39. Newell and Rubio, *Mexico's Dilemma*, p. 101ff.

40. Vernon, *Dilemma*, p. 122.

41. Personal interview with Eduardo Bustamante, Mexico City, July 19, 1984.

42. Basáñez, *La lucha por la hegemonía en México*, p. 173.

43. Newell and Rubio, *Mexico's Dilemma*, p. 103.

44. Ibid., p. 108.

45. Basáñez, *La lucha por la hegemonía en México*, p. 139.

46. Vernon, *Dilemma*, p. 88.

47. Laurence Whitehead, "Mexico from Bust to Boom: A Political Evaluation of the 1976–1979 Stabilization Programme," *World Development* 8 (1980):845.

48. Personal interview with Carlos Abedrop.

49. Kenneth M. Coleman and Charles L. Davis, "Preemptive Reform and the Mexican Working Class," *Latin American Research Review* 18, 1 (1983):19.

50. Edward C. Epstein, "Business-Government Relations in Mexico: The Echeverría Challenge to the Existing Development Model," *Journal of International Law* 12 (Summer 1980):537.

51. John F. Purcell and Susan K. Purcell, "The State and Economic Enterprise in Mexico: The Limits of Reform," in *Nueva Política* 1 (April–June 1976):233.

52. Edward C. Epstein, "Introduction to Recent Developments in Mexican Law: Politics of Modern Nationalism," *Denver Journal of International Law and Policy* 4 (Spring 1974):11.

53. Newell and Rubio, *Mexico's Dilemma*, p. 134.

54. Steven E. Sanderson, *Agrarian Populism and the Mexican State* (Berkeley: University of California Press, 1981), p. 172.

55. Whitehead, "Mexico from Bust to Boom," p. 845 and Epstein, "Business-Government Relations," p. 540.

56. Basáñez, *La lucha por la hegemonía en México*, p. 19.

57. Dale Story, "Trade Politics in the Third World: A Case Study of the Mexican GATT Decision," *International Organization* 36 (Autumn 1982):670; Carlos Arriola, "Las organizaciones empresariales contemporáneas," in Centro de Estudios Internacionales, *Lecturas de política mexicana* (Mexico City: El Colegio de México, 1977), p. 351; and Epstein, "Business-Government Relations," p. 527.

58. Francisco Ortiz Pinchetti, "A la crisis del gobierno corresponde la quiebra de su socio Alfa," *Proceso*, May 17, 1982, p. 7.

59. Steven E. Sanderson, "Presidential Succession and Political Rationality in Mexico," *World Politics* 35 (April 1983):322.

60. Personal interview with Pedro Sánchez Mejorada, Mexico City, August 30, 1983.

61. Newell and Rubio, *Mexico's Dilemma*, p. 202.

62. Basáñez, *La lucha por la hegemonía en México*, p. 193.

63. Leopoldo Solís and Ernesto Zedillo, "A Few Considerations on the Foreign Debt of Mexico," unpublished paper, Bank of Mexico, April 1984, p. 5.

64. Dale Story, "Development Strategies in an Oil-Exporting, Advanced-Developing Nation: the Case of Mexico," paper presented at the International Studies Association, March 24–27, 1982, Cincinnati, Oh., p. 5.

65. William Chislett, "The Causes of Mexico's Financial Crisis and the Lessons To Be Learned," in George Philip, ed., *Politics in Mexico* (London: Croom Helm, 1984), p. 5.

66. Clark C. Reynolds, "Why Mexico's 'Stabilizing Development' Was Actually Destabilizing," *World Development* 6 (1978):1016.

67. Wayne Cornelius, "Political Liberalization in an Authoritarian Regime: Mexico," in Judith Gentleman, ed., *Mexican Politics in Transition* (Boulder: Westview Press, 1987), p. 20.

68. Basáñez, *La lucha por la hegemonía en México*, p. 206 and Carlos Arriola, "Los empresarios tras el estado," *Nexos*, no. 14 (February 1979), pp. 3–4.

69. Dale Story, "Trade Politics in Mexico: GATT and the 'Song of the Sirens'," paper presented at the Annual Meeting of the Southwest Political Science Association, 1981, Dallas, Texas, p. 33 and "Trade Politics in the

Third World: a Case Study of the Mexican GATT Decision," *International Organization* 36 (Autumn 1982):767-793.

70. Alejandro Junco, "Mexico's Private Sector Reels Under Government Control," *Wall Street Journal*, June 29, 1984, p. 29.

71. *Hispano Americano*, February 28, 1983, p. 26.

72. Personal interview with Miguel de la Madrid, Mexico City, July 20, 1984.

73. Personal interview with Bernardo Quintana Arrioja, Mexico City, August 29, 1983.

74. Personal interview with Mauricio Soler Montesinos, Mexico City, February 24, 1983.

75. Wayne Cornelius, "Political Liberalization in an Authoritarian Regime," p. 22.

76. Dale Story, *The Mexican Ruling Party, Stability and Authority* (New York: Praeger, 1986).

77. John Bailey, "The Impact of Major Groups in Policy-Making Trends in Government-Business Relations in Mexico," in Roderic A. Camp, ed., *Mexico's Political Stability, the Next Five Years* (Boulder: Westview Press, 1986), p. 133; Wayne Cornelius, "The Political Economy of Mexico Under de la Madrid, Austerity, Routinized Crisis, and Nascent Recovery," *Mexican Studies* 1 (Winter 1985):83-124.

78. Saúl David Escobar, "Rifts in the Mexican Power Elite, 1976-1986," in Sylvia Maxfield, *Government and Private Sector in Contemporary Mexico* (La Jolla: Center for U.S.-Mexican Studies, 1987), pp. 84-86.

79. Normal Bailey and Richard Cohen, *The Mexican Time Bomb* (New York: Priority Press, 1982), p. 35.

80. William P. Glade, "Economic Analysis: Mexico," unpublished paper, Country Risk Analysis, Fund for Multinational Management Education, May 17-19, 1983, p. 11.

81. Newell and Rubio, *Mexico's Dilemma*, p. 87.

82. Personal interview with Jorge Canales Elorduy, Mexico City, February 28, 1983.

Chapter 3

1. Derossi, *Mexican Entrepreneur*, p. 1971.

2. Albert Lauterbach, *Enterprise in Latin America, Business Attitudes in a Developing Economy* (Ithaca: Cornell University Press, 1966), xi.

3. Aitkens, "The Future of Entrepreneurial Research," *Explorations in Entrepreneurial History* 1 (1963-1964):5.

4. Ibid., p. 6.

5. Lauterbach, *Enterprise*, p. 5.

6. Personal interview with Sealtiel Alatriste, Mexico City, May 27, 1982.

7. Personal interview with Jorge Sánchez Mejorada, Mexico City, May 16, 1985.

8. Personal interview with Rómulo O'Farrill, Mexico City, August 1, 1984. One can argue that this statement is merely a businessman's rhetoric. For many it is. For others it is sincere, but always moderated by the goals of a competitive, quality product.

9. Personal interview with Jorge Sánchez Mejorada.

10. Personal interview with Gabriel Alarćon, Mexico City, May 20, 1985.

11. Oscar Handlin, "A Note on Social Mobility and the Recruitment of Entrepreneurs in the United States," *Explorations in Entrepreneurial History* 8, special number (1956):4.

12. Personal interview with Federico Ortiz Alvarez, Mexico City, May 20, 1985.

13. Personal interview with Ernesto Canales, Mexico City, May 20, 1985.

14. Personal interview with Ernesto Canales; Derossi, *Mexican Entrepreneur*, p. 38.

15. Personal interview with Mauricio Soler Montesinos, Toluca, Mexico, February 24, 1983.

16. Derossi, *Mexican Entrepreneur*, pp. 48, 50.

17. Dale Story, *Industry, the State and Public Policy in Mexico* (Austin: University of Texas Press, 1986), p. 116.

18. Whiting, Jr., "Private Power," p. 21; and Derossi, *Mexican Entrepreneur*, p. 28.

19. Purcell and Purcell, "Mexican Business and Public Policy," p. 214.

20. Personal interview with Mario Segura Quiroz, Mexico City, July 26, 1984.

21. Gabriel Zaid, "Pagar la deuda, como puede repetirse 1982," *Vuelta* 8, no. 89 (April 1984):7.

22. Dilmus D. James, "Mexico's Recent Science and Technology Planning, an Outsider Economist's Critique," *Journal of Inter-American Studies and World Affairs*, 22 (May 1980):163–193.

23. Vernon, *Dilemma*, p. 158.

24. Personal interview with Ernesto Robles Levi, Mexico City, May 21, 1985.

25. Personal interview with Emilio Goicochea Luna, Mexico City, August 24, 1983.

26 Personal interview with Eduardo Bustamante, Mexico City, July 19, 1984.

27. *The Making of a Government, Political Leaders in Modern Mexico*, (Tuscon: University of Arizona Press, 1984).

28. Robert Scott, "Mexico: the Established Revolution," in Lucian Pye and Sidney Verba, eds., *Political Culture and Political Development* (Princeton: Princeton University Press, 1965), p. 373.

29. Personal interview with Emilio Goicochea Luna.

30. Personal interview with Alfonso Pasquel, Mexico City, May 24, 1985.

31. Personal interview with José María Basagoiti, Mexico City, August 24, 1983.

32. Jorge Camerena and Pablo Lasso, *Hacía un estilo propio de dirección de empresas, proyecto piloto, Guadalajara, México* (Washington, D. C.: IDB, 1984), p. 60.

33. Personal interview with Enrique Krauze, Mexico City, May 26, 1982.

34. Lauterbach, *Enterprise*, p. 168.

35. Albert Lauterbach, "Government and Development: Managerial Attitudes in Latin America," *Journal of Inter-American Studies*, 3, no. 2 (April 1965):225.

36. Personal interview with Ernesto Canales.

37. Personal interview with Enrique Krauze.

38. James Wallace Dull, "Effects of Multinational Corporations in Mexico on the Attitudes of Mexican Executives," Ph.D. dissertation, Columbia University, 1981, p. 193.

39. Derossi, *Mexican Entrepreneur*, p. 179.

40. Personal interview with Max Michel Suberville, Mexico City, May 15, 1985.

41. Personal interview with Jorge Sánchez Mejorada.

42. Personal interview with Ernesto Canales.

43. Personal interview with José María Basagoiti.

44. Epstein, "Business-Government Relations, p. 526.

45. Personal interview with Federico Ortiz Alvarez.

46. Personal interview with Jaime Sánchez Montemayor, Mexico City, August 25, 1983.

47. Dale Story, "Industrial Elites in Mexico, Political Ideology and Influence," *Journal of Inter-American Studies and World Affairs* 25, no. 3 (August 1983):366; and "Development Strategies," p. 27.

48. Personal interview with Jorge Sánchez Mejorada.

49. Womack, Jr., "The Spoils of the Mexican Revolution," *Foreign Affairs* 48 (July 1970):682.

50. Derossi, *Mexican Entrepreneur*, p. 187.

51. Presidencia de la República, Coordinación General del Sistema Nacional de Evaluación, "Sonedo de Opinión Pública sobre la Nacionalización de la Banca," November 1982.

52. Derossi, *Mexican Entrepreneur*, p. 188.

53. Dull, "Effects of Multinational Corporations," p. 146.

54. Vellinga, *Economic Development*, p. 84.

55. Carlos Arriola, "Las organizaciones empresariales contemporáneas," in Centro de Estudios Internacionales, *Lecturas de política mexicana* (Mexico City: El Colegio de México, 1977), p. 336.

56. Interview with Max Michel Suberville.

57. Interview with Federico Ortiz Alvarez; Sylvia Maxfield, "Losing Command of the Heights: Bank Nationalization and the Mexican State," paper presented to the National Latin American Studies Association, April 17–22, 1985, Albuquerque, N. M., p. 30.

58. Ricardo Tirado Segura, *Las organizaciones empresariales mexicanas: pérfil y control durante los sesentas* (Mexico City: Instituto de Investigaciones Sociales, Universidad Autónomo de México, 1979), p. 101.

59. Personal interview with Federico Ortiz Alvarez.

60. Personal interview with Guillermo Cantú, Mexico City, May 22, 1985.

61. Segura, *Las organizaciones empresariales mexicanas*, p. 97.

62. Camp, *Making of a Government*, pp. 125–150.

63. Personal interview with Antonio Martínez Báez, Mexico City, October 28, 1976.

64. Austin, "Development of Economic Policy," p. 115.

65. Personal interview with Agustín Salvat Rodríguez, Mexico City, October 20, 1976.

66. Personal interview with Eduardo Bustamante, Mexico City, October 28, 1976.

67. Interview with Jaime Sánchez Montemayor.

68. Personal interview with Hugo B. Margáin, Washington, D. C., March 14, 1977.

69. Personal interview with Miguel de la Madrid, Mexico City, July 20, 1984.

70. Basáñez, *La lucha por la hegemonía en México*, p. 75.

71. Smith, *Labyrinths*, p. 147.

72. Personal interview with Jorge Sánchez Mejorada.

Chapter 4

1. Suzanne I. Keller, *The Social Origins and Career Lines of Three Generations of American Business Leaders* (New York: Arno Press, 1980), p. 59.

2. Albert Lipman, "Social Backgrounds of the Bogota Entrepreneur," *Journal of Inter-American Studies and World Affairs* 7 (April 1965):232.

3. Vernon, *Dilemma*, p. 157.

4. Derossi, *Mexican Entrepreneur*, pp. 164–165.

5. Arthur Liebman, et al., *Latin American University Students: A Six Nation Study* (Cambridge: Harvard University Press, 1972), p. 37.

6. Guy Benveniste, *Bureaucracy and National Planning, A Sociological Case Study in Mexico* (New York: Praeger, 1970), p. 127.

7. Derossi, *Mexican Entrepreneur*, p. 164.

8. Reinhard Bendix and Seymour Martin Lipset, *Social Mobility in Industrial Society* (Berkeley: University of California Press, 1959), p. 125.

9. Thomas R. Dye, *Who's Running America? Institutional Leadership in the United States* (Englewood Cliffs, N. J.: Prentice-Hall, 1976), p. 152.

10. Sidney H. Aronson, *Status and Kinship in the Higher Civil Service* (Cambridge: Harvard University Press, 1964), p. 99; and Kenneth Prewitt, *The Recruitment of Political Leaders: A Study of Citizen Politicians* (Indianapolis: Bobbs-Merrill, 1970), p. 32.

11. Leonard Cohen, "The Social Background and Recruitment of Yugoslav Political Elites, 1918–1948," in Allen H. Barton, et al., eds., *Opinion-Making Elites in Yugoslavia* (New York: Praeger, 1973), p. 47 and Robert C. North and Ithiel de Sola Pool, "Kuomintang and Chinese Communist Elites," in Harold D. Lasswell and Daniel Lerner, eds., *World Revolutionary Elites* (Cambridge, Mass.: MIT Press, 1966), p. 377.

12. Camp, *Mexico's Leader*, p. 42.

13. Camp, *Intellectuals*,

14. Vernon, *Dilemma*, p.157.

15. Derossi, *Mexican Entrepreneur*, p. 137.

16. James W. Wilkie and Paul D. Wilkins, "Quantifying the Class Structure of Mexico, 1895–1970," in *Statistical Abstract of Latin America*, vol. 21 (Los Angeles: UCLA Latin American Center, 1981), p. 589.

17. Lipman, "Social Backgrounds," p. 233.

18. Carl S. Joslyn and Frank W. Taussiug, *American Business Leaders: A Study in Social Origins and Social Stratification* (New York: MacMillan, 1932), p. 241.

19. Paul Duncan-Jones and Rosemary G. Stewart, "Educational Background and Career History of British Managers, with Some American Comparisons," *Explorations in Entrpreneurial History* 9 (December 1956):61; and Stuart Adams, "Trends in Occupational Origins of Business Leaders," *American Sociological Review*, 19 (October 1954):548.

20. Alex M. Saragoza, "Behind the Scenes: Media Ownership, Politics and Popular Culture in Mexico, 1930–1958," in Charles A. Hale, Roderic A. Camp, and Josefina Vázquez, eds., *The State and Intellectual Life in Mexico* (Los Angeles: UCLA Latin American Center, forthcoming).

21. Mark Wasserman, "Patterns of Family Alliances in the Mexican Revolution: The Case of Chihuahua," paper presented to the Annual Meeting of the American Historical Association, December, 1980, Washington, D. C., p. 2.

22. Smith, *Labyrinths*, p. 178.

23. Bendix, *Social Mobility*, p. 122.

24. Joslyn and Taussing, *American Business Leaders*, pp. 233–234.

25. Keller, *Social Origins and Career Lines*, p. 61.

26. Derossi, *Mexican Entrepreneur*, p. 160.

27. Adams, "Trends in Occupation Origins," p. 548.

28. Derossi, *Mexican Entrepreneur*, p. 160.

29. Keller, *Social Origins* p. 150.

30. Joseph S. Szyliowicz, "Elite Recruitment in Turkey: The Role of the Mulkiye," *World Politics* 23 (April 1971):396.

31. Jorge Camarena and Pablo Lasso, *Hacía un estilo propio de dirección de empresas, proyecto piloto, Guadalajara, México* (Washington, D. C.: Inter-American Development Bank, 1984), p. 101.

32. George R. Andrews, "Toward a Reevaluation of the Latin American Family Firm: The Industry Executives of Monterrey," *Inter-American Economic Affairs* 30 (Winter 1976):37.

33. Larissa Lomnitz and Marisol Pérez Lizaur, "The History of an Urban Upper-Class Family in Mexico," *Journal of Family History* (Winter 1978):407.

34. Larissa Lomnitz, "Horizontal and Vertical Relations and the Social Structure of Urban Mexico," unpublished manuscript, 1980, p. 29.

35. Story, "Industrial Elites," p. 359.

36. Derossi, *Mexican Entrepreneur*, p. 144.

37. Lipman, "Social Backgrounds," p. 231.

38. Keller, *Social Origins and Career Lines*, p. 41.

39. Mabel Newcomer, *The Big Business Executive* (New York: Columbia University Press, 1955), p. 43.

40. Personal interview with Emilio Goicochea Luna, Mexico City, August 24, 1983.

41. Personal interview with Carlos Abedrop, Mexico City, August 29, 1983.

42. Personal interview with Jacobo Zaidenweber, Mexico City, August 29, 1983.

43. Bendix, *Social Mobility*, p. 132.

44. Keller, *Social Origins and Career Lines*, Table 19.

45. Arthur S. Banks, *Cross-Polity Times Series Data* (Cambridge, Mass.: MIT Press, 1967), p. 224.

46. Andrews, "Toward a Reevaluation," p. 33.

47. Camarena, *Hacia un proyecto*, p. 47.

48. Keller, *Social Origins and Career Lines*, p. 74.

49. George A. Sand, "An Analysis of Selected Aspects of the Business Administration Programs in Mexico," Ph.D. dissertation, Illinois State University, 1975, p. 100.

50. Richard A. LaBarge and T. Noel Osborn, "The Status of Professional Economics Programs in Mexican Universities," *Inter-American Economic Affairs* 31 (Summer, 1977), p. 9.

51. Ibid. p. 13.

52. Andrews, "Toward a Reevaluation," p. 34.

53. LaBarge, "The Status of Professional Economics Programs," p. 12.

54. Donald Mabry, *The Mexican University and the State*, (College Station: Texas A & M Press, 1982), p. 218.

55. Lipman, "Social Backgrounds," pp. 231–232.

56. Francisco Ortiz Pinchetti, "El grupo Monterrey crea sus propias fábricas de hombres," *Proceso*, June 23, 1980, p. 12.

57. Keller, *Social Origins and Career Lines*, p. 82.

58. Personal interview with Alejandro J. Dumán Urrea, State of Mexico, March 1, 1983.

59. Personal interview with Rómulo O'Farrill, Mexico City, August 1, 1984.

60. Keller, *Social Origins and Career Lines*, p. 82.

61. G. William Domhoff, *The Powers That Be, Processes of Ruling-Class Domination in America* (New York: Random House, 1978), p. 18.

62. Ibid., p. 19.

63. Personal interview with Jorge Sánchez Mejorada, Mexico City, May 16, 1985.

64. Personal interview with Federico Ortiz Alvarez, Mexico City, May 20, 1985.

65. Ibid.

66. Smith, *Labyrinths*, pp. 13–14.

67. Nelson W. Polsby, *Community Power and Political Theory*, (New Haven: Yale University Press, 1974), p. 106.

68. Camp, *Making of a Government*, p. 156.

69. Richard Centers, "Children of the New Deal: Social Stratification and Adolescent Attitudes," in Reinhard Bendix and Seymour Martin Lipset, eds., *Class, Status and Power* (New York: Free Press, 1953), p. 361.

70. Oscar Handlin, "A Note on Social Mobility and the Recruitment of Entrepreneurs in the United States," *Explorations in Entrepreneurial History* 8 (1956):2.

71. Personal interview with Ernesto Canales, Mexico City, May 20, 1985.

72. Vellinga, *Economic Development*, p. 27.

73. Alonso Aguilar Monteverde, "Concentración y centralización del capital," in Alonso Aguilar Monteverde and Fernando Carmona, *México: Riqueza y Miseria* (Mexico City: Editorial Nuestro Tiempo, 1976), p. 76.

74. Andrews, "Toward a Reevaluation," p. 32.

75. Smith, *Labyrinths*, p. 79.

76. Carl Leiden and Karl M. Schmitt, *The Politics of Violence: Revolution in the Modern World* (Engelwood Cliffs, N. J.: Prentice-Hall, 1968), p. 135.

Chapter 5

1. William S. Langston, "Coahuila in the Porfiriato, 1893–1911: A Study of Political Elites," Ph.D. dissertation, Tulane University, 1980, p. 61.

2. Linda Lewin, "Family-based Politics in the Brazilian Northeast," *Comparative Studies in Society and History* 21 (April 1979):292.

3. Large landholders are combined with businessmen because land-ownership was the chief private-sector occupation of individuals with capital in the nineteenth century.

4. Nora Hamilton, for example, has several excellent illustrations, but no evidence that they were typical. See her *Limits of State Autonomy*, p. 33 and "State and National Bourgeoisie," p. 51.

5. Julio Labastida Martín del Campo, "Los grupos dominantes frente a las alternativas de cambio," *El pérfil de México en 1980*, vol. 3 (Mexico City: Siglo XXI, 1972), p. 107.

6. Derossi, *Mexican Entrepreneur*, p. 162.

7. Camp, *Mexico's Leaders*, p. 62.

8. James G. Maddox, "Economic Growth and Revolution in Mexico," *Land Economics* 36 (August 1960):272.

9. Joslyn and Taussiug, *American Business Leaders*, p. 245.

10. Peter J. Freitag, "The Cabinet and Big Business: A Study of Interlocks," *Social Problems* 23 (December 1975):148.

11. Smith, *Labyrinths*, pp. 213–215.

12. Personal interview with Alonso Aguilar Monteverde, Mexico City, July 20, 1984 and his article, "Concentración y centralización del capital," in Alonso Aguilar Monteverde and Fernando Carmona, *México: Riqueza y Miseria* (Mexico City: Editorial Nuestro Tiempo, 1976), p. 79.

13. Whiting, Jr., "Private Power," p. 113.

14. Alonso Aguilar Monteverde, "La oligarquía," in Jorge Carrión and Alonso Aguilar, *La burguesía, la oligarquía y el estado* (Mexico City: Editorial Nuestro Tiempo, 1972), p. 193.

15. Keller, *Social Origins and Career Lines*, p. 178.

16. Andrews, "Toward a Reevaluation," p. 31.

17. Personal interview with Ernesto Canales, Mexico City, May 20, 1985.

18. Vellinga, *Economic Development*, p. 34.

19. Derossi, *Mexican Entrepreneur*, p. 109.

20. Personal interview with Alejandro J. Dumán Urrea, Mexico City, March 1, 1983.

21. Interview with Ernesto Canales.

22. Peter Cheng, "The Japanese Cabinets, 1885–1973: An Elite Analysis," *Asian Survey* 14 (December 1974):1062; Paul H. Lewis, "The Spanish Ministerial Elite, 1938–1969," *Comparative Politics* 5 (October 1972):103; and Joseph Szyliowicz, "Elite Recruitment in Turkey: The Role of the Mulkiye," *World Politics* 23 (April 1971):378.

23. Charles N. Myers, *Education and National Development in Mexico* (Princeton: Princeton University Press, 1965), p. 112.

24. Rafael Segovia, *La politización del niño mexicano* (Mexico City: El Colegio de Mexico, 1975), pp. 36–37, 40.

25. Soledad Loaeza, "Mesocracía o Mediocracía?," *Dialogos*, no. 114 (November–December 1983), p. 34.

26. James C. Abegglen, "Recruitment of Business Leaders," *Business History Review* 29 (March 1955):78.

27. David Barkin, "Education and Class Structure: The Dynamics of Social Control in Mexico," *Politics and Society* 5, no. 2 (1975), p. 188.

28. Rosalio Wences Reza, *El movimiento estudiantil y los problemas nacionales* (Mexico City: Editorial Nuestro Tiempo, 1971), pp. 124–25.

29. Lewis J. Edinger, "Post-Totalitarian Leadership in the German Federal Republic," *American Political Science Review* 54 (March 1960):77.

30. Daniel C. Levy, *Private Education in Latin America* (Chicago: University of Chicago Press, 1986); and Myers, *Education and National Development*, p. 105.

31. Maxfield, "Losing Command," p. 74.

32. *Hispano Americano*, November 5, 1984, pp. 12–13.

33. Personal interview with Emilio Goicochea Luna, Mexico City, August 24, 1983.

34. Personal interview with Alfonso Pasquel, Mexico City, May 24, 1985.

35. Thomas N. Osborn, *Higher Education in Mexico* (El Paso: Texas Western Press, 1976), pp. 56–57.

36. Francisco Suárez Farias, "Composición y comportamiento de la elite política de México (1976–1984)," unpublished paper, UNAM, 1984, p. 23.

37. Theda Skocpol, "Bringing the State Back In: Strategies of Analysis in Current Research," in Evans, Rueschemeyer, and Skocpol, *Bringing the State Back In*, p. 16.

38. Personal interview with Fernando Baqueiro, Mexico City, June 2, 1982.

39. Personal interview with Ernesto Canales, Mexico City, May 20, 1985.

40. Personal interview with Carlos E. Represas, Mexico City, March 3, 1986.

41. Personal interview with Jorge Sánchez Mejorada, Mexico City, May 15, 1985.

42. Personal interview with Hugo B. Margáin, Mexico City, August 26, 1983.

43. Szyliowicz, "Elite Recruitment in Turkey," pp. 389–390.

44. Ellen Kay Trimberger, *Revolution from Above: Military Bureaucrats and Development in Japan, Turkey, Egypt and Peru* (New Brunswick: Transaction Books, 1978).

45. Roderic Ai Camp, "The Technocrat in Mexico and the Survival of the Political System," *Latin American Research Review* 20, no. 1 (1985), pp. 97–118.

46. Personal interview with Antonio Ortiz Mena, Mexico City, January 24, 1984.

47. Larissa Lomnitz and Jacqueline Fortes, "Socialization of Scientists: The Ideal Model," unpublished paper, 1980, p. 4; and Camp, *Intellectuals*, p. 93–94.

48. Mary Matossian, "Ideologies of Delayed Industrialization," in Jason Finkle and Richard Gable, eds., *Political Development and Social Change* (New York: Wiley, 1973), p. 115.

49. "Yale donde vive usted, una perspectiva de los enlaces entre Yale y México," unpublished paper, Mexico City, Graduados de Yale, April 1976, p. 2.

50. Personal interview with Jacobo Zaidenweber, Mexico City, August 29, 1983.

51. Personal interview with Hugo B. Margáin.

52. Personal interview with Gerard Van Heuven, Washington, D.C., September 27, 1983.

53. Angela M. Delli Sante, "The Private Sector, Business Organizations, and International Influence: A Case Study of Mexico," in Richard R. Fagen, ed., *Capitalism and the State in U.S.-Latin American Relations* (Stanford: Stanford University Press, 1979), p. 365.

54. Personal interview with Antonio Armendáriz, Mexico City, May 24, 1982.

55. Personal interview with Ernesto Canales.

56. Personal interview with José María Basagoiti, Mexico City, August 24, 1983.

57. Personal interview with Manuel Hinojosa Ortiz, Mexico City, May 20, 1985.

58. Personal interview with Antonio Martínez Báez, Mexico City, March 6, 1986.

59. Personal interview with Carlos E. Represas.

60. This point is discussed in the Mexican context in Miguel Basáñez, "México ante las cultural combativas y contemplativas, comentarios a *El Hombre Público*," unpublished paper, Universidad Autónoma del Estado de México, 1986, p. 8.

61. Oscar Handlin, "A Note on Social Mobility and the Recruitment of Entrepreneurs in the United States," *Explorations in Entrepreneurial History* 8 (1956):4.

62. Reinhard Bendix and Seymour Martin Lipset, *Social Mobility in Industrial Society* (Berkeley: University of California Press, 1959), p. 143.

63. *Hispano Americano*, April 1, 1986, p. 13.

64. Personal interview with Pedro Sánchez Mejorada.

65. Personal interview with Eugenio Clariond Reyes, Monterrey, March 5, 1986.

Chapter 6

1. Stephen N. Kane, "American Businessmen and Foreign Policy: The Recognition of Mexico, 1920–1923," *Political Science Quarterly* 90 (Summer 1975):296.

2. Mostafa Rejai, "Toward the Comparative Study of Political Decision-Makers," *Comparative Political Studies* (October 1960):351.

3. Guy Benveniste, *Bureaucracy and National Planning, A Sociological Case Study in Mexico* (New York: Praeger, 1970), p. 57.

4. Van Whiting, Jr., "Political and Institutional Aspects of Technology Transfer in Mexico," unpublished paper, 1980, p. 46.

5. Martin H. Greenberg, *Bureaucracy and Development: A Mexican Case Study* (Lexington: D. C. Heath, 1970), p. 57.

6. Wilkie, *Mexican Revolution*, p. 6.

7. Eduardo Suárez, *Comentarios y recuerdos, 1926–1946* (Mexico: Editorial Porrúa, 1977), p. 107.

8. Antonio Carrillo Flores, "Introdución," in Suárez, *Comentariós*, p. xli.

9. Lawrence S. Graham, *Politics in a Mexican Community* (Gainesville: University of Florida Press, 1968), p. 23.

10. Glade and Anderson, *Political Economy*, p. 129.

11. Personal interview with Armando Baqueiro, Mexico City, May 23, 1982.

12. *Proceso*, May 17, 1982, p. 24.

13. Personal interview with Ernesto Robles Levi, Mexico City, May 21, 1985.

14. Personal interview with Carlos Mireles, Mexico City, August 1, 1984.

15. Eveyln Stevens, *Protest and Response in Mexico* (Cambridge, Mass.: MIT Press, 1974), p. 283.

16. Larissa Lomnitz, "The Latin American University: Breeding Ground of the New State Elites," paper presented at the American Association of Anthropological Sciences, January 3–6, 1979, Houston, p. 6.

17. George W. Grayson, *The Politics of Mexican Oil* (Pittsburgh: University of Pittsburgh Press, 1980), p. 58; Story, "Development Strategies," p. 4; and personal interview with Agustín Caso, Washington, D.C., May 28, 1984.

18. Benveniste, *Bureaucracy*, p. 11.

19. James W. Wilkie, *Los Angeles Times*, December 5, 1976, p. 20.

20. Personal interview with Guillermo Sánchez Fábela, Toluca, February 25, 1983.

21. Personal interview with Roberto Arce, Mexico City, July 20, 1984.

22. Personal interview with René Becerra, Mexico City, May 31, 1982.

23. Personal interview with Mario Segura Quiroc, Mexico City, July 26, 1984.

24. Personal interview with Ernesto Robles Levi.

25. Personal interview with Pedro Daniel Martínez García, Mexico City, May 16, 1985.

26. Derossi, *Mexican Entrepreneur*, p. 174.

27. Ibid., p. 40.

28. Aurora Loyo Brambila and Ricardo Pozas Horcasitas, "Notes on the Mechanisms of Control Exercised by the Mexican State over the Organized Sector of the Working Class, A Case Study: the Political Crisis of 1958," Paper presented to the Center for Inter-American Relations, 1975, p. 55 and Purcell, *Mexican Profit-Sharing Decision*, p. 142.

29. Whiting, Jr., "Private Power," p. 17.

30. Story, "Industrial Elites," p. 370.

31. Ibid., pp. 369–370.

32. Purcell and Purcell, "Mexican Business and Public Policy," p. 193.

33. Personal interview with Ernesto Robles Levi.

34. Personal interview with Pedro Sánchez Mejorada, Mexico City, August 30, 1983.

35. Personal interview with Emilio Goicochea Luna, Mexico City, August 24, 1983; and personal interview with Mauricio Soler Montesinos, Toluca, February 24, 1983.

36. Personal interview with José María Basagoiti, Mexico City, August 24, 1983.

37. Personal interview with Andrés Marcelo Sada Zambrano, Mexico City, March 4, 1986.

38. Personal interview with José María Basagoiti.

39. Personal interview with Jorge Canales Elorduy, Toluca, February 28, 1983.

40. Personal interview with Eugenio Clariond Reyes, Monterrey, March 5, 1986.

41. Personal interview with Hugo B. Margáin, Mexico City, August 26, 1983.

42. Personal interview with Antonio Ortiz Mena, Washington, D.C., January 24, 1984.

43. Richard Newfarmer and William Mueller, *Multinational Corporations in Brazil and Mexico* (Washington, D.C.: U.S. Senate, 1975), p. 63.

44. Epstein, "Business-Government Relations," pp. 533–34.

45. Derossi, *Mexican Entrepreneur*, p. 69.

46. Douglas C. Bennett and Kenneth E. Sharpe, "Agenda Setting and Bargaining Power: The Mexican State versus Transnational Automobile Corporations," *World Politics* 32 (1979):88.

47. Interview with Alonso Aguilar Monteverde, Mexico City, July 20, 1984.

48. James D. Cockcroft, *Mexico*, p. 184.

49. Lorenzo Meyer, *Los grupos de presión extranjera en el México*

revolucionario, 1910–1940 (Mexico City: Secretaría de Relaciones Exteriores, 1973), p. 62.

50. Basáñez, *La lucha por la hegemonía en México*, p. 96.

51. Derossi, *Mexican Entrepreneur*, p. 55.

52. Dull, "Effects of Multinational Corporations," p. 121.

53. Ibid., p. 145.

54. Merle Kling, *A Mexican Interest Group in Action* (Englewood Cliffs, N.J.: Prentice-Hall, 1961), p. 19.

55. Dull, "Effects of Multinational Corporations," p. 179.

56. Personal interview with Bernardo Galei, Mexico City, March 3, 1986.

57. Personal interview with Ernesto Robles Levi.

58. Personal interview with Carlos Mireles.

59. Personal interview with Roberto Arce.

60. Personal interview with Cresencio Ballesteros, Mexico City, July 26, 1984.

61. Personal interview with Carlos E. Represas, Mexico City, March 3, 1986 and personal interview with Antonio Martínez Báez, Mexico City, March 6, 1986.

62. Interview with René Becerra.

63. Personal interview with Emilio Alanís Patiño, Mexico City, May 26, 1982.

64. Personal interview with Emilio Goicochea Luna.

65. Personal interview with Jaime Sánchez Montemayor.

66. Personal interview with José Juan de Olloqui, Mexico City, October 4, 1983.

67. Story, "Industrial Elites," p. 366.

68. Derossi, *Mexican Entrepreneur*, pp. 175–176.

69. Cockcroft, *Mexico*, p. 218.

70. Howard Handleman, "The Politics of Labor Protest in Mexico: Two Case Studies," *Journal of Inter-American Studies and World Affairs* 18 (August 1976):272–273.

71. Personal interview with Antonio Ortiz Mena.

72. Rafael Segovia, "Ante las elecciones," *Vuelta* 6, (July 1982):41.

73. Epstein, "Business-Government Relations," p. 532.

74. Shafer, *Mexican Business Organizations*, p. 42.

75. Newell and Rubio, *Mexico's Dilemma*, p. 99.

76. Purcell, *Mexican Profit-Sharing Decisions*, pp. 116, 122 and Frederic Meyers, *Party, Government and the Labor Movement in Mexico: Two Case Studies* (Los Angeles: UCLA Institute of Industrial Relations, 1967), p. 162.

77. Epstein, "Business-Government Relations," p. 539.

78. Personal interview with Emilio Goicochea Luna.

79. Personal interview with René Becerra.

80. Personal interview with Hugo B. Margáin.

81. Personal interview with Antonio Ortiz Mena.

82. Purcell and Purcell, "Mexican Business and Public Policy," p. 193.

83. Personal interview with René Becerra.

84. Personal interview with Jaime Sánchez Montemayor.

85. Dale Story, "Trade Politics in the Third World: A Case Study of the Mexican GATT Decision," *International Organization* 36 (Autumn 1982):780 and "Trade Politics in Mexico," p. 33.

86. Roderic A. Camp, *The Role of Economists in Policy-making, A Comparative Case Study of Mexico and the United States* (Tucson: University of Arizona Press, 1977), p. 56.

87. Kane, "American Businessmen," p. 296.

88. Enrique Krauze, "México: el Timón y la Tormenta," *Vuelta* 6 (October 1982):15 and personal interview with Ernesto Robles Levi.

89. Personal interview with Carlos Tello, Washington, D.C., February 22, 1984.

90. Maxfield, "Losing Command," p. 7.

91. Ibid., p. 54.

92. Personal interview with José Levy, Washington, D.C., May 30, 1984.

93. William P. Glade, "Mexico: Party-Led Development," in Robert Wesson, ed., *Politics, Policies, and Economic Development in Latin America* (Stanford: Hoover Institution Press, 1984), p. 105.

94. Personal interview with Antonio Ortiz Mena.

95. Roderic A. Camp and Miguel Basáñez, "The Nationalization of Banks and Mexican Public Opinion," *The Mexican Forum* 4 (April 1984):1–8.

96. Personal interview with Gabriel Zaid, Mexico City, October 6, 1983.

97. Personal interview with Ernesto Robles Levi.

98. Personal interview with Hugo B. Margáin.

99. William P. Glade, "Economic Analysis: Mexico," pp. 15–16.

100. Interview with Ernesto Canales, Mexico City, May 20, 1985.

101. Derossi, *Mexican Entrepreneur*, p. 183.

102. Nora Hamilton, "State-Class Alliances and Conflicts," *Latin American Perspectives* 11 (Fall 1984):18.

103. Glade, "Economic Analysis," pp. 15–16.

104. Personal interview with Carlos Tello.

105. Newell and Rubio, *Mexico's Dilemma*, p. 263.

106. Glade, "Mexico: Party-Led Development," pp. 105–106.

107. Glade, "Economic Analysis," p. 18.

108. Personal interview with Bernardo Quintana Arrijoa.

109. Personal interview with Carlos Abedrop, Mexico City, August 29, 1983.

110. Personal interview.
111. Personal interview with Carlos Mireles.
112. Personal interview with Antonio Martínez Báez.
113. Purcell, *Mexican Profit-Sharing Decision*, p. 78.
114. Personal interview with Andrés Marcelo Sada Zambrano, Mexico City, March 4, 1986.
115. Personal interview with Eugenio Clariond Reyes, Monterrey, March 5, 1986.
116. Personal interview with Fernando Canales Clariond, Monterrey, March 5, 1986.
117. Personal interview with Eduardo A. Elizondo, March 5, 1986.

Chapter 7
1. Karl Schmitt, "Church and State in Mexico: A Corporatist Relationship," *The Americas* 40 (January 1984):355.
2. Ibid., p. 350.
3. Vernon, *Dilemma*, p. 75.
4. Frank Brandenburg, "Organized Business in Mexico," *Inter-American Economic Affairs* 12 (Winter 1958):30.
5. Vernon, *Dilemma*, p. 21.
6. Frank Brandenburg, "Organized Business in Mexico," p. 36.
7. Personal interview with René Becerra, Mexico City, May 31, 1982.
8. Roderic A. Camp, "Organized Labor and the Mexican State: A Symbiotic Relationship?," *The Mexican Forum* 4 (October 1984):1-8; and *Intellectuals*, p. 223ff.
9. Brandenburg, "Organized Business in Mexico," p. 40.
10. Newell and Rubio, *Mexico's Dilemma*, p. 66.
11. Story, "Industrial Elites," p. 368.
12. Shafer, *Mexican Business Organizations*, p. 133.
13. *Hispano Americano*, February 7, 1983, p. 7.
14. *Hispano Americano*, February 28, 1983, p. 26.
15. *Excélsior*, May 28, 1984, p. 14.
16. Personal interview with Jorge Arrambide, Monterrey, March 5, 1986.
17. Personal interview with Antonio Martínez Báez, Mexico City, March 6, 1986.
18. Story, "Industrial Elites," p. 367.
19. Howard Handelman, "Oligarchy and Democracy in Two Mexican Labor Unions: a Test of Representational Theory," *Industrial and Labor Relations Review* 30, no. 2 (January 1977):205-218; and "The Politics of Labor Protest in Mexico: Two Case Studies," *Journal of Inter-American Studies and World Affairs* 18 (August 1976):267-294.

20. Personal interview with Eduardo Bustamante, Mexico City, July 19, 1984.

21. Nora Hamilton, "The State and the National Bourgeoisie in Post-revolutionary Mexico: 1920–1940," *Latin American Perspectives* 9 (Fall 1982):38.

22. Personal interview with Max Michel Suberville, Mexico City, May 15, 1985; and interview with Eduardo Bustamante.

23. Cockcroft, *Mexico*, p. 210.

24. Shafer, *Mexican Business Organizations*, p. 33; Marco Antonio Alcazar, *Las agrupaciones patronales en México* (Mexico: El Colegio de México, 1970), p. 98 and Segura, *Las organizaciones empresariales mexicanas*, p. 93.

25. Personal interview with Alfonso Pasquel, Mexico City, May 24, 1985.

26. Personal interview with Alejandro J. Dumán Urrea, Naucalpan, state of México, March 1, 1983.

27. Tirado Segura, *Las organizaciones empresariales mexicanas*, p. 35.

28. Personal interview with Emilio Goicochea Luna, Mexico City, August 24, 1983.

29. Tirado Segura, *Las organizaciones empresariales mexicanas*, p. 51.

30. Personal interview with Jorge Arrambide.

31. Basáñez, *La lucha por la hegemonía en México*, p. 161.

32. Personal interview with Alfredo Phillips Olmedo, Mexico City, May 24, 1985.

33. Tirado Segura, *Las organizaciones empresariales mexicanas*, p. 70.

34. Alcazar, *Las agrupaciones patronales*, p. 24.

35. Brandenburg, "Organized Business in Mexico," p. 35.

36. Sergio Zermeño, "De Echeverría a de la Madrid: las clases altas y el estado mexicano," paper presented at the Latin American Program, Woodrow Wilson International Center for Scholars, Smithsonian Institution, 1982, Washington, D.C., p. 25.

37. Vernon, *Dilemma*, p. 20.

38. Labastida Martín del Campo, "De la Unidad Nacional al Desarrollo Estabilizador, 1940–1970," in Pablo González Casanova, ed., *América Latina* 2 (Mexico City: Siglo XXI, 1981), p. 338.

39. Sanford Mosk, *The Industrial Revolution in Mexico* (Berkeley: University of California Press, 1950, p. 21.

40. Ibid., pp. 22, 27, 29.

41. Brandenburg, "Organized Business in Mexico," p. 35.

42. Dale Story, "Trade Politics in the Third World: a Case Study of the Mexican GATT Decision," *International Organization* 36 (Autumn 1982):785 and "Industrial Elites," p. 368.

43. Story, "Industrial Elites," p. 357.

44. Ibid., p. 356.

45. Ibid., p. 358.

46. Delli Sante, "Private Sector," p. 337.

47. Personal interview with Carlos Mireles, Mexico City, August 1, 1984.

48. Carlos Arriola, "Las organizaciones empresariales contemporáneas," in Centro de Estudios Internacionales," *Lecturas de política mexicana* (Mexico City: El Colegio de México, 1977), p. 337.

49. Story, "Industrial Elites," p. 359.

50. Tirado Segura, *Las organizaciones empresariales mexicanas*, p. 16.

51. Shafer, *Mexican Business Organizations*, p. 58.

52. Brandenburg, "Organized Business in Mexico," p. 42.

53. Shafer, *Mexican Business Organizations*, p. 37–38.

54. Coparmex, *Coparmex, su orígen y desarrollo* (Mexico City: Coparmex, 1979), p. 18.

55. Personal interview with José Levy, Washington, D.C., May 30, 1984.

56. Shafer, *Mexican Business Organizations*, p. 59.

57. Basáñez, *La lucha por la hegemonía en México*, p. 198.

58. Personal interview with José María Basagoiti, Mexico City, August 24, 1983.

59. Coparmex, *Coparmex*, p. 16.

60. Tirado Segura, *Las organizaciones empresariales mexicanas*, pp. 5–6.

61. Newell and Rubio, *Mexico's Dilemma*, p. 127.

62. Tirado Segura, *Las organizaciones empresariales mexicanans*, p. 85.

63. Whiting, Jr., "Private Power," p. 51.

64. Personal interview with José Levy.

65. Basáñez, *La lucha por la hegemonía en México*, p. 196.

66. Tirado Segura, *Las organizaciones empresariales mexicanas*, p. 86b.

67. Zermeño, "De Echeverría a de la Madrid," p. 13.

68. *Hispano Americano*, April 30, 1984, p. 19.

69. Basáñez, *La lucha por la hegemonía en México*, p. 204.

70. Delli Sante, "Private Sector," pp. 337–381 and Erwin Rodríguez Díaz, "La Cámara Americana de Comercio," *Estudios Políticos* 1 (April–June 1975):33–63.

71. Maxfield, "Losing Command," p. 29.

72. Consejo Coordinador Empresarial, A.C., *CCE* (Mexico City, n.d.).

73. Personal interview with José Levy.

74. Consejo Coordinador Empresarial, A.C., *CCE*.

75. Arriola, "Las organizaciones empresariales," p. 338.

76. Basáñez, *La lucha por la hegemonía en México*, p. 200.

77. Personal interview with Jorge Sánchez Mejorada, Mexico City, May 15, 1985.

78. Basáñez, *La lucha por la hegemonía en México*, p. 183.

79. Segura, *Las organizaciones empresariales mexicanas*, p. 90.

80. Alan Riding, *Distant Neighbors* (New York: Knopf, 1984), p. 132.
81. Personal interview.
82. Personal interview.
83. Personal interview.
84. Personal interview with Cresencio Ballesteros, Mexico City, July 26, 1984.
85. Personal interview.
86. Personal interview with Antonio Martínez Báez.
87. Story, *Industry, State, and Public Policy*, p. 105.

Chapter 8

1. Nathaniel Leff, "Industrial Organization and Entrepreneurship in the Developing Countries: The Economic Groups," *Economic Development and Cultural Change* 26 (July 1978):661–675.
2. Ibid., p. 663.
3. American Consul, Monterrey, Mexico, "The Monterrey Industrial Groups," unclassified report, June 10, 1975, p. 3.
4. Vernon, *Dilemma*, p. 20.
5. Personal interview with Alfonso Pasquel, Mexico City, May 24, 1985.
6. Jorge G. Castañeda, *Los últimos capitalismos* (Mexico City: Ediciones Era, 1982), p. 87.
7. Personal interview with Guillermo Sánchez Fábela, Mexico City, February 25, 1983.
8. Castañeda, *Los últimos capitalismos*, pp. 88–90.
9. Sanford Mosk, *The Industrial Revolution in Mexico* (Berkeley: University of California Press, 1950), p. 25.
10. American Consul, "Monterrey Industrial Groups," p. 4.
11. Robert T. Aubrey, "Capital Mobilization and the Patterns of Business Ownership and Control in Latin America: The Case of Mexico," in Sidney Greenfield, et. al., *Entrepreneurship in Cultural Context* (Albuquerque: University of New Mexico Press, 1979), pp. 231, 236.
12. Ibid., p. 238.
13. Personal interview with Antonio Ortiz Mena, Washington, D.C., January 24, 1984.
14. Derossi, *Mexican Entrepreneur*, appendix.
15. Ibid., p. 106.
16. Larissa Lomnitz, "Horizontal and Vertical Relations and the Social Structure of Urban Mexico," *Latin American Research Review* 17, no. 2 (1982):70.
17. Letter from Eduardo Bustamante, May 9, 1972, and personal interview, Mexico City, July 19, 1984.
18. Camp, *Intellectuals*, pp. 227–228.

19. Alonso Aguilar Monteverde, "Concentración y centralización del capital," in Alonso Aguilar Monteverde and Fernando Carmona, *México: Riqueza y Miseria* (Mexico City: Editorial Nuesto Tiempo, 1976), pp. 49–81.

20. Enrique Krauze, "Mexico: el Timón y la Tormenta," *Vuelta*, 6 (October 1982), p. 30.

21. Filbert M. Joseph and Allen Wells, "Corporate Control of a Mono-crop Economy: International Harvester and Yucatán's Henequen Industry during the Porfiriato," *Latin American Research Review* 17, no. 1 (1982):77.

22. Joslyn and Taussiug, *American Business Leaders*, p. 238.

23. Domhoff, *Powers That Be*, p. 21; Philip H. Burch, Jr., *The Managerial Revolution Reassessed* (New York: D. C. Heath, 1972); and Earl F. Cheit, "The New Place of Business," in Earl F. Cheit, ed., *The Business Establishment* (New York: Wiley, 1964), p. 172.

24. Derossi, *Mexican Entrepreneur*, p. 101.

25. Ibid., p. 57.

26. Jorge Camarena and Pablo Lasso, *Hacía un estilo propio de dirección de empresas, proyecto piloto, Guadalajara, México* (Washington, D.C.: Inter-American Development Bank, 1984).

27. Personal interview with Mauricio Soler Montesinos, Mexico City, February 24, 1983.

28. Larissa Lomnitz and Marisol Pérez Lizaur, "Retrato de Familia," *Vuelta* 5 (January 1981), p. 29.

29. American Consul, "Monterrey Industrial Groups," p. 5.

30. Robert T. Aubrey, "Capital Mobilization and the Patterns of Business Ownership and Control in Latin America: The Case of Mexico," paper presented at the Annual Meeting of the Rocky Mountain States Council of Latin Americanists, 1975, Glendale, Arizona, p. 17.

31. Personal interview with Guillermo Cantú, Mexico City, May 22, 1985.

32. Personal interview with Cresencio Ballesteros, Mexico City, July 26, 1984.

33. American Consul, "Monterrey Industrial Groups," p. 5.

34. Personal interview with Jorge Canales Elorduy, Mexico City, February 28, 1983.

35. Personal interview with Alfonso Pasquel, Mexico City, May 24, 1985.

36. Personal interview with Mario Segura Quiroc, Mexico City, July 26, 1984.

37. Personal interview with Bernardo Quintana Arrioja and Bernardo Quintana Issac, Mexico City, August 29, 1983.

38. Personal interview with Pedro Sánchez Mejorada, Mexico City, August 30, 1983.

39. Personal interview with Rómulo O'Farrill, August 1, 1984.

40. American Consul, "Monterrey Industrial Groups," p. 5.

41. Francisco Ortiz Pinchetti, "A la crisis del gobierno corresponde la quiebra de su socio Alfa," *Proceso*, May 17, 1982, p. 9.

42. Marlise Simons, "Mexico, The People Next Door," *The Wilson Quarterly*, 3 (Summer 1979), pp. 117–129.

43. Basáñez, *La lucha por la hegemonía en México*, p. 88.

44. Hugh O'Shaugnessy, "A Hive of Private Enterprise," *Financial Times* (London), May 4, 1979, p. 27 and American Consul, "Monterrey Industrial Groups," p. 8.

45. American Consul, "Monterrey Industrial Groups," p. 8.

46. Personal interview with Ernesto Canales, Mexico City, May 20, 1985.

47. Personal interview with Gabriel Zaid, Mexico City, October 6, 1983.

48. Ibid.

49. Derossi, *Mexican Entrepreneur*, p. 54.

50. Ortiz Pinchetti, "A la crisis," p. 9.

51. Ibid.

52. Vellinga, *Economic Development*, p. 81.

53. Personal interview with Antonio Armendáriz, Mexico City, May 24, 1982.

54. Vellinga, *Economic Development*, pp. 80–81.

55. Ariel José Contreras, *México 1940: industrialización y crisis política, estado y sociedad civil en las elecciones presidenciales* (Mexico City: Siglo XXI, 1977), p. 170.

56. Ibid., pp. 167–168.

57. Ortiz Pinchetti, "A la crisis," p. 10.

58. O'Shaugnessy, "Hive of Private Enterprise," p. 27.

59. Basáñez, *La lucha por la hegemonía en México*, p. 90.

60. Tirado Segura, *Las organizaciones empresariales mexicanas*, p. 99; and Julio Labastida Martín del Campo, "De la Unidad Nacional al Desarrollo Estabilizador (1940–1970)," in Pablo González Casanova, ed., *América Latina*, vol. 2 (Mexico City: Siglo XXI, 1981), p. 365.

61. Christopher Buckley, "Mexican Gore: Dona Irma and Her Dirty Little Book," *Esquire*, June 20, 1978, p. 70.

62. *Business Week*, January 30, 1978, p. 86.

63. *Wall Street Journal*, November 12, 1979, p. 41.

64. O'Shaugnessy, "Hive of Private Enterprise," p. 27.

65. Sergio Zermeño, "De Echeverría a de la Madrid: Las clases altas y el estado mexicano," paper presented at the Latin American Program, Woodrow Wilson International Center for Scholars, Smithsonian Institution, 1982, Washington, D.C. and Ortiz Pinchetti, "A la crisis," pp. 10–11.

66. *Wall Street Journal*, June 10, 1982, p. 17.

67. Ortiz Pinchetti, "A la crisis," p. 7.

68. Personal interview with Enrique Krauze, Mexico City, May 26, 1982.

69. Ortiz Pinchetti, "A la crisis," p. 8.
70. Ibid.
71. Also see *Latin American Weekly Report*, December 18, 1981, p. 7.
72. Ibid.
73. Personal interview with Emilio Alanís Patiño, Mexico City, May 26, 1982.
74. Personal interview with Carlos Tello, Washington, D.C., February 22, 1984; a detailed analysis of the Somex case can be found in Douglas C. Bennett and Kenneth E. Sharpe, "The State as Banker and as Entrepreneur: The Last Resort Character of the Mexican State's Economic Intervention, 1917–1970," *Comparative Politics* 12 (January 1980):178.
75. Personal interview with Antonio Armendáriz.
76. Personal interview with Bernardo Quintana Arrioja.
77. Personal interview with Adolfo Guerra Saba, Toluca, February 25, 1983.
78. Personal interview with Carlos Tello.
79. Personal interview with Gabriel Zaid.

Chapter 9

1. Shafer, *Mexican Business Organizations*, p. 126.
2. Theda Skocpol, "Brining the State Back In: Strategies of Analysis in Current Research," in Evans, Rueschemeyer, and Skocpol, eds., *Bringing the State Back In*, p. 21.
3. Ibid., p. 9.
4. Whiting, Jr., "Private Power," p. 39.
5. Personal interview, Washington, D.C., September 27, 1983.
6. Basáñez, *La lucha por la hegemonía en México*, p. ii.
7. Douglas Bennett and Kenneth Sharpe, "The State as Banker and Entrepreneur: The Last Resort Character of the Mexican State's Intervention, 1919–1976," *Comparative Politics* 12, no. 2 (January 1980):168.
8. Purcell and Purcell, "Mexican Business and Public Policy," p. 221.
9. Ibid., p. 195.
10. Felipe Leal, "The Mexican State: 1915–1973, A Historical Interpretation," *Latin American Perspectives* (Summer 1975):55.
11. Arnold Rose, *The Power Structure* (Oxford: Oxford University Press, 1967), p. 23.
12. Domhoff, *Powers That Be*, p. 13.
13. Ibid., p. 22.
14. Smith, *Labyrinths*, p. 215.
15. Kay Trimberger, *Revolution from Above: Military Bureaucrats and Development in Japan, Turkey, Egypt and Peru* (New Brunswick: Transaction Books, 1978).

16. Susan K. and John F. Purcell, "Estada y sociedad en México: debe un sistema político estable, institucionalizarse,?" *Foro Internacional* 20 (January–March 1980):456.

17. Labastida Martín del Campo, "Los grupos dominantes frente a las alternativas de cambio," p. 103.

18. Personal interview with Alfredo Phillips Olmedo, Mexico City, May 24, 1985.

19. Whiting, Jr., "Private Power," p. 39.

20. N. Stephen Kane, "American Businessmen and Foreign Policy: The Recognition of Mexico, 1920–1923," *Political Science Quarterly* 90 (Summer 1975):293.

21. Luis Villoro, *Signos políticos* (Mexico City: Editorial Grijalbo, 1974), p. 92.

22. Whiting, Jr., "Private Power," p. 46.

23. Story, "Industrial Elites," p. 357 and *Industry, State, and Public Policy* p. 195.

24. William P. Glade, "Mexico: Party-Led Development," in Robert Wesson, ed., *Politics, Policies, and Economic Development in Latin America* (Stanford: Hoover Institution Press, 1984), p. 95.

25. Nora Hamilton, "The State and the National Bourgeoisie in Postrevolutionary Mexico: 1920–1940," *Latin American Perspectives* 9, no. 4 (Fall 1982), p. 25.

26. Basáñez, *La lucha por la hegemonía en México*, p. 11.

27. Glade, "Mexico," p. 96.

28. Ibid., p. 95.

29. William P. Glade and Charles W. Anderson, *The Political Economy of Mexico* (Madison: University of Wisconsin, 1963), p. 117.

30. Bennett and Sharpe, "State as Banker," p. 183.

31. Ibid., p. 165.

32. Personal interview with Ernesto Canales, Mexico City, May 20, 1985.

33. Glade and Anderson, *Political Economy*, p. 163.

34. I am indebted to Richard A. Nuccio for this idea.

35. Glen Dealy, *The Public Man: An Interpretation of Latin American and Other Catholic Countries* (Amherst: University of Massachusetts Press, 1977).

36. Rafael Segovia, *La politización del niño mexicano* (Mexico City: El Colegio de México, 1975), p. 124 and Robert E. Scott, "Mexico: the Established Revolution," in Lucian Pye and Sidney Verba, eds., *Political Culture and Political Development* (Princeton: Princeton University Press, 1965), p. 358.

37. John A. Booth and Mitchell A. Seligson, "The Political Culture of Authoritarianism in Mexico: A Reexamination," *Latin American Research Review* 19, no. 1 (1984):106–124.

38. Newell and Rubio, *Mexico's Dilemma*, p. 33.

39. Leopoldo Solís, "Mexican Economic Policy in the Post-War Period: The Views of Mexican Economists," *The American Economic Review* 61 (June 1971):54.

40. Vernon, p. 75.

41. Albert L. Michaels, "Mexican Politics and Nationalism from Calles to Cárdenas," Ph.D. dissertation, University of Pennsylvania, 1966, p. 218.

42. Personal interview with Antonio Carrillo Flores, Mexico City, June 26, 1975.

43. Antonio Carrillo Flores, *La técnica, la iniciativa privada y al productividad en la industrialización de México* (Mexico City: Banco de México, 1952), p. 49.

44. Camp, *Making of a Government*, pp. 1134–35.

45. Personal interview with Raúl Cardiel Reyes, Mexico City, July 25, 1974.

46. William B. Quandt, *Revolution and Political Leadership: Algeria, 1954–1968* (Cambridge, Mass.: MIT Press, 1969), p. 267.

47. Camp, *Mexico's Leaders*, p. 193.

48. Vernon, *Dilemma*, p. 23.

49. Ibid., p. 44.

50. Data are from my study of Mexican firms.

51. Basáñez, *La lucha por la hegemonía en México*, p. 95 and Fernando Fajnzylber and Trinidad Martínez Tarrago, *Las empresas transnacionales (expansión a nivel mundial proyección en la industria mexicana)* (Mexico City: Fondo de Cultura Económica, 1976), pp. 154, 165.

52. Newfarmer and Mueller, *Multinational Corporations in Brazil and Mexico*, p. 62.

53. Epstein, "Business-Government Relations," p. 533.

54. Glade and Anderson, *Political Economy*, p. 120.

55. Personal interview with Cresencio Ballesteros, Mexico City, July 26, 1984.

56. Dilmus D. James, "Mexico's Recent Science and Technology Planning, An Outsider Economist's Critique," *Journal of Inter-American Studies and World Affairs* 22 (May 1980):178.

57. Angela M. Delli Sante, "The Private Sector's Business Organizations, and International Influence: A Case Study of Mexico," in Richard R. Fagen, ed., *Capitalism and the State in U.S.-Latin American Relations* (Stanford: Stanford University Press, 1979), p. 339.

58. Basáñez, *La lucha por la hegemonía en México*, pp. 204–205.

59. Personal interview with Dr. Pedro Daniel Martínez García, Mexico City, May 16, 1985.

60. Newell and Rubio, *Mexico's Dilemma*, p. 135.

61. Personal interview with Jorge Sánchez Mejorada, Mexico City, May 16, 1985.

62. Personal interview with Sealtiel Alatriste, Mexico City, May 27, 1982.

63. Personal interview with Jorge Sánchez Mejorada.

64. Delli Sante, "Private Sector's Business Organizations," p. 373.

65. Solís, "Mexican Economic Policy," p. 60.

66. Edward J. Williams, "Mutation in the Mexican Revolution: Industrialism, Nationalism and Centralism," *Secolas Annals* (March 1976), pp. 38–39.

67. Purcell, *Mexican Profit-Sharing Decision*, p. 30.

68. Personal interview with Ernesto Canales.

69. Camp, *Intellectuals*, pp. 214–215.

70. Personal interview with Ernesto Canales.

71. Personal interview with Ernesto Robles Levi, Mexico City, May 21, 1985.

72. Newell and Rubio, *Mexico's Dilemma*, p. 153.

73. Basáñez, *La lucha por la hegemonía en México*, p. 193.

74. Personal interview with Alejandro J. Dumán Urrea, Mexico City, March 1, 1983 and John D. Harbron, "The Dilemma of an Elite Group: The Industrialist in Latin America," *Inter-American Economic Affairs* 19, no. 2 (Fall 1965):52.

75. Personal interview with José Juan de Olloqui, Mexico City, October 4, 1983.

76. Vernon, *Dilemma*, p. 25.

77. Roger D. Hansen, *The Politics of Mexican Development*, (Baltimore: Johns Hopkins University Press, 1971), p. 35 and Glade and Anderson, *Political Economy*, p. 110.

78. Epstein, "Business-Government Relations," p. 526.

79. Alejandro Junco, "Mexico's Private Sector Reels Under Government control," *Wall Street Journal*, June 29, 1984, p. 29.

80. Personal interview with Ernesto Robles Levi.

81. Camp, *Intellectuals*, p. 177ff.

82. Susan K. and John F. Purcell, "State and Society in Mexico: Must a Stable Polity Be Institutionalized," *World Politics* 32 (January 1980), p. 206.

83. Personal interview with Ernesto Robles Levi.

84. Personal interview with Alfonso Pasquel, Mexico City, May 24, 1985.

85. Marco Antonio Alcazar, *Las Agrupaciones patronales en México*, (Mexico City: El Colegio de México, 1970), p. 100; and Purcell and Purcell, "Mexican Business and Public Policy," p. 193.

86. Hansen, *Politics of Mexican Development*, p. 5.

87. Hugh O'Shaugnessy, "A Hive of Private Enterprise," *Financial Times* (London), May 4, 1979, p. 27.

88. Wayne Cornelius, "Mexico and the United States in the 1980s,"

paper presented at the Symposium on Orozco and the Mexican Revolution, Dartmouth College, October 12–13, 1984, Hanover, N.H., p. 16.

89. Epstein, "Business-Government Relations," p. 541.

90. Vernon, *Dilemma*, pp. 149, 153.

91. Basáñez, *La lucha por la hegemonía en México*, p. 206.

92. Purcell and Purcell, "Mexican Business and Public Policy," p. 193.

93. Roderic A. Camp, "Opposition in Mexico, A Comparison of its Leadership," in Judith Gentleman, ed., *Mexican Politics in Transition*, (Boulder: Westview Press, 1986), pp. 251–52.

94. See the Mexican press, especially *Excélsior*, for November 9, 1985.

95. Personal interview.

96. Basáñez, *La lucha por la hegemonía en México*, p. 207.

97. Carlos Arriola, "Las organizaciones empresariales contemporáneas," Centro de Estudios Internacionales, *Lecturas de política mexicana* (Mexico City: El Colegio de México, 1977), pp. 351–352.

98. Dale Story, "Trade Politics in Mexico: GATT and the 'Song of the Sirens'."

99. Interview with Jorge Sánchez Mejorada.

100. Personal interview, Toluca, México, May 16, 1985.

101. Camp, *Intellectuals*, pp. 198ff.

102. *Hispano Americano*, November 26, 1985, pp. 23–24.

103. Sergio Zermeño, "De Echeverría a de la Madrid: Las clases altas y el estado mexicano," paper presented at the Latin American Program, Woodrow Wilson International Center for Scholars, Smithsonian Institution, 1982, Washington, D.C., p. 39.

104. Fatima Fernández Christlieb, "Prensa y poder en México," *Estudios Políticos* 2, no. 2 (July–September 1975):33, 54–55.

105. Ibid., pp. 32, 63.

106. Ibid., pp. 30, 50, 56.

107. Personal interviews with Rómulo O'Farrill, Mexico City, August 1, 1984 and Gabriel Alarcón, Mexico City, May 20, 1985.

108. Robert N. Pierce, *Keeping the Flame, Media and Government in Latin America*, (New York: Hastings House, 1979), p. 98.

109. Basáñez, *La lucha por la hegemonía en México*, p. 12.

110. Enrique León Martínez, *La televisión en el proceso político de México* (Mexico City: Federación Editorial Mexicana, 1975), pp. 73–74.

111. Raul H. Mora, "Educación y cultura expulsadas, pero no la indoctrinación," *Proceso*, May 17, 1982, pp. 46–47.

112. Basáñez, *La lucha por la hegemonía en México*, p. 103.

113. Personal interview with Alfonso Pasquel.

114. Personal interview with Bernardo Quintana Arrioja and Bernardo Quintana Issac, Mexico City, August 29, 1983.

115. Maxfield, "Losing Command," p. 71.

116. E. V. K. Fitzgerald, "Mexico, A New Direction in Economic Policy?," *Bank of London & South America Review* 12 (October 1978):535.

117. Vellinga, *Economic Development*, p. 34.

118. Hamilton, "State and National Bourgeoisie," p. 39.

119. Lauterbach, *Enterprise in Latin America*, pp. 166–167.

120. "Mexico's President Answers Critics," *Wall Street Journal*, September 10, 1984.

Bibliographic Essay

Anyone who attempts to describe and analyze Mexican entrepreneurs and their political activities, as distinct from the economic policy decisions of the Mexican government, will encounter little secondary literature. Although various studies have focused on specific entrepreneurial activities, none has attempted to paint a broad and complete portrait of how Mexican entrepreneurs see themselves, how they define their role, who they are, the characteristics of their informal and formal relationships with the state, and the consequences of these characteristics for private-public sector relations.

As I suggested in the Introduction, I found two theoretical approaches helpful in exploring this topic: elite theory and state theory. A prolific literature exists for both, although typically, most of it has more relevance to highly industrialized societies than to countries like Mexico, which even among Third World cultures is politically unique. Consequently, an eclectic and selective approach to this literature is helpful. Among elite theorists, I found three works most useful: G. William Domhoff, *The Powers That Be, Processes of Ruling-Class Domination in America* (New York: Random House, 1978)—which provides excellent revisions of C. Wright Mills' classic, *The Power Elite* (New York: Oxford University Press, 1959)—and Philip H. Burch, *Elites in American History*, 3 vols. (New York: Holmes and Meier, 1981). Burch provides an insightful discussion in vol. 1 of the problems the scholar faces with this type of research.

A plethora of literature exists on state theory. The reader should keep in mind that the focus of this book is on entrepreneurs' relationship to the state, rather than the reverse. Whereas one might consult the works of Robert MacIver, Grant McConnell, Robert Jessop, and others, as well as classics like Plato's Republic and Hegel's *The Philosophy of Right*, by far the most useful general work was Martin Carnoy's *The State and Political Theory* (Princeton: Princeton University Press, 1984) and Peter Evans, Dietrich Rueschemeyer, and Theda Skocpol, eds., *Bringing the State Back In* (Cambridge: Cambridge University Press, 1985), especially Skocpol's chapter on strategies in current research. These books are useful because they avoid esoteric philosophical jargon and raise essential contemporary questions. The two most lucid explanations of general state theory, with applications appropriate to Mexico, are articles by Clas Offe and Volker Ronge, "Theses on the Theory of the State," *New German Critique*, no. 6 (1975), pp. 137–147, and J. P. Nettl, "The State as a Conceptual Variable," *World Politics* 20 (July 1968):559–592.

For Mexico, the most insightful interpretations on the role of the state are numerous articles by Nora Hamilton, including "The State and the National Bourgeoisie in Postrevolutionary Mexico: 1920–1940," *Latin American Perspectives* 9 (Fall 1982):31–54, and her book, *The Limits of State Autonomy, Post-revolutionary Mexico* (Princeton: Princeton University Press, 1982). A more general survey, with a state-oriented focus, is James D. Cockcroft's *Mexico, Class Formation, Capital Accumulation, and the State* (New York: Monthly Review Press, 1983); *La formación del estado mexicano* (Mexico City: Porrúa, 1984) is much less useful. Several excellent but different interpretations by Mexicans of the evolution of the state are: Juan Felipe Leal, "The Mexican State: 1915–1973, A Historical Interpretation," *Latin American Perspectives* 2 (Summer 1975):48–63; Manuel Camacho, "El poder: estado a 'feudos' políticos," *Foro Internacional* 14 (1974):331–351; Julio Labastida Martín del Campo, "Algunas hipótesises sobre el modelo político mexicano y sus perspectivas," *Revista Mexicana de Sociología* 36 (July-September 1974):629–642; Miguel Basáñez, *La lucha por la hegemonía en México, 1968–80* (Mexico City: Siglo XXI, 1981); and Roberto Newell and Luis Rubio, *Mexico's Dilemma, the Political Origins of Economic Crisis* (Boulder: Westview Press, 1984). Finally, Douglas C. Bennett and Kenneth E. Sharpe offer an insightful if more focused look in their "The State as Banker and as Entrepreneur: The Last Resort Character of the Mexican State's Economic Interventions, 1917–1970," *Comparative Politics* 12 (January 1980):165–189.

For an historical understanding of the state's relationships to various groups, and the applicability of corporatist models to Mexico, the most helpful sources are John W. Sloan, "The Mexican Variant of Corporatism," *Inter-American Economic Affairs* 38 (Spring 1985):3–18; Karl Schmitt, "Church and State in Mexico: A Corporatist Relationship," *The Americas* 40 (January 1984):349–376; and Ruth Berins Collier and David Collier, "Inducements versus Constraints: Disaggregating Corporatism," *American Political Science Review* 73 (December 1979):967–986.

Elite studies of entrepreneurs, strangely, are not readily available. Other than Burch's work, the most useful elite analyses of businessmen, which provide helpful comparisons with Mexico, are Suzanne Infeld Keller's *The Social Origins and Career Lines of Three Generations of American Business Leaders* (New York: Arno Press, 1980) and Carl S. Joslyn and Frank Taussiug's earlier work, *American Business Leaders: A Study of Social Origins and Social Stratification* (New York: Macmillan, 1932).

For historical background on the private-public sector relationship, excluding the policy context, Mexican and United States periodicals and newspapers offer very little. The same is true for data about entrepreneurs and their holdings. The reason for this is that many of the most important features of the structural relationship between the state and the private sector are informal and personal. Consequently, oral interviews provide the richest source of information. However, care must be taken to interview both politicians and entrepreneurs, and among entrepreneurs to interview capitalists and professional managers, interest-group leaders and chief executive officers, regional and Mexico City entrepreneurs, and individuals from a variety of economic sectors. Still, some information can be found in *Excélsior*, which has a running economic commentary, similar to its "Frentes Politicos" column about politics. *Hispano Americano*, until it changed orientation in the mid-1980s, provides an excellent, balanced, and consistent source of information about private-sector attitudes and even some information about leading business figures since publication began in the 1940s. For the 1970s and 1980s the most helpful source is *Proceso*, despite its ideological bias, and *Expansión*, which represents a private-sector viewpoint.

General works by economists abound, but only a few have focused on the political aspects of Mexican development. Each of these works provides a helpful overview, and some important historical comparisons from the 1960s. They are Raymond Vernon, *The Dilemma of Mexico's Development* (Cambridge: Harvard University Press, 1963); William P. Glade and Charles W. Anderson, *The Political Economy of Mexico* (Madison: University of Wisconsin Press, 1963); and Roger D. Hansen, *The Politics of Mexican Development* (Baltimore: Johns Hopkins University Press, 1971). The only recent work in this vein, but by a political scientist, is the unpublished manuscript by Van R. Whiting, Jr., "Private Power in Mexico," Brown University, 1983.

The most serious scholarship on the Mexican private sector focuses on interest-group organizations. Whereas North American scholarship initially led the way, Mexicans now dominate the field. The classic work in this field, both for its breadth and the originality of its sources, is Robert F. Shafer's *Mexican Business Organizations* (Syracuse: Syracuse University Press, 1973). For the preceding decades, two other articles proved helpful. Frank Brandenburg, in addition to his well-known book, published "Organized Business in Mexico," *Inter-American Economic Affairs* 12 (Winter 1958):26–52. Shortly after that, in the only case study of a specific Mexican interest group, Merle Kling examined *A Mexican Interest Group in Action* (Engelwood Cliffs: Prentice-Hall, 1961). In the 1970s, Julio Labastida, Martín del Campo, and Marco Antonio Alcazar published two studies, respectively, "Los grupos dominantes frente a las alternativas de cambio," in *El pérfil de México en 1980*, vol. 3 (Mexico City: Siglo XXI, 1972), pp. 99–155, and *Las agrupaciones patronales en México* (Mexico City: El Colegio de México, 1970). More recently, more detailed and empirically sophisticated work has appeared in Mexico. Ricardo Tirado Segura has published several books and articles; among the most important are his *Las organizaciones empresariales mexicanas: pérfil y control durante los sesentas* (Mexico City: Instituto de Investigaciones Sociales, 1979), and "Semblanza de las organizaciones empresariales mexicanas," *Estudios Políticos* 3 (January–March 1984), and the work by Carlos Arriola, including his "Las organizaciones empresariales contemporáneas," in Centro de Estudios Internacionales, *Lecturas de política mexicana* (Mexico City: El Colegio de México, 1977), pp. 323–354, and "Los empresarios tras el Estado?" *Nexos*, no. 14 (February 1979):3–5.

Three Mexican authors have enriched this literature with analyses of the North American business organizations: Angela M. Delli Sante's excellent study, "The Private Sector, Business Organizations, and International Influence: A Case Study of Mexico," in Richard R.

Fagen, ed., *Capitalism and the State in U.S.-Latin American Relations* (Stanford: Stanford University Press, 1979), pp. 337–381; Lorenzo Meyer's *Los grupos de presión extranjeros en el México revolucionario, 1910–1940* (Mexico City: Secretaría de Relaciones Exteriores, 1973); and Erwin Rodríguez Díaz's "La Cámara Americana de Comercio," *Estudios Políticos* 1 (April–June 1975):33–63.

Interestingly, although the interest-group associations have attracted significant scholarly attention, entrepreneurs themselves have been almost entirely ignored. The major exception to this is the classic work by Flavia Derossi, *The Mexican Entrepreneur* (Paris: Development Center of the Organization for Economic Cooperation and Development, 1971), which examines industrialists through detailed interviews, and Dale Story's recent work, which includes some of the best insights on industrial organizations. His most relevant work is his article, "Industrial Elites in Mexico, Political Ideology and Influence," *Journal of Inter-American Studies and World Affairs* 25 (August 1983):351–376, and his book, *Industry, the State, and Public Policy in Mexico* (Austin: University of Texas Press, 1986). The only study of a contemporary group of entrepreneurs, based on a thorough questionnaire, is Jorge Camarena and Pablo Lasso's examination of prominent Guadalajara businessmen, *Hacía un estilo propio de dirección de empresas, proyecto piloto, Guadalajara, México* (Washington, D.C.: Banco Inter-Americano de Desarrollo, 1984).

Background information on Mexican entrepreneurs is very difficult to come by, whether social, educational, or economic. The data in Chapter 8 on family and firms come from hundreds of disparate sources, many of them periodicals, some of them unpublished, still others oral, and much of it from local and regional genealogical sources at the Library of Congress. Some general literature on North American businessmen, specifically on their origins and recruitment, is available, but little of it is recent. The best theoretical focus on social background variables is Lewis J. Edinger and Donald Searing's "Social Background in Elite Analysis: A Methodological Inquiry," *American Political Science Review* 61 (June 1967):428–445. For businessmen specifically, see the articles by James C. Abegglen, "Recruitment of Business Leaders," *Business History Review* 29 (March 1955):75–78; Oscar Handlin, "A Note on Social Mobility and the Recruitment of Entrepreneurs in the United States," *Explorations in Entrepreneurial History* 8 (1956): 1–15; Albert Lipman, "Social Backgrounds of the Bogota Entrepreneur," *Journal of Inter-American Studies and World Affairs* 7 (April 1965): 227–236; Stuart Adams,

"Trends in Occupational Origins of Business Leaders," *American Sociological Review* 9 (October 1954):541-548; John D. Harbron, "The Dilemma of an Elite Group: The Industrialist in Latin America," *Inter-American Economic Affairs* 19 (Fall 1965):43-62; and Fritz Redlich, "Business Leadership: Diverse Origins and Variant Forms," *Economic Development and Cultural Change*, 6 (April 1958):177-190.

Whereas almost no literature exists on the background of Mexican entrepreneurs, Mexicans—and some North Americans—have been fascinated by industrial groups, particularly the Monterrey Group. Two excellent theoretical pieces on industrial groups exist. The first, by Nathaniel Leff, "Industrial Organization and Entrepreneurship in the Developing Countries: The Economic Groups," *Economic Development and Cultural Change* 26 (July 1978):661-675, provides a broad overview, and Robert T. Aubrey, "Capital Mobilization and the Patterns of Business Ownership and Control in Latin America: The Case of Mexico," in Sidney Greenfield, et al., eds., *Entrepreneurship in Cultural Context* (Albuquerque: University of New Mexico Press, 1979), pp. 225-242, aptly discusses Mexico. Studies of the Monterrey Group, which identify many of its peculiarities, include Abraham Nuncio, *El Group Monterrey* (Mexico City: Editorial Nueva Imágen, 1982); American Consul, Monterrey, "The Monterrey Industrial Groups," unpublished report, June 10, 1975; and George R. Andrews, "Toward a Re-evaluation of the Latin American Family Firm: The Industry Executives of Monterrey," *Inter-American Economic Affairs* 30 (Winter, 1976):23-40; and Alex M. Saragoza's dissertation, "The Formation of a Mexican Elite, the Industrialization of Monterrey, Nuevo León, 1880-1920," University of California, San Diego, 1978, and his book.

Economic ownership, as I have suggested, must be examined from disparate and incomplete sources. An approach that combines biographical with financial research is most useful. These sources are too numerous to enumerate, but several are essential. Two reference works, which annotate hundreds of Mexico biographical collections used in this project, are a must for biographical research on any group in Mexico; Juan B. Iguíñiz, *Bibliografía biográfica mexicana* (Mexico City: Universidad Nacional Autónomo de México, 1969), and Sara de Mundo Lo, *Index to Spanish American Collective Biography* (Boston: G. K. Hall, 1982). Also the annual issue of *Expansión*, which lists the five hundred most important firms in Mexico, is a place to start for firms. The stock market must now provide firm ownership information, but the vast majority of Mexican firms are not publicly traded.

The best single analysis of firm ownership, focused on companies in the state of México, is Mario Ríos Villegas and Alexander N. Naime's *Los grupos empresariales en el estado de México* (Toluca: Secretaria de Trabajo, Gobierno del Estado de México, 1983). On a national level, two authors have provided invaluable information on wealthy families and firm ownership. They are Alonso Aguilar Monteverde, whose "Concentración y centralización del capital," in his *México: Riqueza y Miseria* (Mexico City: Editorial Nuestro Tiempo, 1976), pp. 49–81, is essential reading; and Salvador Cordero, who has published *Concentración industrial y poder económico en México* (Mexico City: El Colegio de México, 1977), and with Rafael Santín, *Los grupos industriales: una nueva organización económica en México* (Mexico City: El Colegio de México, 1977). The most useful source on board membership over time—but only for banks, insurance companies, financial institutions, and selected firms—is the authoritative *Anuario Financiero de México*, published annually since 1940 by the Asociación de Banqueros de México, available in the Library of Congress.

Among the numerous biographical dictionaries and genealogical works I consulted, most of which are cited in the two biographical reference books just mentioned above, several deserve special mention. They are Rosario Sansores Pren, *Libro azul de la sociedad mexicana* (Mexico City, 1946), which has excellent information on children, club memberships, and spouses for an older generation of central figures in Mexico. Even more useful, but dealing only with Monterrey, is *Quien es cada quien en Monterrey* (Monterrey, 1952). The best single geneological work is Torsten Dahl's, *Linajes en México* (Mexico City, 1967). Readers may encounter another work, the privately printed *Quien es quien en la empresa mexicana* (Mexico City, 1985), but biographies of living entrepreneurs, researched for this study, are now available in my *Who's Who in Mexico Today* (Boulder: Westview Press, 1988).

In addition to the analyses of economic groups, historians have added substantial information to our knowledge of local economic and political groups, especially their intermarriage, through microhistory. Some of the most useful studies include the work of Allen Wells and Filbert Joseph in Yucatán, "Corporate Control of a Monocrop Economy: International Harvester and Yucatán's Henequen Industry during the Porfiriato," *Latin American Research Review* 17 (1982):69–100; Allen Wells, "Family Elites in a Boom-and-Bust Economy: The Molinas and Peóns of Porfirian Yucatán," *Hispanic American Historical Review* 62 (May 1982):224–253; Héctor Aguilar Camín

292   BIBLIOGRAPHIC ESSAY

in Sonora, *La frontier nomada: Sonora y la revolución mexicana* (Mexico City: Siglo XXI, 1977); William S. Langston in Coahuila, "Coahuila in the Porfiriato, 1893–1911: A Study of Political Elites," Ph.D. dissertation, Tulane University, 1980; Mark Wasserman in Chihuahua, "Patterns of Family Alliances in the Mexican Revolution: The Case of Chihuahua," Paper presented to the Annual Meeting of the American Historical Association, December 29, 1980, Washington, D.C., as well as his *Capitalists, Caciques and Revolution: The Native Elite and Foreign Enterprises in Chihuahua, México, 1854–1911* (Lincoln: University of Nebraska Press, 1984); and Stuart Voss in northwestern Mexico, in Stuart F. Voss, et al., *Notable Family Networks in Latin America* (Chicago: University of Chicago Press, 1984).

For Monterrey, and its environs, several excellent studies exist, and they have more relevance than other regional works because Monterrey produced a disproportionate group of future economic elites. Among the most helpful are Isidro Vizcaya Canales, *Los orígenes de la industrialización de Monterrey* (Monterrey: Librería Tecnológico, 1971); Menno Vellinga, *Economic Development and the Dynamics of Class, Industrialization, Power and Control in Monterrey, Mexico* (Netherlands: Van Gorcum Assen, 1979); and Mario Cerutti's work, especially "Madero en la economía de Monterrey, *Cathedra* 8 (April–June 1978):29–93, and "Monterrey y el desarrollo del capitalismo en el noreste de México," *Cathedra* 4 (January–March 1968):3–30. Also, of course, is Alex Saragoza's Ph.D. dissertation, and his book, *The Mexican Elite and the Mexican State, 1880–1940* (Austin: University of Texas Press, 1988), unpublished at the time of this research.

Very little research exists on the attitudes of entrepreneurs in Latin America, and Mexico specifically. The books by Story, Derossi, and Camarena provide important empirical findings on selected businessmen. Wilber A. Chaffee, Jr., in his "Entrepreneurs and Economic Behavior: A New Approach to the Study of Latin American Politics," *Latin American Research Review* 11, no. 3 (1976):55–68, has approached the topic more theoretically, but basically is concerned only with development. Albert Lauterbach has published the only general work, *Enterprise in Latin America—Business Attitudes in a Developing Economy* (Ithaca: Cornell University Press, 1966). The only other study, which provides a revealing portrait of Mexican management employed in multinational corporations, is James Wallace Dull's "Effects of Multinational Corporations in Mexico on the Attitudes of Mexican Executives," Ph.D. dissertation, Columbia University, 1981.

Numerous works discuss the economic influence of transnational corporations in Mexico. Among the best general works, although they exclude the impact on state-private sector relations, are Fernando Fajnzylber and Trinidad Martínez Tarrago, *La empresas transnacionales* (Mexico City: Fondo de Cultura Económica, 1976), and Richard Newfarmer and William Mueller, *Multination Corporations in Brazil and Mexico* (Washington, D.C.: U.S. Senate, 1975). A work which bridges this gap in Van R. Whiting, Jr., "Transnational Enterprise and the State in Mexico," unpublished manuscript, 1981. However, the best single study, because of its insights on state-private sector relations, is Douglas C. Bennett and Kenneth E. Sharpe's *Transnational Corporations Versus the State, The Political Economy of the Mexican Auto Industry* (Princeton: Princeton University Press, 1985) and their earlier "Agenda Setting and Bargaining Power: The Mexican State versus Transnational Automobile Corporations," *World Politics* 32 (1979):57–89.

On the Mexican private-public relationship a few studies do exist. Susan and John Purcell initially pursued this topic in the early 1970s, publishing several articles, the most important of which was "Mexican Business and Public Policy," in James Malloy, ed., *Authoritarianism and Corporatism in Latin America* (Pittsburgh: Pittsburgh University Press, 1977), pp. 191–226. In the 1980s Edward C. Epstein followed with several more articles, the most useful of which is "Business-Government Relations in Mexico: The Echeverría Challenge to the Existing Development Model," *Journal of International Law* 12 (Summer 1980):525–547. In 1986, Sylvia Maxfield organized an excellent conference on government and the private sector at the Center for U.S.-Mexican Studies, University of California at San Diego (UCSD). The results of that conference have been published in *Government and Private Sector in Contemporary Mexico* (La Jolla: Center for U.S.-Mexican Studies, UCSD, 1987). Federico Rafael Cabrera Amescua, in an excellent communications thesis, "La Empresa privada y el gobierno en México," Universidad de Anahuac, 1986, offers some useful insights.

Mexican political leaders have fared much better. Several books provide data on their backgrounds, so comparisons between private- and public-sector leadership can be drawn, and their degree of interchange measured. Among these studies are Peter H. Smith, *The Labyrinths of Power: Political Recruitment in Twentieth Century Mexico* (Princeton: Princeton University Press, 1979); my own *Mexico's Leaders, Their Education and Recruitment* (Tuscon: University of Arizona

Press, 1980) and *The Making of a Government, Political Leaders in Modern Mexico* (Tucson: University of Arizona Press, 1984); and Emilio Salim Cabrera's "Clase política mexicana, rasgos y pérfiles," unpublished study, 1986. Finally, my work on cultural elites, *Intellectuals and the State in Twentieth Century Mexico* (Austin: University of Texas Press, 1985), especially in terms of the similar structural characteristics of intellectuals and politicians, suggests many parallels with entrepreneurs.

In addition to the more general analyses of the private-public relationship, several case studies exist of specific policy decisions involving the private sector. The most notable have been Susan K. Purcell, *The Mexican Profit-Sharing Decision, Politics in an Authoritarian Regime* (Berkeley: University of California Press, 1975); Sylvia Maxfield, "Losing Command of the Heights: Bank Nationalization and the Mexican State," paper presented to the National Latin American Studies Association, April 17–22, 1985, Albuquerque, N.M., Dale Story's articles on the initial rejection of GATT; and my own early work on Mexico's decision to join the Latin American Free Trade Association, entitled *The Role of Economists in Policy-making: A Comparative Case Study of Mexico and the United States* (Tuscon: University of Arizona Press, 1977).

Finally, education has played an important role in my analysis of entrepreneurs and their present and future relationship with public figures. A number of studies exist of the major universities, and of higher education, but very few scholars have examined curriculum and values in private colleges. Actually, most of the current attention to this subject is by a group of reporters working for *Proceso*. Among a series of articles published in the 1980s, the best are Francisco Ortiz Pinchetti's "El grupo Monterrey crea sus proprias fábricas de hombres," June 23, 1980, pp. 10–13 and Rául H. Mora's "Educación y cultura expulsadas, pero no la indoctrinación," May 17, 1982, pp. 46–49. The best scholarly analysis is Richard A. LaBarge and T. Noel Osborn, "The Status of Professional Economics Programs in Mexican Universities," *Inter-American Economic Affairs* 31 (Summer 1977):3–24 and a recent work by Peter Cleaves, which puts economics in the larger context of the leading professions; *Professions and the State: The Mexican Case* (Tuscon: University of Arizona Press, 1987). The best general overview can be found in Daniel Levy's *Higher Education and the State in Latin America* (Chicago: University of Chicago Press, 1986), especiallly the section on function in his case study of Mexico.

Index